INTERNATIONAL
POLITICAL ECONOMY
AND GLOBALIZATION

INTERNATIONAL
POLITICAL ECONOMY
AND GLOBALIZATION

Javed Maswood
Griffith University, Australia

World Scientific
Singapore • New Jersey • London • Hong Kong

※ 420 72091

Published by

World Scientific Publishing Co. Pte. Ltd.

P O Box 128, Farrer Road, Singapore 912805

USA office: Suite 1B, 1060 Main Street, River Edge, NJ 07661

UK office: 57 Shelton Street, Covent Garden, London WC2H 9HE

Library of Congress Cataloging-in-Publication Data
Maswood, Javed.
    International political economy and globalization / Javed Maswood.
       p.   cm.
    Includes bibliographical references and index.
    ISBN 9810238541 (alk. paper). -- ISBN 981023855X (pbk. : alk.
paper)
    1. International economic relations. 2. Economic development.
  3. Economic policy. 4. International business enterprises.
  HF1359.M378 1999
  337--dc21   2000   99-40240
                                              CIP

British Library Cataloguing-in-Publication Data
A catalogue record for this book is available from the British Library.

Printed in Singapore by World Scientific Printers

PREFACE

This book is the result of a research which began several years ago, and it has gone through several incarnations. I started writing it when I was on leave from Griffith University and teaching in the Department of Japanese Studies, National University of Singapore. As a result of the many revisions and rewrites, this is not the book I had originally wanted to write, at least in terms of structure and content. The chapters on foreign investment and labor standards were late additions and with each new draft, I also tinkered on the balance between theoretical content and empirical discussion. I am certain that the finished product is better than the task I had assigned myself when I began writing, and hopefully, I have managed to achieve the right balance between theory and factual detail. Through the lengthy writing process, my objective in writing this book had remained the same; to provide a clear and coherent analysis of the key issues in international political economy.

The emergence of economic globalization is the main new feature of international political economy. Admittedly, this is not the consensus position and skeptics remain convinced that the economic globalization is not substantively different from international interdependence. I maintain that globalization is real, and in this book, I have tried to look at its impact on economic relations between states. Some of the consequences of economic globalization, for example, the Asian financial crisis and the erosion of state control over national economies, will be obvious to the readers but globalization ought not to be associated only or primarily with negative outcomes. Globalization is also a source of economic efficiency, but does require a process of adaptation and adjustment to maximize the gains and minimize potential disruptions to economic activity.

Writing is a lonely experience, but still requires the positive intervention of friends and colleagues. At the National University of Singapore, the acting Head of the Department of Japanese Studies, Professor Hayden Lesbirel, was a source of constant encouragement and advice. Other colleagues at the National University, in particular Professor Eyal Ben-Ari and Dr Kanishka Jayasuriya, helped create a wonderful work environment and facilitated the writing of this book. At Griffith University, I would like to thank Professor Bob Elson. He may not know it but his prodding and friendly "barbs" encouraged me to stay committed. Each successive draft of this book benefited from the feedback of my students at Griffith University. They suffered through the successive drafts and offered useful comments. Many others read different parts of the book and were generous in their comments and criticism. I would like to thank Dr John Ravenhill at the Australian National University, Dr M. Ramesh at Sydney University, and Dr Leong Liew and Professor Bill Shepherd at Griffith University. To them I owe a debt of gratitude, for they graciously gave their time and helped improve the overall quality of the manuscript. I am certain that there remain many errors of omission and commission for which I alone am responsible.

CONTENTS

Chapter One

INTRODUCTION TO INTERNATIONAL POLITICAL ECONOMY

International political economy (IPE) is a study of interactions between states and markets at the international level. More specifically, IPE is a study of how political and economic variables facilitate or obstruct international economic transactions. IPE assumes that pure markets, unencumbered by political intervention and regulation, do not exist and that it is impossible to demarcate the empirical contents of economics and politics.

Through much of the post-war period, the discipline of international politics was narrowly focused on issues of international security and conflict. This was understandable in the context of insecurity generated by the Cold War between the United States and the Soviet Union. In the 1970s, however, a *détente* in US–Soviet relations pushed security issues to the background, and a series of economic crises — including the collapse of the Bretton-Woods monetary regime, the oil crisis, and stagflationary[1] pressures — led to a better understanding of the linkages between politics and economics.

IPE is concerned primarily with identifying and analyzing the underlying order that governs international economic transactions. It also assumes that the structure of order is derivative either of political decisions of independent states, or of the international political structure. For example, the hegemonic stability thesis asserts that order is a function of

1

a skewed distribution of power within the international system. Empirical evidence for this include the two periods of mid to late nineteenth century and the post-war period. Britain and the United States were hegemonic powers in the two respective periods, and contributed to the maintenance of relatively free international trade patterns. Conversely, hegemonic stability thesis assumes that when power is relatively evenly distributed, mercantilism[2] and trade protectionism may be the dominant practices. Empirical evidence for this is found in the period between the fifteenth and eighteenth centuries when the European political system was dominated by England, France, Spain, Sweden, Prussia, and Russia. Joan Spero explains that relative power parity meant that each state was sensitive to even minor changes that could potentially alter the balance of power and this resulted in an economic system that was intensely competitive, dominated by mercantilist and protectionist ideas.[3]

In the post-war period, progressive liberalization of trade, together with other conditions, has produced a high level of global economic inter-dependence. A concommitant strengthening of global economic forces has, allegedly, diminished national economic autonomy and produced a new condition of economic globalization. According to Kevin Kelly, the ordering principle for the new global IPE is pluralist, which means that while there continues to be some sort of management [order], no one is in charge.[4] The new structure is still in a process of "becoming," but it is useful to trace the path to this pluralist order; how regimes were created and, in turn, became the progenitors of economic globalization.

Regimes in IPE

In the immediate aftermath of the Second World War, the primary objective of the framers of the post-war order was to eliminate the self-destructive protectionism that had marked the pre-war period and to pave the way for a more liberal economic order. This was, to some extent, predicated on an assumption that competitive protectionism had contributed to a spiralling of international political conflict and war. The post-war liberal economic order consisted of negotiated rules and regulations to manage international trade and monetary relations. The General

Agreement on Tariffs and Trade (GATT) was the primary institution
dealing with trade issues, whereas monetary relations were governed
through the Bretton-Woods agreement.

Regime theory is generally identified with American scholarship, and
regimes have been defined as formal or informal principles, rules, and
norms of behavior within specific issue areas. According to Arthur Stein,
"A regime exists when the interaction between the parties is not
unconstrained or is not based on independent decision making."[5]
Similarly, according to Stephen Krasner, regimes are "implicit or explicit
principles, norms, rules, and decision-making procedures around which
actors' expectations converge in a given area in international relations."[6]

An important qualification, however, is that such rules are not
strictly enforceable. Instead, while compliance remains voluntary, regimes
provide enough positive inducements to elicit conformity. The advantage
of operating within regimes is that they facilitate transactions by ordering
environmental uncertainty. Essentially, regimes restrict the menu of
choice available to actors to mitigate, but not eliminate, the element of
uncertainty in international politics. As "fix rule" institutions, with agreed
behavioral guidelines, they enable wholesale advance coordination of
state and non-state activities and preclude the need for costly and time-
consuming negotiations each time the behavioral path of actors intersect.
The costliness of separate bilateral negotiations, for example, can be
avoided within a regime structure. This also helps to explain the interest
of the Chinese government in securing membership of the GATT and its
successor institution, the World Trade Organization (WTO). If approved,
the WTO membership will obviate the need for maintaining, and
periodically renegotiating, the 90 bilateral trade agreements between
China and other countries.

The significance of regimes as filters of international behavior has led
to a growing body of theoretical literature on the creation and maintenance of regimes. The IPE literature on regimes focuses mainly on the
supply of regimes; to complete the demand side of the equation, it is
possible to borrow and build on the basic principles derived from
transaction costs economics.

The Supply of Regimes

A systemic explanation for the supply of regimes was provided by Realists who argued that regime creation required a powerful state, a hegemon, to provide initiative and leadership. This was presumed to follow from the public goods nature of regime and the concomitant incentives to free ride. This proposition was formulated as the hegemonic stability thesis (HST).

According to HST, a skewed distribution of power is essential to regime creation and maintenance because it is the hegemon that bears the costs of regime creation, enforces internal discipline, and serves as a model for other states to follow. In a trade regime, for instance, the importance of a hegemonic actor is predicated on the systemic need for a large and open economy to balance periodic global supply and demand imbalances, without which protectionist tendencies might prove difficult to contain (see further below).[7]

In ascribing motives to the hegemon, the Realists discount pure altruism and benevolence. Instead, the emphasis is on opportunistic behavior. While Charles Kindleberger — who first articulated the hegemonic stability thesis — viewed regime creation as an economically responsible act, he nonetheless argued that the hegemon received recompense for pursuing this cosmopolitan goal, albeit in an intangible currency, such as power and prestige. Gilpin attributed similar reasoning to the hegemon. He wrote that, "The United States has assumed leadership responsibilities [in the post-war period] because it has been in its economic, political, and even ideological interest to do so, or at least it has believed this to be the case."[8]

An alternative to hegemonic stability thesis is the suggestion by liberal and interdependence theorists, like Robert Axelrod,[14] Robert Keohane[15] and Charles Lipson,[16] that cooperation may be possible even in the absence of a hegemon, or that regime creation can proceed on the basis of demonstrated gain for members. Axelrod, for example, found that cooperation between individuals [states] was possible even "... without the aid of a central authority [hegemon] to force them to cooperate with each other."[17] The claim extends beyond functionally specific and technical regimes, such as in telecommunications and air traffic control, where rules and standards are formulated simply on the basis of particular needs and collective benefits. Interdependence theorists argue that cooperative behavior may emerge even in functionally diffuse regimes when members recognize, and act on, their individual gain, even in the absence of a hegemon to minimize "free ride."

The logic underpinning the liberal approach can be demonstrated using game theory and prisoner's dilemma. In a two-player prisoner's dilemma, each player is assumed to have the option to either cooperate or defect, and the payoffs are structured such that defection yields higher payoffs, but mutual defection produces an outcome worse than mutual cooperation. The realists have used this to affirm that despite the benefits of mutual cooperation, each egoistic player will choose to defect and produce mutually sub-optimal results. Thus, by likening international politics to the prisoner's dilemma, Realists have made cooperation a derivative of hegemonic leadership. According to liberal and interdependence theorists, however, the prisoner's dilemma can produce a completely different outcome, if it is assumed that the game is "infinitely iterated"[18] or involves "repeated transactions."[19] The importance of iteration to cooperation is that it produces a learning effect which, according to Axelrod, can be used to maximize the potential for cooperation through a tit for tat strategy.[20]

The Demand for Regimes

The demand for international regimes can be traced to the transaction costs of international economic exchange in the absence of rules of conduct. Transaction costs economics is associated with the works of Oliver Williamson, who built on a framework proposed originally by Robert Coase in 1937. Williamson argues that it is heroic to assume, as does neoclassical economics, that the costs of transacting in the market-place are negligible and close to zero. In reality, he suggests, market-based transactions, in the absence of rules and procedures, may be costly and this — independently of monopoly considerations — may drive firms to pursue vertical integration. Explaining the options available to firms,

Williamson writes that if transactions are assumed as the centerpiece of the theory of the firm, then "[i]nterfirm contracting is well suited for some transactions; intrafirm contracting is well suited for others. Hybrid modes are superior in still others. The object is to establish which transactions go where."[9]

Transaction costs economics asserts that contracting in the market is a costly activity because of the unpredictability of the future, the opportunistic behavior of agents, and the bounded rationality[10] of the principals. The only constraint to infinite size expansion and vertical integration, he suggests, is the difficulty of exercising control in a large governance structure.

The essential insight of transaction costs economics is that economic activity can be organized differently, with different costs structures, and that the final choice can be explained in terms of the efficiency objective of the firm. Transaction costs economics provides useful insight in explaining demand for political regimes. The approach is useful in highlighting the fact that activities can be differently organized and that the criterion for organizational differences can be attributed to variations in costs and economies involved. As examples of transaction-coordination through international regimes, we can include the post-war GATT trading system and the IMF-centered international monetary order. These two examples of trade and monetary regimes immediately highlight the important point that not all regimes are alike. Regimes vary greatly in terms of their organizing principle. Thus, regimes may either be highly institutionalized or, as in the case of the GATT, possess minimal institutionalization. Moreover, apart from the organizing principle, regimes may also vary in terms of the prescribed and proscribed rules and norms of behavior.

As suggested by transaction costs economics, regimes have been characterized by general incompleteness, resulting either from failure to anticipate future problems or from expediency. Even contemporaries involved in regime creation recognized the partial nature of agreements without necessarily being aware of the precise deficiencies. For example, at the Savannah Conference held in March 1946 to give concrete shape to the Bretton-Woods agreement on international monetary arrangements

— which was ratified by 34 countries the previous December — the French delegate, Mr Mendes France, stated that "we are aware that these resolutions are not perfect. They are the result of transactions, and like all transactions, include provisions which do not thoroughly fit together."[11] The incompleteness of contracts can be attributed to the bounded rationality of actors and as a result, the original principles, rules and norms have been subject to revision as conditions changed. All long-term contracts, or regimes, will necessarily be incomplete as long as they are contracted under conditions of uncertainty. According to Williamson, uncertainty affects contracting in the following three ways[12]:

1. Not all future outcomes which require adjustment can be anticipated beforehand.
2. The appropriate adjustment itself will not be apparent until the condition materializes.
3. States may disagree on future changes, unless changes are completely unambiguous. This may preclude complete contracting.

In summary, the demand for regimes is more likely when any one of the following three conditions are met:

1. lack of a clear legal framework establishing liability for actions;
2. information imperfections; and
3. positive transaction costs.[13]

International Regimes and Economic Globalization

Globalization has occurred at two levels. The first is the process of inclusionary expansion through the collapse of the non-market economies and the emergence — for the first time in the post-war period — of a global political economy. By contrast, during the Cold War period, economic exchange between the two blocs was limited. As a western institution — the GATT for instance — had approximately 90 member countries at the end of the 1980s; its successor — the World Trade Organization, which was established in 1995 — has a membership base of 130 in the late 1990s with another 30 countries, including Russia and China, in the process of obtaining membership. With the inclusion of new members, the WTO will cover virtually all of world trade and investment.[21]

At the second, more complex level, globalization means the rapid transformation of economic activity and the emergence of a single global market alongside strategies of global production. It is the latter form of globalization, defined as the internationalization of production, distribution and marketing of goods and services,[22] or as the emergence of a single, undifferentiated, global market, that has been identified as the key to understanding contemporary international political economy.

The post-war exercise in institution and regime formation assumed that regime members would be both national economies and autonomous political units. By the 1970s, however, as a result of successful liberalization through regime-based negotiations, the separate national economies have become more interdependent. The main impact of interdependence is to leave national economies more sensitive and vulnerable to external developments. More recently, scholars have labeled contemporary developments as a process of globalization, which is replacing national economies with a global economy. The difference between globalization and interdependence is that while the latter was essentially an exchange-based linking of economies, the former includes an integration of economies through production and financial networks. Globalization points also to a conjunction of segmented political entities and a single global economy wherein market forces are less easily subject to regulation. As such, globalization suggests a diminishing role for state actors within IPE.

The End of the Cold War

Although not hermetically sealed, the post-war international political economy was divided into two separate groupings; one dominated by the United States and the other by the Soviet Union. Competing with the western liberal international economic order, the Soviet-dominated economic regime (the Council for Mutual Economic Assistance, or CMEA) was based on the principles of centralized decision making and control. It was founded by the USSR, Poland, Czechoslovakia, Hungary, Romania and Bulgaria in January 1949. Until the early 1960s, it was an agglomeration of East European countries. Mongolia, in 1962, was the first non-European country to be granted full participation in the CMEA. Others, like Cuba and Vietnam, became participating members in the 1970s.

In its early years, the CMEA was essentially a mechanism for extending Soviet control over the other members through coercive policies but, as Michael Marrese writes, the Soviets "... soon realized that the allegiance of East European countries could no longer be secured effectively via the stick and resorted to a new policy that employed a combination of the carrot (trade subsidization) and the stick (the threat of armed intervention)."[23] Thereafter, the East European countries posted significant economic gains as the Soviet Union became an exporter of raw materials at below world market prices and an importer of (allegedly shoddy) manufactured goods at internationally uncompetitive prices.[24] This enabled the Soviet Union to demand political loyalty and subservience in exchange for economic privileges, but proved detrimental to the Soviet economy, which was essentially subsidizing living standards in Eastern Europe and elsewhere (such as Cuba), through the supply of cheap minerals and fuels as well as monetary aid.

The collapse of Communism in Eastern Europe and the disintegration of the Eastern bloc was precipitated by Soviet economic reforms and the retraction of the Brezhnev Doctrine. The Brezhnev Doctrine emphasized socialist unity and the right of the Soviet Union to intervene elsewhere in defense of socialism. Its retraction removed the specter of Soviet military intervention in East European countries in defense of socialism, as had happened in Hungary in 1956 and in Czechoslovakia in 1968 when they initiated reforms and began to gravitate out of the Soviet sphere of influence. Following the retraction of the Brezhnev Doctrine, the centralized political and economic structures of East European countries gave way to a greater reliance on market mechanisms and political competition.

Similar reforms were also introduced in the Soviet Union, in the mid-1980s, in response to a worsening economic crisis. The economic crisis, in turn, was the product of an intensified Cold War rivalry in the early 1980s and the diversion of economic resources away from productive sectors to military programs. The increased military demand had exposed the vulnerability and inefficiencies of a command economy, but the reform agenda quickly snowballed and led to the abandonment of Communism.

Economic Globalization

The fall of Communism has created an ideologically and politically unitary global political economy. However, the rapid formation of global markets that transcend national borders has greater significance for IPE. The overall effect of globalization is not uniform across all aspects of international economic relations. Globalization is most pronounced in trade and financial relations, but not in labor market relations. Labor remains relatively confined to national jurisdictions even though there have been attempts, led by the advanced economies, to standardize global labor market conditions. Not surprisingly, this project has met with considerable resistance from developing countries, which fear that harmonization of labor regulations will erode their competitive advantage and prove detrimental to their growth prospects. In this book, I will deal with globalization and its impact on each of the three aspects of trade, finance, and labor relations.

The impact of globalization on state autonomy has attracted considerable attention. It is suggested, for example, that globalization has rendered states obsolete, since they are unable to preserve traditional patterns of international relations any longer, in the face of global market forces. Even if this is debatable and the state system unlikely to disappear, globalization has complicated the task of national economic management. In many instances, global economic forces are beyond the control of national governments, even when governments act collusively. In practical terms, what this means is that globalization has raised the costs of bad governmental policies that lead to fiscal deficits, over-regulation of the economy, and labor market rigidities.[25]

One evidence for globalization is taken to be the rapid increase in the share of trade (exports plus imports) in the Gross Domestic Product (GDP) of a country, a rapid increase in the flow of capital across borders, and foreign direct investment. For example, in the ten-year period between the mid-1980s and mid-1990s, the share of trade in GDP for the developing countries increased from around 33 percent to around 43 percent, whereas for the high-income developed countries, the same ratio increased from around 24 percent to about 33 percent.[26] World trade growth has also, throughout the post-war period, outpaced the growth in production. Average annual growth of world merchandise trade between 1950 and 1994 was around 6 percent, whereas the growth in world output was around 4 percent. The value of world merchandise trade in 1994 was slightly more than US$4 trillion, an increase of 13 percent over 1993.

Globally, in the 1980s, the increase in foreign direct investment (FDI) outpaced the growth in world trade. Between 1983 and 1988, world trade grew by 5 percent, whereas direct investment grew by 30 percent in real terms. Despite the rapid growth of FDI, however, global merchandise trade still vastly overshadowed investment flows. In 1990, for instance, global flow of merchandise was US$3.5 trillion, and the flow of FDI income stood at US$115 billion.[27] FDI, however, has acquired new significance within the context of globalization.

Foreign investment within a globalized operating structure is geared not only to supply demand within the host country, as per the product-cycle theory, for example, but is also part of a global marketing strategy. This has, consequently, increased the share of intra-firm trade in total world trade. This has been particularly pronounced for European and Japanese multinational corporations (MNCs), whereas the share of intra-firm trade to total US trade has remained relatively stable. Between 1977 and 1989, intra-firm exports of US firms were relatively stable at around 35 percent and intra-firm US imports, too, were stable at around 40 percent.[28] The increased role of MNCs in world trade can be gauged by the presence of approximately 35 000 multinational corporations, the largest 300 of which accounted for one-quarter of all developing country corporate assets.[29] This was a clear reflection of the growing importance of MNCs in the developing countries, and of the push by these firms to gain cost advantage by shifting some productive activities to low-cost countries.

Globalization has also significantly blurred distinctions between trade and investment. It is a fact that many countries, while encouraging foreign investment, also impose performance criteria to force foreign firms to comply with local content requirements or minimum export requirements. Both have major implications for international trade, and it was soon obvious that investment issues could not be dealt with separately from trade issues, or that the GATT (later, WTO), as the machinery to deal with trade issues, could not ignore investment issues. The earliest proposal, however, was to develop a separate and independent regime on investments. In 1970, Goldberg and Kindleberger, for example, recommended establishing a new body, similar to the GATT, to formulate a set of rules and dispute settlement procedures for foreign investment flows.[30] Instead, when the Uruguay Round opened, foreign direct investment was brought under the GATT purview. Thus, as will become clear in Chapter five, one obvious consequence of globalization has been to push the GATT into new areas.

The range of globalized activities in manufacturing covers not only production bases in other countries but also the sourcing of spare parts and components on a global scale rather than only from domestic suppliers. An example of global manufacturing is the Ford Escort, which is produced in the United Kingdom by an American automobile company with components and raw materials sourced from 11 countries.[31] Where trade used to be in finished commodities, the nature of trade is being increasingly transformed by the growing importance of trade-in components and intermediate goods. Other instances of globalization include American companies that handle telephone inquiries through operators in the Caribbean, or Swiss Air — which has some of its accounting done in New Delhi.[32] Given all these new developments, Susan Strange, citing Peter Drucker, suggests that the "world economy is 'in control', superseding the macroeconomics of the nation-state on which much economic theory, whether Keynesian, monetarist or Marxist, still anachronistically focuses."[33]

There are, of course, sceptics who are less convinced of the reality of globalization. Richard Harris, for example, argues that globalization is still some way off because of the natural limits posed by "politics, culture, language, and distance."[34] Even less sympathetic to globalization is P. Bairoch, who finds that globalization is not the significant new development that it is claimed to be. He argues that, historically, periods of high internationalization (globalization) have alternated with periods of low internationalization, and that contemporary globalization is simply an aspect of this long-term cyclical trend (see Table 1.1 below). This leads him to conclude that "... even for the country [the US] where the process of globalization seems the most obvious, the process is not a new one."[35] This view is shared by Paul Krugman, who writes that "... historians of the international economy date the emergence of a truly global economy to the forties — the 1840s — when the railroads and steamships reduced transport costs to the point where large-scale shipment of bulk commodities became possible."[36]

The statistical evidence presented below, however, conceals important undercurrents of change in the contemporary period. As the example of the Ford Escort demonstrates, manufactured products are no longer traded largely as consumer goods or capital goods, but increasingly also as intermediate goods. This feature of contemporary trading patterns has produced a much higher level of economic integration than in the

Table 1.1. Merchandise exports as percentage of GDP.

	Western Developed Countries	United States	Western Europe	EEC (12 members)	Japan
1890	11.7	6.7	14.9	–	5.1
1913	12.9	6.4	18.3	–	12.6
1929	9.8	5.0	14.5	–	13.6
1938	6.2	3.7	7.1	–	3.0
1950	7.8	3.8	13.4	12.9	6.8
1970	10.2	4.0	17.4	16.7	9.7
1992	14.3	7.5	21.7	21.1	8.8

Note: The figures are three-year averages, except for 1950.
Source: Bairoch, P., "Globalization Myths and Realities: One Century of External Trade and Foreign Investment," in Boyer, R. and Daniel Drache (eds.), *States Against Markets: The Limits of Globalization,* Routledge, London, New York, 1996, p. 179.

past. It is not simply an increase in exports and imports; globalization of production processes has added a unique new dimension to the contemporary period. Robert Boyer and Daniel Drache acknowledge that, "today's globalization is qualitatively and quantitatively different from previous periods."[37]

Globalization, according to Miriam Campanella, involved a mix of three factors: the entrance of powerful new actors such as multinational corporations (MNCs); the rapid diffusion of communication and information technologies; and economic liberalization, symbolized in a withdrawal of the state from the market in several OECD countries.[38] Paradoxically, however, protectionism in key markets also contributed to globalization of business. Increased protectionism in the 1980s in important consumer markets encouraged manufacturers to establish production facilities in their export markets in order to retain market share. This explains Japanese investment in the United States in, for example, the automobile industry. Prior to the 1981 restrictions of Japanese automobile exports to the US, Japanese car manufacturers had relied exclusively on exports to service demand in the United States.

The globalization of business has also been influenced by the imperative to improve cost and competitive position in a recessionary economic climate. Japanese and European investment in the developing countries can be classified as part of this competitiveness drive. The emergence of Japanese MNCs is evidenced in the rapid growth of foreign direct investment in the 1980s. The Japanese foreign investment boom of the 1980s was sustained by trade surpluses and asset (primarily land) price inflation, which created instant surplus liquidity.

The trend toward globalization has generated considerable debate and discussion on the relationships between the state and the newly configured global market, on one hand, and between trade and investment, on the other. As regards the first aspect of globalization, the existing literature can be classified into two groups. The first emphasizes the transformation or the "transformation potential" of globalization.[39] Ruggie, for example, argued that globalization has not only enhanced the role of multinational and transnational corporations within the international political economy, but has also unleashed forces which could alter the way we conceptualize world politics and international political economy, especially in regard to territoriality and state sovereignty. He argued that the relationship between transnationalism and the contemporary state system was not unlike that between medieval trade fairs and feudal authority structures. While the feudal lords encouraged trade fairs as a source of revenue, these fairs also "... contributed significantly to the demise of feudal authority relations,"[40] by initiating the capitalist revolution.

If true, globalization has initiated a transformation of world politics, away from a system of segmented — though interlinked — political and economic units to one of political segmentation alongside a single global economy. This raises questions as to the emerging relationship between national states and a single global economy. Kenichi Ohmae, for example, highlights the expanded horizon of producers and consumers alike and popularized the concept of a "borderless" economy. He heralded the emergence of a "nationalityless" global market with a significantly diminished role for national governments. He relegated the government to the "... backseat, not the driver's position ...," and its role to ensuring that the country benefited "... fully from the best-performing corporations and producers in the world, at the lowest possible cost to their people on a long-term basis."[41]

The second view is exemplified by, for example, Kapstein, Hirst, and Thompson. Kapstein argued that, despite globalization, there has been no significant change to contemporary structures and that states have retained their full economic and political sovereignty.[42] Throughout history, he argues, states have shown a remarkable ability to adapt to changing circumstances, and there is no reason to assume that they will not adjust to the challenges of globalization and remain the pre-eminent actors on the international stage. Similarly, according to Hirst and Thompson, globalization is not yet an extant reality.[43] Unlike advocates of globalization, they assert a basic continuity in international political economy. Hirst and Thompson argue that the international economy was equally integrated at the beginning of the twentieth century: that while satellite communication has brought markets closer together, it has not fundamentally altered their operation; and that there are few true MNCs, with most companies still operating in a small number of countries, or at most regionally.

The truth probably lies somewhere in between these two polar positions. The real implication of the first view is to reclaim the autonomy of economics by denying that politics matters. I believe this to be mistaken, not because it denies the validity of political economy as a field of inquiry, but rather because it is unreasonable to assume that states will passively reconcile to market constraints without attempting to influence market outcomes. Moreover, if globalization has undermined, or is tending to undermine, the effectiveness of national policy instruments, it may also have created new opportunities for the state at the international level. This is so because while globalization is — at least partly — a response to cost pressures and the imperative to reduce production costs, the net result of globalization has been to increase transaction costs for firms. According to John Dunning, the advent of globalization has led "... to an increase in the relative significance of transaction to production costs of doing business ... ."[44]

Economic liberalization and advances in communications technology facilitated the process of globalization, but operating within a global market still requires coordination of market-segmented regulatory policies. It would be an exaggeration to conclude that globalization implies an all-embracing unitary regulatory structure, despite a general trend toward economic liberalization and more relaxed entry conditions to foreign capital in many developed and developing countries. The transaction costs encountered by global corporations may be a new source for regime formation, and might also be viewed as an important factor in the contemporary push for regionalization, given that the objective of regionalism is to harmonize economic and regulatory policies. The reality of segmented regulatory practices and the desirability of uniform regulatory codes are also a source of conflict. Conflict here is the result of disagreement as to the "model" for harmonization of regulations across countries. The US, for example, insists on certain labor codes which the developing countries resist, and also demands unity in dealings with so-called "rogue" states which has placed it in conflict with other developed economies, such as the European Union (see Chapter two).

The significance of non-state and societal actors has also increased. Multinational corporations, for example, have become major new players and played an important part in the Uruguay Round negotiations. Globalization has led to a blurring of inter-regimes boundaries and to a more complex political reality. Trade decisions are no longer resolved only in their own terms, but are affected by other considerations of human rights, environment and sustainable development. Globalization has also dramatically altered the nature of international trade and produced a pattern of trade which is increasingly dominated by intra-firm transactions across national boundaries. This "incestuous" trade pattern has produced powerful new actors on the international stage.

In this complex new reality of globalization, the relevance of regimes is in providing useful conceptual tools to simplify and order existing reality. The regime theory approach isolates specific issue areas, such as trade and money but, as suggested by de la Mothe and Gilles Paquet, "It is not clear that an approach in terms of trade, investment, technology or multinationals, one at a time, is sufficient to untangle the complex patterns we observe and to reconstruct the operating networks that underpin them. It may well be that persuasive explanations will require an integrative look — a recasting of economic, social, and political activities into different molds [sic]."[45]

In this book, I will use such an integrative approach to highlight the interconnections between the various issue areas.

References

1. Stagflation refers to the unlikely combination of economic stagnation and inflation that marked the decade of the 1970s following the quadrupling of oil prices in 1973.
2. Mercantilism is an economic doctrine that identifies national economic wealth to national treasure and the available stock of gold and precious metals. When this has dominated trade policies, states have encouraged exports (to induce an inflow of precious metals) and discouraged imports (to reduce the outflow of precious metals).

3. Spero, Joan E., *The Politics of International Economic Relations*, 4th ed., Routledge, London, 1992, pp. 4–5.
4. See de la Mothe, J. and Paquet, G., "In Search of a New International Political Economy", in de la Mothe, J. and Gilles Paquet (eds.), *Evolutionary Economics and the New International Political Economy*, Pinter, London, 1996, pp. 55ff.
5. Stein, A. A., "Coordination and Collaboration: Regimes in an Anarchic World," *International Organization*, Vol. 36, No. 2, Spring 1982, p. 301.
6. Krasner, S. D., "Structural Causes and Regime Consequences: Regimes as Intervening Variables," *International Organization*, Vol. 36, No. 2, Spring 1982, p. 186.
7. In other issue areas, say environmental management, leadership may not necessarily depend on a hegemon, and may even be exercised by non-state actors.
8. Gilpin, R., *The Political Economy of International Relations*, Princeton University Press, Princeton, 1987, p. 88.
9. Williamson, O. E., "The Firm as a Nexus of Treaties: An Introduction," in Aoki, M., Bo Gustafsson and Oliver E. Williamson (eds.), *The Firm as a Nexus of Treaties*, Sage Publication, London, 1990, p. 8.
10. The concept of bounded rationality originated with Herbert Simon who defined it as behavior that is "intendedly rational, but only limitedly so." Cited in Williamson, O. E., "Transaction Cost Economics Meets Posnerian Law and Economics," *Journal of Institutional and Theoretical Economics*, Vol. 149, No. 1, March 1993, p. 109.
11. Van Dormael, A., *Bretton Woods: Birth of a Monetary System*, The Macmillan Press Ltd., London and Basingstoke, 1978, p. 290.
12. Williamson, O. E., *The Economic Institutions of Capitalism: Firms, Markets, Relational Contracting*, The Free Press, New York, 1985, p. 70. See also p. 178.
13. Keohane, R. O., "The Demand for International Regimes," *International Organizations*, Vol. 36, No. 2, Spring 1982, p. 338.
14. Axelrod, R., *The Evolution of Cooperation*, Penguin Books, New York, 1984.

15. Keohane, Robert, O., *After Hegemony: Cooperation and Discord in the World Political Economy*, Princeton University Press, Princeton, 1984.

16. Lipson, C., "International Cooperation in Economic and Security Affairs", *World Politics,* October 1984.

17. Axelrod, R., *The Evolution of Cooperation*, Penguin Books, New York, 1984, p. 6.

18. Axelrod, R., *The Evolution of Cooperation*, Penguin Books, New York, 1984.

19. Lipson, C., "International Cooperation in Economic and Security Affairs," *World Politics*, Vol. 37, No. 1, October 1984, p. 1.

20. A tit for tat strategy is defined as "... voidance of unnecessary conflict by cooperating as long as the other player does, provocability in the face of uncalled for defection by the other, forgiveness after responding to a provocation, and clarity of behavior so that the other player can adapt to your pattern of action." See Axelrod, R., *The Evolution of Cooperation*, Penguin Books, New York, 1984, p. 20.

21. Hart, M., "The WTO and the Political Economy of Globalization," *Journal of World Trade*, Vol. 31, No. 5, October 1997, p. 84.

22. Harris, R. G., "Globalization, Trade, and Income," *Canadian Journal of Economics*, Vol. 26, No. 4, November 1993, p. 755.

23. Marrese, M., "CMEA: Effective but Cumbersome Political Economy," *International Organization*, Vol. 40, No. 2, Spring 1986, pp. 290–291.

24. Marrese, M., "CMEA: Effective but Cumbersome Political Economy," *International Organization*, Vol. 40, No. 2, Spring 1986, p. 299.

25. Blackhurst, R., "The WTO and the Global Economy," *The World Economy*, Vol. 20, No. 5, August 1997, p. 531.

26. Qureshi, Z., "Globalization: New Opportunities, Tough Challenges," *Finance & Development*, Vol. 33, No. 1, March 1996, pp. 30–32.

27. Hoekman, Bernard M., "New Issues in the Uruguay Round and Beyond," *The Economic Journal,* Vol. 103, No. 421, November 1993, p. 1529.

28. Bonturi, M. and Küichiro Fukusaku, "Globalization and Intra-Firm Trade: An Empirical Note," *OECD Economic Studies*, Vol. 20, No. 1, Spring 1993, see Table 1.

29. Harris, R. G., "Globalization, Trade, and Income", *Canadian Journal of Economics,* Vol. 26, No. 4, November 1993, p. 758. These 35 000 TNCs own or control about 150 000 foreign affiliates. See, Dunning, John H., "How Should National Governments Respond to Globalization?", *The International Executive,* Vol. 35, No. 3, May/June 1993, p. 188.

30. See McCulloch, R., "Investment Policies in GATT," *The World Economy,* Vol. 13, No. 4, December 1990, p. 344.

31. Simon, Dennis F., "The International Technology Market: Globalization, Regionalization and the Pacific Rim," *Business & The Contemporary World,* Vol. 5, No. 2, Spring 1993, p. 53.

32. See, Lindbaek, J. and Jean–Francois Rischard, "Agility in the New World Economy," *Finance & Development,* Vol. 31, No. 3, September 1994, p. 34.

33. Strange, S., *States and Markets: An Introduction to International Political Economy,* Pinter Publishers, London, 1988, p. 63.

34. Harris, R. G., "Globalization, Trade, and Income", *Canadian Journal of Economics,* Vol. 26, No. 4, November 1993, p. 773.

35. Bairoch, P., "Globalization Myths and Realities: One Century of External Trade and Foreign Investment," in Boyer, R. and Daniel Drache (eds.), *States Against Markets: The Limits of Globalization,* Routledge, London, New York, 1996, p. 180.

36. Krugman, P., *Peddling Prosperity: Economic Sense and Nonsense in the Age of Diminished Expectations,* W. W. Norton and Co., Inc., New York, 1994, p. 258.

37. Boyer, R. and Daniel Drache, "...", in Boyer, R. and Drache, D. (eds.), *States Against Markets: The Limits of Globalization,* Routledge, London, New York, 1996, p. 13.

38. Campanella, M. L., "The Effect of Globalization and Turbulence on Policy-Making Processes," *Government and Opposition,* Vol. 28, No. 2, Spring 1993, p. 192. Others have written about globalization in similar terms. See, for example, Wang Xinhua, "Trends Towards Globalization and a Global Think Tank," *Futures,* Vol. 24, No. 3, April 1992; and Harris, R. G., "Globalization, Trade, and Income," *Canadian Journal of Economics,* Vol. 26, No. 4, November 1993, p. 763.

39. See, Ruggie, John G., "Territoriality and Beyond: Problematizing Modernity in International Relations," *International Organization*, Vol. 47, No. 1, Winter 1993.

40. Ruggie, John G., "Territoriality and Beyond: Problematizing Modernity in International Relations," *International Organization*, Vol. 47, No. 1, Winter 1993, p. 155.

41. Ohmae, K., *The Borderless World: Power and Strategy in the Interlinked Economy*, Fontana, London, 1990, p. 16.

42. Kapstein, Ethan B., "We are US: The Myth of the Multinational," *The National Interest*, Winter 1991–1992. See also Kapstein, Ethan B., *Governing the Global Economy: International Finance and the State*, Harvard University Press, Cambridge, Mass, 1994, Chapter 1.

43. Hirst, P. and Grahame Thompson, "The Problem of 'Globalization': International Economic Relations, National Economic Management and the Formation of Trading Blocs," *Economy and Society*, Vol. 21, No. 4, November 1992, p. 369.

44. Dunning, J. H., "How Should National Governments Respond to Globalization?," *The International Executive*, Vol. 35, No. 3, May/June 1993, p. 192.

45. De la Mothe, J. and G. Paquet, "Conclusion," in de la Mothe, J. and Gilles Paquet (eds.), *Evolutionary Economics and the New International Political Economy*, Pinter, London, 1996, p. 278.

Chapter Two

INTERNATIONAL TRADE: FROM THE GATT TO THE WTO

As a source of dynamism and development, international trade was a solvent of feudalism, a catalyst for the industrial revolution in Europe and is, today, a key to understanding economic globalization. The benefits of trade, in terms of employment growth and prosperity, are well recognized in economic theory, but states have never sanctioned unimpeded exchange of goods and services across borders. Alternatives, such as mercantilism, protectionism, and economic nationalism, have, instead, obstructed the passage of free trade. The best that has been achieved are periods of liberal trade or freer trade.

Mercantilist theories dominated and informed trade practices for several hundred years until the 1800s. For mercantilists, economic growth and welfare were contingent on expanding the domestic supply base of monetary metals to fuel a concomitant increase in money supply. Contraction in the availability of monetary metals was, on the other hand, associated with reduced money supply and downward pressure on prices, lower growth, lower incomes, and reduced welfare.[1] Mercantilists viewed international trade as a zero-sum activity and, consequently, emphasized the importance of trade controls to benefit the national economy. According to Kristof Glamann, under mercantilist principles, how to "acquire the largest share of what was commonly seen as a more or less fixed volume of international trade, and how so to manage the national share as to produce a favorable balance of trade and a net import of bullion and precious metals, were the twin tasks to which governments of the day addressed themselves."[2] This meant limiting imports and generating exports to accumulate precious metals, like gold and silver.

Adam Smith (1723–1790) provided the earliest liberal critique of mercantilism in his book *An Inquiry into the Wealth of Nations*. He defended free trade and criticized mercantilists for confusing national wealth with national treasure, suggesting instead that wealth and welfare could be maximized if a country specialized in the production of some goods and exchanged the surplus production for the surplus production of other countries producing different commodities. Liberal economic theory defends free trade from narrow considerations of national interest, but in the conviction that free trade *is* in the national interest of all countries. At an empirical level, this may be demonstrated by looking at how nations fared in the age of mercantilism, given that different countries pursued it with more or less vigor. According to Fellner, "Even during the era of mercantilism there was much less regulation and control in England than in some of the Continental countries. At the end, the more rigorously 'mercantilistic' nations [such as France] fared worse."[3] France had a larger population and was better endowed with natural resources, but it was England that emerged as the leading industrial power in the nineteenth century. Fellner acknowledged that while it may be impossible to be certain that French mercantilism caused it to lag behind Britain, the possibility that it did cannot be ruled out either.

In the contemporary period, protectionists are not so naive as to equate wealth with national treasure but still argue that some protection from imports may be desirable for reasons of international strategy, protecting specific, and desirable, sectors from foreign competition, or for employment considerations. Apart from protectionist pressures, trade policies are also regularly swayed by political ambitions and objectives. Recent politicization of international trade include American threats in 1993—1994 to withdraw China's Most Favoured Nation (MFN) status if it failed to improve domestic human rights conditions. Similarly, the United States also served notice on Indonesia to improve labor and human rights by February 1994 or risk losing trade concessions under the Generalized

System of Preferences (GSP).[4] Politicization of trade, however incongruous with theories of free trade, is inevitable, and states that can, will always seek to use trade to their political and economic advantage or to influence international developments.

Once we accept the harsh reality that the logic of free trade has failed to silence its critics, it is useful to identify the circumstances that are conducive to freer trade. Reductionist explanations concentrate on national decision-makers to explain the vagaries of free trade. The transition to liberal trade after the Second World War might be linked to the rise of liberal internationalists, like the American Secretary of State, Cordell Hull, to positions of influence in government. Other reductionist explanations may concentrate on domestic political and economic factors conducive to, or detrimental to, free trade policies, including domestic electoral politics, infant industry arguments, or simply national prestige. It might be noted here that consumers, the beneficiaries of free trade, rarely ever organize to advocate free trade whereas producers frequently attempt to secure protection from foreign competitors.

At a systemic level, a standard explanation for the presence or absence of liberal trade is the hegemonic-stability thesis. It asserts that relative free trade is likely only under circumstances of asymmetric distribution of power. This is supported by the evidence that international free trade became a reality, for the first time, under *Pax Britannica* in the nineteenth century and, again, under *Pax Americana* in the twentieth century.[5] Neither Britain nor the US, however, moved to a position of free trade immediately after achieving hegemony in the international system.

Free Trade in Practice

In Britain, free trade made slow headway following the industrial revolution which began around 1780. The industrial revolution was characterized by a shift away from the dominance of mercantile capital to fixed industrial capital, and away from labor intensive to capital intensive manufacturing.[6] It was not a single cataclysmic event that changed the shape of British society and economy but rather a process that, between 1780 and 1860, gradually transformed Britain from an agricultural to an industrial economy. The reasons for the industrial revolution cannot be ascertained with any certainty but population growth and increased availability of productive tools were important factors.[7] Together they increased the level of domestic demand and the economic capacity to respond to higher demand.

The growth in manufacturing opened up new trade possibilities, given that consumption of manufactured goods had high income elasticity.[8] However, in the early period of industrialization, Britain actually introduced higher tariffs to protect its declining agricultural sector. This was done through price supports, and restrictions on agricultural imports until domestic prices had crossed certain threshold levels. Fielden writes that the "British tariff of 1815 was harsher than the eighteenth century's. In that year also, the final great Corn Law excluded foreign wheat until home prices reached 80 shillings per quarter."[9] There were also export controls and the British government restricted the export of machinery and technology to preserve its own manufacturing advantages.

Despite the prohibition, however, machinery continued to be smuggled out of the country and there was a constant flow of foreigners into Britain trying to learn and master the latest technology, especially after 1815. The French, German and American industrialization started around this time and they made rapid progress as they could implement quickly what Britain had worked out over a longer period of time.

Britain moved to free trade policies, by ending import restrictions and export controls, in the mid-1840s. Hegemonic stability thesis explains this transition with reference to Britain's emergence as a hegemonic power. Britain was the pre-eminent industrial power, a strength that was symbolized by the global dominance of British textile. The textile industry, merchants and manufacturers, stood to benefit from free trade and played a leading role in the Anti-Corn Law League, which lobbied for free trade. It helped that the textile industry was highly organized, which Cheryl Schonhardt-Bailey explained as being due to the geographical concentration of the industry in Manchester.[10] Being geographically concentrated meant that the costs of organizing for lobbying activities were small and that the benefits of free trade, expected to be substantial, would also concentrate in the same geographical area.

As a result of the activities of the League, the prohibition on the export of machineries was lifted in 1843 and in 1846, the Corn Laws were repealed. The attraction of free trade policies can be explained in terms of the potential gains from trade and, no doubt, there was also an awareness that other countries had to have the opportunity to sell to Britain if they were to continue importing British manufactured goods. For the export-oriented textile industry in Britain, the transition toward free trade was a logical product of their international competitiveness. The lifting of the ban on export of machineries, however, also contributed to the spread of industrialization to more remote parts, such as Russia, where the process of industrialization had not yet begun.[11]

The foreign reaction to British free trade policy was that it was a clever move designed to preserve Britain's position as the premier industrialized country. Reminiscent of recent debates, nineteenth century critics of free trade in Europe and America argued that it would establish a system of unequal development, since a country specializing in manufacture — a dynamic sector — could expect to grow faster than another country specializing in primary production. The American economist Henry Carey (1793–1879) and the German economist Friedrich List (1789–1846), denounced British free trade as a ploy aimed at "... keeping the rest of the world occupied in subordinate pursuits — mere hewers of wood and drawers of water for an industrial England."[12] More recently, Marcello de Cecco argued that Adam Smith and David Ricardo did not "seem to realize that the division of labor resulting from their scheme implie[d] a faster rate of development for Britain than for those countries which [did] not specialize in the production of industrial commodities."[13]

What the critics presented as inevitable, however, failed to materialise. Instead, by the early twentieth century, Britain was a country in economic decline. This was followed by general retreat from free trade practices during the First World War and rampant protectionism during the interwar period. Disruptions to normal trade during the First World War had encouraged many countries to embark on domestic industrial production in order to satisfy unmet import demand. After the war, these new industries, threatened by resumption of imports, lobbied for, and obtained, protection from foreign competition.

In 1922, the United States introduced the Fordney–McCumber tariffs which raised average tariff levels on dutiable imports from 27 percent to 39 percent. Despite the increase in tariff levels, the Fordney-McCumber Act introduced a single tariff rate applicable to all countries. The US government, with some justification, could claim that this new was, at least, nondiscriminatory and accorded each trading partner "MFN" treatment.[14] The US also used it to extract similar MFN treatment from other countries. For example, France was pressured into granting the US the same preferential tariff rate that it extended to Germany under the Franco–German treaty of 1927. According to Cony-beare, "The Fordney-McCumber tariff from 1922 to 1929 may be regarded as a successful example of hegemonic predation that probably raised the national income of the United States by obtaining tariff concessions from the rest of the world ... ."[15]

These gains were more than reversed when the United States introduced the infamous Smoot–Hawley Tariff Act in 1930 and increased tariff levels to 53 percent. This quickly provoked widespread retaliation against American exports. As access to the American market became more restrictive, other countries introduced retaliatory tariffs. The net result was a spiralling of tariff levels and average tariff in major countries increased to around 50 percent. Some examples of post-Smoot–Hawley retaliation are listed below:

- In April 1930, Australia increased tariff levels beyond an earlier increase in June 1929.
- In July 1930, Spain, concerned with Smoot–Hawley tariffs on grapes, oranges, cork and onions, passed new prohibitive legislation.
- In June 1930, Italy increased tariffs on American and French automobile in retaliation for higher tariffs on olive oils and hats, etc.
- In September 1930 and in 1932, Canada introduced new tariffs in retaliation of American restrictions on timber and agricultural products.
- Switzerland introduced a boycott on American exports in response to American tariff on watches, shoes, etc.

Due partly to the tariff war, total world trade, between 1929 and 1933, shrank from about US$3 billion to US$1 billion,[16] and the world was plunged into the Great Depression. This may also have facilitated the march toward the Second World War, because trade contraction, declining production and rising unemployment were important factors that led states to switch idle industrial capacity to military production and to draft the army of unemployed into national armed forces. This fuelled an arms race that sent the world down the slippery slope of hostility and war. Another factor in the inexorable drift towards war was the punitive peace that had been imposed on Germany as part of the Versailles Agreement that ended the First World War. The terms of the peace agreement inflamed German discontent, which the nationalist forces exploited to their advantage. German disinterest in preserving international stability was an important factor in the escalating crisis of the period.

Even as the world hurtled towards the precipice of war, the view that free trade was beneficial for national economic welfare and for world peace was becoming part of the accepted logic. The American Secretary of State, Cordell Hull, was a leading advocate of free trade. He stated that, "... enduring peace and the welfare of nations [were] indissolubly connected with friendliness, fairness, equality and the maximum practicable degree of freedom in international trade."[17]

Still, national governments found it difficult to extricate themselves in time from their own folly. Only after the devastation of the Second World War was there a concerted attempt, on the part of British and American leaders, to create a lasting structure for a post-war liberal trading regime. The US commitment to liberal trade was especially significant. US government and business leaders recognized that free trade was in their interest, because American industry had survived the war-time destruction and could be expected to dominate world trade. National interest proved a powerful incentive for the US to assume leadership in creating a liberal trade structure. Other countries, too, had a stake in liberal trade as they hoped to rebuild their economies, and benefit by exporting to a relatively open American market.

The Post-War Structure of Liberal Trade

In the post-war period, support for liberal trade was boosted by the view that free trade was essential to world peace and prosperity.[18] The move toward free trade had begun even before the close of the Second World War. For example, in the Atlantic Charter, signed in August 1941, the Allied Powers committed themselves to "... endeavor ... to further the enjoyment of all States, great or small, victor or vanquished, of access on equal terms to trade and raw materials of the world which are needed for their economic prosperity."[19]

Multilateral negotiations on promoting liberal trade began in 1946. At the final negotiating conference known as the Havana Conference (1948), 56 countries were represented and agreed to the Havana Charter. The Havana Charter emphasized the "balanced growth" of the world economy and a revival of the world economy based on market forces. It agreed to establish an International Trade Organization (ITO) which would supplement the International Monetary Fund and the International Bank for Reconstruction and Development that had been established following the Bretton-Woods (New Hampshire) agreement. The ITO was to be a rule-oriented institution that would strictly enforce trade liberalization. Deviant members could be expelled from the ITO and subject to sanctions. It was felt that the force of sanctions would compel all states to abide by the rules. The ITO stipulated that a free trade regime was to be realized by 1952. It was agreed that voting within the ITO would be based on "one state one vote," despite American demands for weighted voting that would ensure its dominance over the ITO. This was rejected by 35 of the 56 countries at the Havana Conference.

Almost immediately, the ITO came under intense criticism within the US. Business groups objected that the ITO would regulate private business practices. Others objected that the ITO rules would not apply equally to the developing countries which could introduce and maintain protectionist policies in their development objectives. Much weightier was the criticism that the ITO was a supranational organization that would compromise US sovereignty and independence by making American trade policy subject to an international organization not controlled by the United States. The US Congress indicated its disapproval of the International Trade Organization and this effectively scuttled its establishment, because the Congress, not the president, had jurisdiction over matters of international trade. According to Jeffrey Schott, the Havana Charter was subject to criticism "both from the 'perfectionists' who thought its provisions are flawed, and from the 'protectionists' who increasingly clamored for safeguards for national trading interests."[20] Because of strong domestic opposition to the ITO, the US government decided against submitting the agreement to the Congress for ratification, knowing that Congress would not approve it.[21] Instead of the ITO, the General Agreement on Tariffs and Trade (GATT) became the main vehicle for liberalization of international trade after the War.

The General Agreement on Tariffs and Trade

The GATT was signed in October 1947 by eight countries and its primary function was to record the ITO agreements. Unlike a formal organization that states might join as members, it was simply a treaty with contracting parties. Over time, however, the GATT acquired a small secretariat and became both a multilateral agreement and an "international organiza- tion."[22] The function of the GATT Secretariat was to provide support facilities for the various negotiating rounds to reduce trade barriers. Accession to the GATT was open to countries that embraced the dual principles of open markets and decentralized decision making. Since it was only intended as a temporary mechanism until the ITO had become a reality, it inevitably was a less complete document.[23]

The GATT system was based on two main rules. The first was its insistence on multilateral Most Favored Nation treatment (Article 1) which proscribed bilateral deals in favor of multilateral agreements which did not discriminate against any contracting party of the GATT.

To promote multilateralism and non-discrimination, Article One, the most favored nation (MFN) clause, required that where bilateral negotia- tions and agreements lowered tariffs between two countries, the reduced tariff should be multilateralized and available to all exporters of that product. This was to prevent trade benefits from being granted on a preferential basis to only a few countries. It ensures, what Kenneth Dam called, the "spillover effect." Thus, all contracting parties of the GATT benefited when one country lowered its tariffs as a result of negotiations with another country. The same principle, of course, also applied when one country decided to increase existing tariff levels. Provision for increasing tariff levels was contained in Article 19 of the Agreement, known as the safeguard clause.[24] The MFN clause had three exceptions:

1. pre-existing preferential trading arrangements were excluded from the MFN clause. Thus Britain was allowed to maintain preferences granted to former colonies under the British imperial preferences. The GATT also allowed for new preferences to be granted to developing countries, such as the GSP privileges granted by the US and other developed countries;
2. customs unions and free trade areas were also exempted from the MFN conditions. The reason behind this was the assumption that free trade areas would gradually expand and facilitate the establishment of global free trade. Under this exclusion, free trade agreements within the EC, for example, need not be extended to non-EC countries;
3. a new contracting party to the GATT could also be denied the MFN privileges by existing members. When Japan joined the GATT in 1955, 14 member countries denied the MFN privileges on grounds of undesirable low wage competition.

The second important rule was that of national treatment (Article 3) which prohibited states from discriminating against imports once these had entered the domestic market. Needless to say the rules and norms of behavior were not always faithfully observed by the the GATT-contracting parties. The US, for example, has had a long standing dispute with the Japanese governments on grounds that the Japanese government procurement policies discriminated against imported goods.

In so far as adjustments to trading imbalances were concerned, the American negotiators obtained their preferred outcomes. The rules on trade adjustment formed part of the Bretton Woods agreement which established the postwar monetary order. During the negotiations, Lord Keynes, the British negotiator, had argued that adjustment should be required of both surplus and deficit countries, that surplus countries should use monetary or fiscal policies to increase imports and that deficit countries should use policies to reduce domestic demand and increase exports. The US resisted this suggestion, fully expecting the US to continue as the surplus country, and forced a decision rule that required only deficit countries to implement adjustment policies. The US was thus spared, at least for the time being, from having to alter the level of domestic economic activity and from having to implement painful adjustment policies for reasons of international trade. The burden of adjustment was conveniently shifted to deficit countries. Ironically however, when the US trade balance moved into deficit in the 1960s, there was no attempt to introduce adjustment policies to correct the payments imbalance. Instead, the US government argued that its deficits were the result of closed foreign markets rather than uncompetitive American products. The obvious solution, then, was to pry open foreign markets which would restore the US trade to a surplus position. This belief was one reason why the US pressed ahead with the Kennedy Round of trade negotiations to further reduce global tariff levels (see below).

Like the abortive ITO before it, the GATT had a "one state, one vote" principle and decisions required a majority vote. In practice, however, trade negotiations observed the rule of general consensus. Amendments to the GATT required a two-third majority of the contracting parties except in the case of the MFN clause; the escape clause (Article 19) and the amendments clause (Article 30) which required unanimity. Despite the egalitarian nature of the GATT, it was more palatable to the US because it contained clear assurances that western interests would dominate. It did not contain provisions favored by the developing countries and which had been included in the Havana Charter, such as the provisions on economic development, commodity agreements and business practices considered unfavorable by the developing countries.[25] In 1965, however, an amendment and addition to the GATT, Part 4 of the Agreement, did provide for special consideration to be given the developing countries in, for example, stabilizing commodity prices and improving access to markets in developed countries for their processed and manufactured exports.

One of the principal objectives of the GATT was to replace the more pernicious quota restrictions with tariffs, which were less restrictive of international trade. Thus, as Bhagwati stated, the GATT was based on a "fix rule" principle rather than on "fix quantity" principle. Of course, there were clear expectations that tariff levels would be progressively reduced. Two exceptions to this, however, permitted states to introduce quota restrictions.

The GATT negotiators chose to consider agricultural commodities separately and focused mainly on manufactured goods trade. The GATT principles were not extended to agricultural commodities and many countries, like Japan, continued to maintain strict quota restrictions on some agricultural products. The GATT also allowed states to introduce quota restrictions for balance of payments reasons, because quotas were considered more effective in reducing imports and, therefore, in achieving payments balance. The US had originally insisted that all quotas be abolished. If accepted, this would have been advantageous to the US since it was also the largest exporter of primary products. Other countries, however, rejected this for balance of payments reasons. The result was a compromise in which all states agreed to end quota restrictions eventually but were permitted such restrictions as long as these could be justified on grounds of payments imbalance.[26]

Apart from the exceptions, an "escape clause" (Article 19) permitted a country to re-introduce higher tariffs, albeit on a nondiscriminatory basis, if it could demonstrate that an earlier tariff concession had resulted in serious injury to domestic industry. It was intended as a temporary relief although most tariff increases under Article 19 were, in fact, never rescinded. Article 19 also provided that if negotiations were unsuccessful, the country seeking to invoke Article 19 could unilaterally suspend tariff concessions. In this case, however, the affected party also had the right to suspend concessions of approximate equal value. To invoke Article 19, a country had to demonstrate causation between a tariff concession and injury to domestic industry. The burden of proof was difficult to establish and, consequently, led to unilateral or bilateral measures, outside of the GATT, to restrict trade, as in the case of the US–Japan auto dispute of the early 1980s which resulted in a Japanese decision to exercise voluntary export restraint (VER).

Trade Liberalizing Achievements of the GATT

The GATT's liberal achievements have come from eight multilateral tariff negotiating rounds. As a measure of its success, it might be mentioned

Table 2.1.   The GATT negotiating rounds.

Round	Year	Countries	Trade Covered
Geneva (Switzerland)	1947	23	US$10 b
Annecy (France)	1949	33	N.A.
Torquay	1950–1951	34	N.A.
Geneva	1955–1956	22	US$2.5 b
Dillon (Geneva)	1961	45	US$4.9 b
Kennedy	1962–1967	48	US$40.0 b
Tokyo	1973–1979	99	US$155.0 b
Uruguay	1986–1993	107	[1]

Note: [1] It has been estimated that, over a ten-year period, the Uruguay Round will lead to annual global GNP expansion of US$230 billion and merchandise trade expansion of US$745 billion.

that whereas, in 1947, average tariff on manufactured goods in developed countries was roughly 47 percent, in the 1980s, this was reduced to under 5 percent.

The Kennedy Round was the first major attempt to liberalize world trade. It began with an across the board tariff cut of 50 percent followed by negotiations to adjust tariff levels. The end result was that 30 percent of the dutiable imports of the major participants were left untouched by tariff reductions and approximately a third of the reductions on the remaining imports were of less than 50 percent.

The US government pushed for the Kennedy Round in the belief that freer trade would help the US overcome its weak export position and restore confidence in the US dollar. It successfully persuaded the Congress to accept the "fast track" option to ensure quick ratification of any resulting agreement without amendments to any individual aspect of the trade deal. This made Congressional ratification of any agreement more of a formality and reassured other negotiating countries that difficult negotiations, once completed, would not be doomed by a recalcitrant Congress insisting upon specific amendments and changes.

The Kennedy Round was followed by the Tokyo Round which began in 1973 and was scheduled for completion in 1975. The Tokyo Round took much longer to conclude because of the difficult nature of issues and because of global economic turbulence, such as the two oil crises, currency devaluation and general stagflationary conditions. Moreover, because of persistent American trade deficits, the domestic support base that had been instrumental in the success of earlier rounds had weakened and there was little political will to pursue liberalization. Between 1967 and 1975, the American Congress refused to give the president the authority to press ahead with a trade deal and, consequently, trade negotiations made little headway during this period.[27] Only later when fast track was approved did negotiations begin in earnest. The Round was only brought to a successful completion in April 1979.

The primary concern of negotiators in the Tokyo Round was non-tariff barriers (NTBs). Although tariff cuts were also significant in percentage terms, tariff levels were generally low to begin with. Tariff rates for all industrial products for the United States, the European Community and Japan were between 5.5 percent to 6.6 percent and tariff cuts for industrial goods was about 33 percent to be phased in over an eight-year period.

The Tokyo Round also resulted in a number of agreements and understanding among select group of countries on issues of specific interest to them. For example, the Agreement on Trade in Civil Aircraft involved only 39 countries. Some of the other Agreements were on technical barriers to trade (66 countries), government procurement (56 countries), and import licensing procedures (66 countries). Seven of the agreements contained precise obligations on the countries that had agreed to ratify them and these are referred to as "codes."

The government procurement code detailed the rules/procedures for competitive bidding on government contracts with a view to give foreign contractors national treatment. However, not all areas of government procurement were covered by these codes, the main exception being in the areas of national security and defense. The target country for opening up the process of government procurement was Japan, which had a long history of denying foreign companies treatment equal to domestic suppliers. At one time, the Chairman of Nippon Telephone and Telegraph (NTT), the domestic telecommunications giant had arrogantly brushed aside criticisms, and American pressure to buy US telecommunication products by saying that all the US had to offer were "mops and buckets." After the Tokyo Round agreements, NTT procurements were gradually opened up to foreign competitions.

The issue of state subsidy was important in the interest of ensuring a level field for exporters from all countries. Government subsidies to industries and firm essentially enhance the competitiveness of a firm or industry by socializing some of the costs. This gives exporters of subsidized products the ability to undercut competitors without subsidies. The problem is that nearly all countries provide some form of subsidy to domestic producers.

The subsidies code agreed to in the Tokyo Round distinguished between export subsidies and subsidies "for the promotion of social and economic policy objectives."[28] Whereas the existing GATT subsidy clause stipulated that no new subsidies were to be allowed for non-primary products, the new code prohibited export subsidies for non-agricultural products. This modestly strengthened the GATT. Although no export subsidies are allowed, it remained difficult to distinguish between the two types and subsidies, in various forms, continued to be offered. The following examples give an indication of the subsidies problem in the contemporary period:

- In the five-year period to 1982, the EC gave US$30 billion in subsidies to the steel industry.
- In 1982, Japan announced a US$750 million plan to develop the next generation computer.
- Both the US and the EC provided extensive and increasing subsidies to agricultural products.

Uruguay Round

The period from the late 1970s to the end of the 1980s was marked by a resurgence of protectionist sentiment in some western industrialized countries, most prominently the United States. Protectionism in the US stemmed from a persistent trade deficit and perceptions that other trading countries were exploiting relative open markets in the US while denying American exporter access to their own markets. Sections of the business community, displaced workers, and legislators chafed at the "unfairness" of international trade and sought to rectify the situation by demanding a level playing field. Disaffected groups insisted that the US government, for instance, abandon its commitment to liberal trade in favor of reciprocity and protection for domestic sectors adversely affected by foreign imports.

The protectionist sentiment was strongest in the Congress, sections of the public, business, and mass media. The US administration, however, remained committed to liberal trade principles. While there were some deviations from the established rules of liberal trade, there was no wholesale questioning of the trade regime. The US government recognized that any reversal of the hard fought gains would be detrimental to the long-term prospects of the US, as well as the world economy.

To stem the tide of protectionism, in September 1986, trade ministers from 90 countries, meeting at Punta del Este, Uruguay, issued a declaration launching the Uruguay Round of trade negotiations.[29] In doing so, the objective was to restore confidence in the GATT as relevant to trade in the 1990s. It was expected that negotiations would help contain the crisis of protectionism that threatened to erode the achievements of the past, incorporate into the GATT system those sectors, like agriculture, that had previously been excluded from the GATT purview, and formulate new rules and guidelines to deal with a more complex and globalized trading world.

The Round began with an agreement on "standstill" and "rollback." A Surveillance Body was set up to maintain a moratorium (standstill) on trade restriction and facilitate the dismantling (rollback) of protectionist measures. The agreement, however, was only partially respected. In the period between September 1986 and November 1990, 25 possible violations of the standstill commitment were brought to the attention of the Surveillance but only six were successfully resolved. The process of the GATT initiated rollback of protectionism produced even fewer results.[30] Even if less than salutary, standstill and rollback were worthy principles in focusing the attention of the world community and as a moral deterrent to flagrant violations. The Punta del Este Declaration set up three specialized committees to oversee the negotiating process:

1. Trade Negotiations Committee (TNC). This body had overall responsibility for the Round;
2. Group of Negotiations on Goods (GNG). This committee oversaw the 14 negotiating committees established in January 1987 to lower trade restrictions on goods trade. It reported to the TNC;
3. Group of Negotiations on Services (GNS). The mandate of this group was to promote liberalization of services trade. This group also reported to the TNC.

The negotiating agenda was an ambitious attempt to broaden the scope of the GATT and to include international trade in services and agricultural commodities. The wide negotiating agenda, however, complicated the work of the trade negotiators and while the Round was scheduled to conclude in 1990, agreement was delayed until 1993. One explanation for the delay might be the large membership base of the GATT and the attendant difficulties of reaching consensus. At the time of the Kennedy Round, the GATT members numbered 53 countries but the Uruguay Round negotiations involved around 100 countries. However, although the expanded membership base complicated the task of negotiators, agreement in the Uruguay Round, was held up not by a majority of the members but by a few, yet large and influential, trade actors.

The Uruguay Round was completed in December 1993. If the provisions are faithfully implemented by the signatory countries, it is estimated that over a ten-year period, the deal would add US$230 billion to world GNP and lead to a merchandise trade expansion of US$745 billion.[31] There was agreement also by the developed countries to phase out the Multifibres Arrangement (MFA) over a ten-year period, on the proviso that developing countries, like India, phased out tariffs on Western imports. The MFA had regulated trade in textiles by establishing quotas on exports and its inclusion in the liberal trade system was a major breakthrough for developing countries. Unlike in earlier Rounds, the developing countries played a much more active role in the Uruguay Round in order to realize some of their objectives. The GATT had operated much like a rich man's club because while it offered some concessions to developing countries, such as the Generalized System of Preferences (GSP),[32] it failed to promote liberalization in areas of greatest interest, such as textiles. Developing country interest in promoting a more balanced liberal trade structure can be partly attributed to the debt crisis of the early 1980s and the IMF structural adjustment programs, which had forced them to liberalize their trade policies. In turn, this encouraged them to try and secure a better deal, through the GATT, for their own export commodities.

Another important achievement was in agriculture which had previously been kept out of the GATT system. Negotiations on agricultural liberalization were the most contentious and came close to completely undermining any agreement. Finally, there was agreement on the establishment of the World Trade Organization (WTO), as a successor to the GATT and to police the accord and settle trade disputes.

Liberalization of Agricultural Trade

As a trading sector, agricultural products constitute only around 13 percent of total world trade. However, with the incorporation of agriculture into the GATT framework, agriculture trade is expected to grow significantly and it is not surprising that much of the anticipated welfare gains of the Uruguay Round liberalization will be the result of liberalization of agriculture trade.

The previous exclusion of agriculture from the GATT negotiations was necessitated by domestic political sensitivities in the European Union (EU),[33] the United States, and Japan. The Japanese government, for example, insisted on protecting domestic rice production on grounds of food security — a critical component of Japan's so-called "comprehensive national security." The EU also was highly protectionist and provided generous subsidies to farmers under the Common Agriculture Policy (CAP). The CAP helped maintain high domestic prices through state purchase of agricultural outputs and through other subsidies, which encouraged farmers to produce in excess of domestic demand. The resulting surplus production was, in turn, disposed in third country market with the help of export subsidies.

The aggressive EU export strategy became a source of irritation for American farm producers who found their traditional export market undercut by aggressive European policies. In retaliation, the US government increased subsidy payments to its farmers to counter sub-sidized exports from the EU. With the help of these subsidies, American exporters, poached traditional export markets of Australian and other agricultural exporters. Unable to match the EU or the US in subsidies, these countries, in 1986, formed the Cairns Group of Fair Traders[34] to campaign for subsidy-free liberal trade in agriculture.

This subsidy war was costly and, according to OECD calculations, agriculture support policies, in 1989, cost consumers and tax payers in OECD countries roughly US$251 billion.[35] Neither side, however, had the political will to step back. In December 1990, the deadline for completing the Uruguay Round expired with a wide chasm separating the US and the EU. Intermittent negotiations continued even after the deadline had expired but produced no real breakthrough. The US government, supported by the Cairns Group, insisted on a 75 percent cut in internal support and border protection and a 90 percent cut in export subsidies whereas the EU was willing to concede no more than a 30 percent reduction. The two sides were also locked in disagreement on the appropriate base years for these reductions.[36]

European resistance was spearheaded by France, the world's second largest exporter of agricultural products. For employment reasons, the French government felt compelled to defend and protect its farming community from more efficient agricultural producers. Agriculture was also an important source of employment for several other EU countries and not easy to liberalize, given existing high levels of unemployment. The importance of agriculture as a source of employment is shown in the table below.

Eventually, the American Congress, frustrated by lack of progress established a new deadline of 15 December 1993 for fast-track approval of any agreement. Fast track authority is considered important in inter-national negotiations because without it, the Congress can examine and veto specific aspects of an agreement and jeopardize ratification of a complex set of agreements. The threat to withdraw Congressional fast-track authority from the President renewed international efforts to reach an agreement. In the shadow of this "ultimatum," it was ironically an American concession that made agreement possible. Negotiations were

Table 2.2. Agriculture in EU countries.

West Germany	Percent of Population in Agriculture in 1986	Contribution of Agriculture to National Output in 1986
France	7.3	4.0
West Germany	5.3	2.0
UK	2.6	2.0
Netherlands	4.8	4.0
Portugal	21.9	10.0
Spain	16.1	6.0
Italy	10.9	5.0
Ireland	15.8	14.0
Greece	28.5	17.0
Denmark	6.2	6.0
Belgium	2.9	2.0
Luxemborg	4.0	–

Source: El-Agraa, A.M., "The Common Agricultural Policy," in El-Agraa, A.M. (ed.), *Economics of the European Community*. 3rd ed., Philip Allan, Hertfordshire, 1990, p. 189.

concluded by the December deadline and the final agreement was signed by the GATT member countries in April 1994 in Morrocco.

The final accord stipulated that non-tariff barriers to agriculture trade be replaced by tariffs and that all tariffs, including existing tariffs, be reduced by an average of 36 percent, over six years, in the case of developed countries and 24 percent, over ten years, in the case of developing countries. The developed countries also agreed to reduce budgetary outlays on export subsidies to a level 36 percent below the 1986–1990 base period over six years and to reduce volume of subsidized exports by 21 percent over six years.[37] Developing countries had to reduce export subsidies by 24 percent and subsidized exports by 14 percent over the same period.

On new issues, the Uruguay Round extended the GATT to include services trade, foreign investments (TRIMs, or Trade Related Investment Measures), and intellectual property rights (TRIPs, or Trade Related Aspects of Intellectual Property Rights). These were issues of particular concern to developed OECD countries because they account for 84 percent of all services exports and 90 percent of all investment flows. The developing countries, on the other hand, opposed the inclusion of these sectors, firstly, because of a fear that their inefficient domestic services sector, such as banking, insurance and telecommunications, would be swamped by western multinationals; and secondly, because they considered investment controls and other TRIMs as essential to their developmental objectives. The issue of TRIMs is discussed in Chapter six but, briefly, the agreement specified that developed countries had to remove all non-conforming TRIMs within two years, the developing countries within five years, and the least developed countries within seven years.[38]

The importance of services trade had increased progressively through the postwar period and in 1990, global services trade was worth US$820 billion, or 23 percent of total merchandise trade. Moreover, for individual developed countries, the services component of economic output and exports had increased substantially to alter the structure of their economy. In 1993, for example, services generated 74 percent of American gross domestic product, and produced a balance-of-trade surplus of US$55.7 billion against a deficit of US$132.4 billion for goods trade.[39] For developed countries, in particular, a more liberalized regime of services trade was essential to enhance GATT, not only because services were an important trading category, but also because services and goods trade had become interlinked, with services accounting for a sizeable component of the value of all goods. This meant that export competitiveness of goods, depended on liberalized services trade.

On services, the Uruguay Round produced a *quid pro quo* agreement giving developing countries more liberal rules on textiles trade in exchange for agreement to include services, and foreign investment, within GATT. The General Agreement on Trade in Services (GATS) emphasized the dual principles of transparency of trade regulations and most favored nation treatment. At the same time, countries were permitted to exempt certain services from the MFN treatment, provided that exemptions were reviewed at the end of five years and limited to no more than ten years. The agreement on services was modest compared to initial expectations but significant in, progressively, realizing a more complete trade regime. Separate negotiations later produced a Basic Telecoms Agreement and an Information Technology Agreement.

The issue of intellectual property rights had been a running sore in relations between developed and developing countries because of allegation that developing countries failed to respect property rights, such as trademarks and copyright, resulting in loss of incomes for owners of such rights. Treaties guaranteeing such rights have existed since the 1960s[40] but enforcement has always been a problem. In the Uruguay Round Agreement on the Trade Related Aspects of Intellectual Property Rights, countries agreed to make wilful trademark counterfeiting and infringement of commercial copyright criminal offences. The Agreement covered a range of intellectual property such as copyright, computer programs, trade marks, designs, patents and layout of integrated circuits but also geographical indications (to identify area of origin, especially for wines).

GATT Reform and the WTO

The Uruguay Round agreement also resulted in institutional reforms in the GATT structure. The necessity of institutional overhaul can be traced to a number of factors. According to Lutz, reform was an important step toward minimizing the "de-liberalization of international trade."[41] The rise of protectionism and retreat from liberal achievements provided useful incentives to reinvigorate free trade principles by strengthening the rules.

Also, as institutional economics points out, the effectiveness of institutions in facilitating economic transactions depends on their congruity with existing realities. In the trade regime, GATT attempted to fill the void left by the ITO and progressively acquired a semi-institutional status but as a loosely structural body, it was not the ideal mechanism for managing global economic relations. A more formal institutional arrangement was considered appropriate to deal with the new realities. Blackhurst argued that with globalization, "... multilateral organizations which provide the institutional and legal frameworks for these cross-border commercial activities need to evolve in ways that allow them to continue to keep pace with the changing conditions."[42] Bringing the GATT into the global age was, therefore, another reason for changes to the structure of liberal trade.

It was obvious also that the GATT had failed a majority of the developing countries whose main exports such as textiles, continued, regulated by mechanisms outside the GATT.[43] In its conceptualization and practice, the GATT operated essentially as a rich man's club. As developing economies became more organized and active and with the addition of new transitional economies, reform was inevitable. Finally, an important source for reform of the international trade structure was a dispute settlement mechanism that did not inspire confidence in GATT's ability to deal with trade disputation. These factors combined to create a push for change. In the previous section, I have already discussed the push to contain protectionism and expand the coverage of trade rules by incorporating new sectors like agriculture trade, services, and textiles. In this section, I will limit myself mainly to the following 2 items on the reform agenda. These were how to:

1. internalize dispute settlement procedures, and;
2. ensure transparency of, and compliance with, rules.

Several scholars have presented possible reform measures to strengthen the rules-oriented GATT regime.[44] Jackson suggested that the GATT had to be empowered to function as an independent and active player in trade matters. He emphasized the importance of strengthening the dispute settlement procedures of the GATT which would encourage dispute settlement "primarily by reference to the existing agreed rules rather than simply by reference to the relative economic or other power which the disputants possess."[45]

Jackson argued that the main weakness of the GATT was the provisional nature of the agreement. To overcome this weakness Jackson emphasized an umbrella organization for international trade, like a World Trade Organization (WTO) which could focus on institutional and procedural issues while leaving all substantive matters to the GATT. The WTO could also serve as a service and support structure for the GATT trade negotiations.[46] To ensure that the WTO did not suffer the same fate as the International Trade Organization in the early postwar period, Jackson proposed that the WTO should possess only an administrative function rather than be responsible for substantive trade obligations. As such, a WTO would not replace the GATT but rather supplement it in ways that gave it greater organizational and structural cohesion.

In the Uruguay Round discussions on GATT reform, both the European Community and Canada tabled proposals for a WTO.[47] The outcome was to approve the establishment of a WTO to replace the GATT. Of course, a new organization and stricter rules may not be the complete solution to protectionism but as The Economist observed, "... a purposeful and influential [WTO] can put up more of a fight than one that is badly run and lacking in confidence."[49] To facilitate the operations of the WTO, established in January 1995,[48] many of the existing rules were revised to encourage the contracting parties to rely on formally sanctioned dispute resolution procedures.

In keeping with the original distaste for legalism, the GATT's dispute settlement procedures had relied on negotiations and conciliation rather than on legal adjudication. According to Edward McGovern, "In the first decades of its existence, particularly under the tutelage of its Director-General, Eric Wyndham-White, there was a deliberate attempt to avoid anything smacking of legalism, an approach illustrated by the complete absence until recent years of any post of legal advisor in the GATT secretariat."[50] This system may have suited the early GATT, when it was a small institution composed largely of western countries, with similar cultural, social, political and economic backgrounds, but the increase in membership and compositional diversity created a need for more rule-based adjudication procedures.

The GATT dispute settlement mechanism was contained in Articles XXII and XXIII of the General Agreement. Until the end of 1986, Article XXII dispute settlement procedures had been used only on about ten occasions whereas 100 complaints had been filed under Article XXIII.[51] Under Article XXIII, a dispute arose when one country alleged another to be guilty of nullification or impairment of a GATT benefit or an impediment to realization of a GATT benefit. In the initial stages of a dispute, Article XXIII provided for bilateral consultations but if the dispute persisted, a special panel could be set up to examine the complaint. The panel report was submitted to the GATT Council for formal adoption if the panel failed to convince the disputants to accept its ruling. The panel report had to be unanimous and the adoption of the report by the GATT Council also required unanimity. This meant that the "losing" party could easily prevent adoption of the report by the Council. However, insofar as success of the dispute settlement procedures was concerned, of the 100 cases referred to a panel, only two eluded successful resolution.

Nevertheless, dissatisfaction remained that the procedures were time-consuming and cumbersome and that by the time a report had been prepared, the affected industry could suffer serious injury. This explains the resort to dispute settlement outside of GATT, such as bilaterally negotiated voluntary export restraint agreements and other neoprotectionist measures. Another source of problem was the proliferation of dispute settlement procedures which led to confusion. As part of the Tokyo Round agreements, various countries agreed on Codes governing specific areas and many of these Codes had their own dispute settlement procedures that varied from those specified in the GATT.

The WTO streamlined dispute resolution by establishing the Dispute Settlement Body (DSB) to hear disputes between members. To expedite the resolution of disputes, it also imposed time limits on the establishment of a panel to hear a dispute and on the adoption of a panel report by the DSB. The agreement stripped members of their earlier right to veto the establishment of a panel or to decline to abide by rulings handed down by a GATT panel on dispute resolution. There is, however, an appeals mechanism which can be invoked by either the winning or losing party. Although the WTO was given no enforcement powers, the agreement provided for retaliation if a member country failed to comply with rulings within a specified time limit.[52] In 1995, the DSB was asked to rule on 20 trade disputes, a number that was far greater than what GATT ever had to deal with in one year.[53] On average, the GATT dealt with six disputes a year but the WTO, in its first two years, dealt with 40 disputes a year. In 1997, the total number of consultations, panels, and appeals of trade disputes numbered around 70. This is clear testimony of the effectiveness of the dispute resolution process of the WTO.

It would be naive to assume that reform of GATT rules and procedures alone might prevent a resurgence of protectionism. The Director General of the GATT, Peter Sutherland, hailing the establishment of the WTO as a victory for liberal trade, acknowledged that we "have not heard the last of 'managed trade,' an idea which is the antithesis of an open multilateral system." The appeal of protectionism is inevitable under adverse economic conditions and the fact that modern states have assumed special roles in achieving certain employment and inflation objectives. The founders of the GATT recognized that protectionism could not be entirely avoided and allowed for temporary protectionist measures under Article 19. However, they attached strict conditions which rendered Article 19, the so-called "safeguard clause," relatively unattractive to member states. To invoke article 19 and protect a domestic industry from trade-related injury, a state had to demonstrate serious injury and compensate the affected country by providing trade liberalization of equivalent value in a different product category. In the absence of suitable compensation, Article 19 permitted the affected country to impose retaliatory and countervailing trade restriction. Moreover, Article 19 required that resort to protectionism had to be on a multilateral basis rather than targeted against specific exporting countries.

In order to simplify Article 19 and pre-empt states from bypassing the GATT provisions, Joachim Zietz suggested relaxing the requirement on a claimant to demonstrate "serious injury" as a result of imports before safeguards could be invoked. Instead of trying to grapple with the nebulous concept of "serious injury," he argued that a more productive approach would be to allow each country to define injury but, at the same time, restrict retaliation to tariff measures that were also temporary. This, he argued, would make the GATT more comprehensive, not only in promoting liberal trade but also in sanctioning deviations from it.[54]

The agreement that was reached established criteria which must be considered in assessing the impact of imports. The agreement defined "serious injury" or the "threat of serious injury" as significant or clearly imminent "overall impairment in the position of a domestic industry," which had to be based on facts and not on allegations, conjecture or remote possibility. On the process of determining injury, it was decided that the criteria had to be clearly defined and made public, and that all interested parties had to be given the opportunity to give evidence before the relevant national authority charged with determining the applicability of safeguard action. The agreement suspended the automatic right to retaliate for the first three years of a safeguards measure, "... providing an incentive for countries to use GATT safeguard rules when import-related, serious injury problems occur."[55]

The agreement also contained injunctions upon states to discontinue measures like voluntary export restraints and orderly marketing agreements, which bypassed GATT-sanctioned protection (Article 19). Instead, members agreed to rely on sanctioned mechanisms if protection for domestic industry became necessary. The agreement required existing VERs to be phased out within a four-year period and prohibited their future use. Another achievement was to tighten the safeguard clause by requiring that safeguard actions not exceed a maximum of eight years. This was to prevent states from resorting to Article 19 protection for indefinite time periods.

The anti-dumping provisions of the GATT were also strengthened. The main users of anti-dumping measures, such as countervailing duties, were the US, the European Union, Canada, and Australia, which together accounted for more than 90 percent of anti-dumping measures in the 1980s.[56] The frequent, and arbitrary, resort to anti-dumping measures gave the impression that the main purpose was not to retaliate against actual dumping but to protect domestic industries. The new WTO anti-dumping codes are more stringent and designed to ensure that anti-dumping proceedings were conducted in an "unbiased and objective" way. However, in contrast to dispute resolution mechanisms, the agreement refused to empower the WTO to overrule a national finding of dumping even if a panel reached a different conclusion. Nonetheless, the amended code did tighten rules in other areas. It requires national authorities to affirmatively ascertain the degree of support for a petition to begin anti-dumping investigation. Under the new conditions, anti-dumping investigation can only begin if at least a quarter of the affected industry supported such a move. It also provided for a fairer method for constructing values for anti-dumping purposes.[57] In the past, the United States for example, assumed an 8 percent profit margin in constructing the value of a product, which was high even by domestic standards and disadvantaged foreign manufacturers that operated on lower profit margins. The new code requires countries to use actual data in constructing value but left ambiguous what a state could do when actual data was unavailable. The anti-dumping code also stipulates that anti-dumping measures can be introduced only if the dumping margin was greater than 2 percent of the export price.[58] The standard American practice had been determine dumping if the margin exceeded 0.5 percent. The new rules mean that products with low dumping margins will escape anti-dumping duties.

It is obvious that the newly formed WTO has many additional responsibilities and functions than its predecessor. However, its administrative support structure was deliberately kept small and its funding was not increased commensurate to its additional tasks. Richard Blackhurst noted two main reasons why the larger member countries were unwilling to empower the WTO with a larger secretariat. First, a larger secretariat would require an increase in their financial contribution, based on shares of world trade, and second, the benefit of a larger and more active WTO would accrue mainly to the smaller countries which, in the absence of an activist WTO to champion all the diverse interest, were more pliant and susceptible to western influence.[59]

Moreover, the US, because of budgetary constraints and domestic political reasons, such as Congressional hostility to funding large multilateral institutions, refused to countenance any increase in funding for the WTO. Funding for WTO was frozen in 1995 at 118 million Swiss francs, which the US insisted should continue into the next century. In terms of absolute and relative funding, the WTO is dwarfed by both the International Monetary Fund (IMF) and the World Bank. The WTO has an administrative budget of US$140 000 per employee compared with US$280 000 for the World Bank and US$230 000 for the IMF.[60] It is clear that the WTO cannot expect an improved budgetary situation in the near future, but will still have to prove itself to be an effective and credible trade institution.

Conclusion

The World Trade Organization marks a new beginning for global liberal trade. There is a better system in place but its success will obviously depend on voluntary compliance, by the key trading countries, of the existing rules and regulations. In the absence of enforcement powers for the WTO, the future of liberal trade depends on political commitment and readiness to eschew deviant and arbitrary practices. Still, by making trade liberalization a permanent feature of international political economy, the WTO may help restrain protectionism. In the past, in between trade negotiating rounds, the GATT was inactive, and this, according to GATT Director-General Peter Sutherland, effectively vacated the policy space to protectionists who were able to berate liberal trade principles. The WTO is, consequently, a better check against deviant tendencies.[61]

In the Uruguay Round, global corporations emerged as advocates of global liberalism in order to create a uniform operating environment across national borders. In the process leading to American ratification of the Uruguay Round agreement, global corporations played an important role, against antagonists who tried to create an impression that the agreement infringed American sovereignty by denying the US the right to resolve trade disputes according to its trade laws. For global corporations, the advantage of the Uruguay Round agreement and the GATT was partly the tariff reductions, but more important was the protection it promised against a fragmentation of the trade regime. The failure to successfully conclude the GATT round would have added to their transactions costs as a result of having to cope with segmented international regulatory regimes. Global corporations recognized the advantages of standardized regulatory policies in ensuring easier market access and argued forcefully for successful completion of the Uruguay Round negotiations.

References

1. Not surprisingly, the logic of mercantilism became less convincing as governments devised other ways of regulating money supply through credit management and monetary policies.

2. Glamann, K., "European Trade 1500–1750," in Cipolla, C. M. (ed.), *The Fontana Economic History of Europe: The Sixteenth and Seventeenth Centuries*, Collins/Fontana Books, Glasgow, 1974, p. 430.

3. Fellner, W., *Emergence and Content of Modern Economic Analysis*, McGraw-Hill Book Co. Ltd., New York, 1960, p. 37.

4. MFN and GSP are explained further below.

5. It should be mentioned that not all periods of hegemonic dominance coincide with free trade. During the seventeenth and eighteenth centuries when Dutch hegemony was unchallenged, international trade was largely governed by the dominant ideology of mercantilism. In the twentieth century, the period between the two world wars was a period of intense economic nationalism despite the fact that the US was, by all indications, a hegemonic economic power.

6. Musson, A. E., *The Growth of British Industry*, Batsford Academic and Educational Ltd., London, 1981, p. 66. There is no precise dating of when the industrial revolution started or even whether the process was more evolutionary than revolutionary.

7. On the increased availability of productive tools see, for example, McCloskey, D., "The Industrial Revolution 1780–1860: A Survey," in Mokyr, J. (ed.), *The Economics of the Industrial Revolution*, George Allen & Unwin, London, 1985, p. 57.

8. Income elasticity refers to the ratio of the percentage increase in the demand for goods or services (in our case, manufactured goods) to an increase in income.

9. Fielden, K., "The Rise and Fall of Free Trade," in Bartlett, C. J. (ed.), *Britain Pre-eminent: Studies of British Influence in the Nineteenth Century*, Macmillan, London, 1969, p. 81. The import of corn without licence had been prohibited in 1463. Restrictions on the export of corn had been introduced even earlier.

10. Schonhardt-Bailey, C., "Lessons in Lobbying for Free Trade in 19th Century Britain: To Concentrate or Not," *American Political Science Review*, Vol. 85, No. 1, March 1991.

11. Stearns, P. N., "Britain and the Spread of the Industrial Revolution," in Bartlett, C. J. (ed.), *Britain Pre-eminent: Studies of British World*

Influence in the Nineteenth Century, Macmillan and Co. Ltd., London, 1969, p. 13.

12. Semmel, B., *The Rise of Free Trade Imperialism: Classical Political Economy, the Empire of Free Trade and Imperialism 1750–1850*, Cambridge University Press, 1970, p. 207.

13. de Cecco, M., *The International Gold Standard: Money and Empire*, Frances Pinter (Publishers), London, 1984, pp. 5–6. Historically, countries that depend on production and export of primary products have fared consistently poorer than countries that produce and export manufactured goods. This is partly because prices for primary products are more unstable and susceptible to periodic or sustained slump and decline, resulting in declining terms of trade for primary producers. In 1991, for example, non-fuel commodity prices fell 15 percent in real terms which meant that these countries, to be able to maintain import levels of the previous year, would have had to export 15 percent more compared to the year before. See *World Economic Survey*, United Nations, New York, 1991, p. 57.

14. Most Favored Nation (MFN) treatment refers to a practice of nondiscriminatory trade and constitutes a central pillar, also, of the post-war GATT regime. The difference is that whereas the Fordney-McCumber tariffs introduced MFN treatment at higher levels of tariffs, the GATT system is based on MFN treatment at progressively lower levels of trade restrictions.

15. Conybeare, J. A. C., *Trade Wars: The Theory and Practice of International Commercial Rivalry*, Columbia University Press, New York, 1987, p. 240.

16. Kindleberger, C. P., *The World in Depression*.

17. See Tussie, D., 1987, pp. 9–10.

18. This proposition requires some qualification. While it may be that economic interdependence is a force for peace, it cannot be positively asserted that interdependence alone has the powers to preempt the more capricious aspect of human nature, ethnic and national conflict. In the establishment of a liberal trade regime after the war, the architects of the GATT were driven by the lessons of the Second World War. Yet, less than 50 years earlier, growing interdependence had

failed to avert the First World War. Barbara Tuchman, in her brilliant account of the onset of the First World War, stated that, "… the interlocking of finance, commerce, and other economic factors — which had been expected to make war impossible failed to function when the time came. Nationhood, like a wild gust of wind, arose and swept them aside." See Tuchman, Barbara W., *The Guns of August*, The Macmillan Company, New York, 1962, pp. 310–11. The degenerative impact of ethnic conflict remains relevant in the 1990s.

19. See, for example, Nicholson, D. F., *Australia's Trade Relations: An Outline History of Australia's Overseas Trading Arrangements*, F. W. Cheshire, Melbourne, 1955, p. 140.

20. Schott, J. J., "US Policies Toward the GATT: Past, Present, Prospective," in Rode, R. (ed.), *GATT and Conflict Management*, Westview Press, Boulder, CO, 1990, p. 25.

21. Congress did, however, ratify the Bretton-Woods agreement because it allowed for weighted voting within the IMF and IBRD. On the other hand, ITO held open the possibility that the US might be dictated upon by others and worse, by the developing countries which had been the most vocal critic of weighted voting.

22. The GATT secretariat is staffed by a relatively small staff. In the mid 1960s, the GATT Secretariat had only 179 full-time employees compared to the 773 staff members of the IMF. In 1984, the IMF Secretariat had 1 750 employees, the World Bank had 5 700 employees and GATT only 283. In 1986, the GATT Secretariat was staffed by about 400 employees.

23. The American Congress did not accept the General Agreement as a treaty obligation and while it did not object to it, there were limits to how far Congress would accept constraints on American policy making.

24. Some countries have devised ingenious ways of circumventing the non-discriminatory principle of the GATT. Japanese imports of plywood used to be classified under the two categories of "hardwood plywood" and "softwood plywood." The lower tariffs for softwood plywood effectively discriminated against the developing countries because softwood plywood, made from pine, came essentially from the

developed countries of the US and Canada. Under criticism that this was discriminatory, Japan abolished this categorization but instead introduced differential tariffs depending on the thickness of plywood, with lower tariff levels for thick plywood. This is as discriminatory as before because softwood plywood tends to be thicker than hardwood plywood. In general, developing countries criticize the developed countries for discriminating against their exports.

25. Kousoulas, D. G., *Power and Influence: An Introduction to International Relations*, p. 179.
26. See Dam, K., p. 150.
27. Kousoulis, D. G., *Power and Influence: An Introduction to International Relations*, p. 181.
28. *The GATT Negotiations and US Trade Policy*, US Congress, 1987, p. 34.
29. When the Round was brought to a completion in mid December 1993, the number of participating countries had increased to 117 countries.
30. *GATT Activities 1990*, General Agreement on Tariffs and Trade, Geneva, Switzerland, July 1991, p. 28.
31. Islam, S., "A Deal, of Sorts," *Far Eastern Economic Review*, 23 December 1993, p. 54.
32. Under the GSP program, developed countries unilaterally offered to permit duty free imports of selected commodities from developing countries. Over time, as overall tariff structures in developed countries came down to insignificant levels, duty-free status for developing countries lost most of the potential advantages.
33. In the Uruguay Round, the EC, not the individual European countries, has the negotiating authority. This is in keeping with the decision to establish a Common Market that would maintain a common external policy.
34. The Cairns Group includes Australia, Argentina, Brazil. Canada, Chile, Colombia, Fiji, Hungary, Indonesia, Malaysia, New Zealand. the Philippines, Thailand, and Uruguay.
35. *World Economic Survey 1991*, United Nations, Department of International Economic and Social Affairs, New York, 1991, p. 63.

36. *GATT Activities 1990*, General Agreement on Tariffs and Trade, Geneva, 1991, p. 35.

37. "The Final Act of the Uruguay Round — A Summary," *International Trade Forum*, No. 1, 1994, pp. 6–8.

38. The GATT Secretariat, "The Final Act of the Uruguay Round: A Summary," *International Trade Forum*, No. 1, 1994, p. 10.

39. Henkoff, R., "Service is Everybody's Business," *Fortune*, Vol. 129, No. 13, 27 June 1994, p. 33.

40. The specific treaties include the International Convention for the Protection of Performers, Producers of Phonograms and Broadcasting Organizations (Rome, 1961); the Paris Convention for the Protection of Industrial Property (Paris, 1967); and Treaty on Intellectual Property in Respect of Integrated Circuits (Washington, 1989).

41. See Lutz, James M., "GATT Reform or Regime Maintenance: Differing Solutions to World Trade Problems," *Journal of World Trade*, Vol. 25, No. 2, April 1991, p. 112.

42. Blackhurst, R., "The WTO and the Global Economy," *The World Economy*, Vol. 20, No. 5, August 1997, p. 543.

43. It should be pointed out that the aversion of developing countries to the GATT may have entered a period of diminished significance as these countries carry out trade liberalizing reforms and seek to integrate themselves into the world trading system. Some of their earlier concerns with the GATT can be related to their import substitution development strategies which are being replaced by export-oriented industrialization.

44. See, for example, Jackson, John H., *Restructuring the GATT System*, Pinter Publishers, London, 1990, and Jackson, John H., "Reflections on Restructuring the GATT," in Schott, Jeffrey J. (ed.), *Completing the Uruguay Round: A Results-Oriented Approach to the GATT Trade Negotiations, Institute for International Economics*, Washington, DC, September 1990.

45. Jackson, John H., *Restructuring the GATT System*, Pinter Publishers, London, 1990, p. 75.

46. Jackson, John H., "Reflections on Restructuring the GATT," in Schott, Jeffrey J. (ed.), *Completing the Uruguay Round: A Results-Oriented*

Approach to the GATT Trade Negotiations, Institute for International Economics, Washington, DC, September 1990, pp. 219–220.

47. Schott, Jeffrey, J., "Uruguay Round: What Can be Achieved?" in Schott, Jeffrey J. (ed.), *Completing the Uruguay Round: A Results-Oriented Approach to the GATT Trade Negotiations, Institute for International Economics*, Washington, DC, September 1990, p. 37.

48. In early 1997, the WTO had a membership of 131 countries. It had also established 28 working parties to consider membership applications from Russia, China and other countries.

49. "Son of GATT: The New World Trade Organization Needs the Right Priorities and the Right Boss," *The Economist*, 6 August 1994, p. 12.

50. McGovern, E., "Dispute Settlement in the GATT — Adjudication or Negotiation?" in Hilf, M., Francis G. Jacobs and Ernst–Ulrich Petersmann (eds.), *The European Community and GATT*, Kluwer Law and Taxation Publishers, The Netherlands, 1986, p. 74.

51. Van Bael, I., "The GATT Dispute Settlement Procedure," *Journal of World Trade*, Vol. 22, No. 4, 1988, pp. 68–69.

52. Main, Ann M., "Dispute Settlement Understanding", *Business America*, January 1994, p. 21.

53. Ruggiero, R., "Growing Complexity in International Economic Relations Demands Broadening and Deepening of the Multilateral Trading System," *WTO Focus*, No. 6, October/November 1995, p. 10.

54. Zietz, J., "Negotiations on GATT Reform and Political Incentives," *The World Economy*, Vol. 12, No. 1, March 1989, p. 46.

55. Goddin, Scott R., "Safeguards," *Business America*, January 1994, p. 18.

56. Steele, K. (ed.)., *Anti-Dumping Under the WTO: A Comparative Review*, Kluwer Law International Ltd., London, 1996, p. 3.

57. In the absence of available data on the cost structure of a commodity, which firms guard as a trade secret, national governments would resort to "constructed values" based on approximations in order to determine whether a country was guilty of dumping. Given the laxity of regulations, constructed values could easily be manipulated to

produce a positive finding of dumping which could then justify the introduction of anti-dumping measures.

58. See, for example, Leidy, M., "Antidumping: Unfair Trade or Unfair Remedy," *Finance and Development*, Vol. 32, No. 1, March 1995, p. 29. The dumping margin is defined as the percentage by which export price is below the constructed value calculated by national authorities.

59. Blackhurst, R., "The WTO and the Global Economy," *The World Economy*, Vol. 20, No. 5, August 1997, p. 539.

60. "WTO Skating on Thin Ice with Budget Freeze," *The Australian*, 7 April 1998, p. 31.

61. See *GATT Focus*, No. 105, January–February 1994, p. 6.

Chapter Three

INTERNATIONAL MONETARY RELATIONS: BRETTON WOODS AND BEYOND

A s discussed in Chapter two, the establishment of the GATT after the Second World War was designed to contain protectionism and promote negotiated trade liberalization among member countries. In the interwar period, protectionism had disrupted trade relations and, arguably, contributed to the outbreak of violence. But protectionism was not the only demon to be exorcised. Trade disruptions had resulted also from restrictions on currency convertibility, cycles of competitive devaluation, and general volatility of exchange rates. The period between the two world wars witnessed three separate exchange rate regimes: floating exchange rates between 1922–1926; fixed exchange rates between 1927–1931; and managed floating exchange rates between 1932–1936. Nominal exchange rates were four times as volatile under floating rate system as under the managed float and the rates under managed float were four times as volatile as under the fixed rate system. Real exchange rates were similarly volatile.[1] This had detrimental economic consequences because when exchange rates fluctuate wildly, prices lose their reference point, markets cease to function efficiently, and resource allocations and trade, consequently, are distorted.[2]

To prevent future recurrence of destructive competition, the British and American governments initiated discussions to create international financial stability even before the war had ended. This led to the

Bretton-Woods agreement and a regime of stable exchange rates and liberalized capital transactions to facilitate trade expansion. This system lasted until 1973, when fixed exchange rates were abandoned in favor of floating exchange rates. In the new system, exchange rates were to be determined by market forces but, in reality, governments intervened persistently to protect exchange rates they considered desirable and appropriate. Because of the pervasiveness of political intervention, the floating rate system was better known as "dirty" or "managed" float. In the mid-1980s, western governments experimented with coordinated intervention in order to achieve specific outcomes, such as a devaluation of the dollar from the high levels it had reached in the early 1980s. This restored some stability without completely sacrificing flexibility.

In this chapter, I will consider the main features of the three post-war monetary regimes, the reasons for the collapse of fixed exchange rate system, the promise and performance of flexible exchange rates, and finally the institutionalization of periodic, but imperfect, exchange rate cooperation and macroeconomic management.

The Bretton-Woods system was modeled on the gold standard of the nineteenth century, in the belief that it would introduce both certainty and stability to the international monetary system. The adoption of fixed exchange rates around a narrow band was reminiscent of fixed exchange rates under the gold standard. To understand the gold-exchange standard adopted after the Second World War, it is necessary to explain the operation of international gold standard.

The International Gold Standard

Great Britain adopted the gold standard in 1821 but gold did not become the international standard until the 1870s. Under the gold standard, individual governments agreed to abide by the following three rules:

1. define national currency units in terms of weight of gold;
2. where notes were issued in addition to gold coins, the notes had to be freely convertible into gold; and
3. allow free import and export of gold.[3]

The advantage of the gold standard, in its pure form, as pointed out by David Hume in the eighteenth century, was that it produced automatic adjustments to trading imbalances. In the deficit country, a surplus of imports over exports meant that the additional imports had to be financed out of available gold stock. The decline in gold reserves would reduce the supply of money, reduce consumption and imports and by reducing prices of domestic products, increase their international competitiveness. Over time, exports would increase and imports decline to hasten trade adjustment. The reverse would happen in the surplus country where the inflow of gold would increase the supply of money and domestic prices which would consequently reduce export competitiveness and increased domestic income would boost imports, reducing the level of surplus. Another advantage of the gold standard was its anti-inflationary bias since money supply could not increase without a concomitant increase in gold reserves. By the same logic, trade growth, under the gold standard, was theoretically limited by growth in international liquidity. Fortuitously, in the nineteenth century, world gold stocks kept pace with demand for liquidity, mainly due to new discoveries of gold in the United States, Russia, Australia and South Africa. Otherwise, shortage of gold supply might have impeded economic growth and growth of world trade.

The drawback of the gold standard was that international monetary stability was achieved at the expense of domestic economic stability because national policy makers could not insulate their economy from shocks and deflationary pressures resulting from movements in gold reserves. As a result, governments tried to avoid the discipline of market forces and, according to Ian Drummond, "The rules of the game were frequently ignored, and ... most though not all central banks had no intention of playing the gold-standard game by any particular rules."[4]

In the early twentieth century, Britain consistently avoided adjusting to trade deficits, relying instead on other countries' willingness to hold sterling as a reserve currency. The sterling had, indeed, become an acceptable reserve apart from gold.[5] The final blow to the gold standard was dealt by the First World War. Most governments, with the exception of Britain, suspended the gold standard in order to protect their domestic economy. However, Britain's adherence to the gold standard was merely a legal formality as the policies of the British government had begun to deviate from the essential rules of the gold standard even before the outbreak of the War in 1914. Moreover, although the British government introduced no formal barriers to the export of gold, it discouraged this through moral suasion, appeals to patriotism, cumbersome procedures at the Bank of England and various other measures.[6]

During the war, Britain's position as the premier economic power was irrevocably lost due to concentration on the war effort. With disruptions to British exports, other countries turned to alternative sources or began import substitution industrialization. The war was a boon to the US as the alternative source of supply and also led to nascent industrialization in Latin America, Canada and several other former markets for British exports. Britain failed to regain these markets after the war and domestic economic problems and structural adjustment delayed its return to the gold standards until 1925. In 1931, however, Britain was forced to abandon the gold standard altogether after it sustained gold losses.

Although the US was ideally placed to replace Britain after the First World War, American policies did not reflect its international responsibility. Worse still, the US government insisted that Britain and France repay their war debts to the US because domestic opinion in the US would not countenance any loan cancellation. Both France and Britain, in turn, insisted that Germany pay war reparations. For a while, the resulting pressure on the international monetary system was kept in check by large flow of funds from the US to Germany, which enabled it to continue payment of reparations. Unfortunately, many of the investment loans made by financial institutions in New York, the new international financial center, turned out to be speculative and without sound commercial viability. Consequently, when the stock market crashed in 1929 and flow of funds from New York dried up, Germany's problems were further compounded as it "... still had heavy reparations obligations along with sizeable debts to US bondholders."[7] Repayment of debt by Germany, Britain and France was made more difficult by American trade policy and creeping protectionism which denied these countries' an opportunity to export manufactured goods to the United States, earn dollars and repay their foreign debts. The decade of the 1930s was marked by fluctuating exchange rates and competitive devaluations as countries jostled with each other for trade advantages.[8]

Constructing a Monetary Regime

A monetary regime, according to Richard Cooper, is a "set of rules or conventions governing monetary and financial relations between countries ... A monetary regime specifies which instruments of policy may be used and which targets of policy are regarded as legitimate, including, of course, the limiting cases in which there are no restrictions on either."[9]

Negotiations between the United States and the United Kingdom were led by Lord Keynes and Harry Dexter White respectively, and began in the early 1940s. The starting point for the talks were the two plans drafted by Keynes and by White for an International Clearing Union and a Stabilization Fund.[10] Each plan reflected the respective interests of the two countries.

International Clearing Union

The ICU was intended as an international central bank with the power to issue its own currency, the bancor, that would be traded among national central banks. Each member country was to be allowed to borrow bancor, up to a specified limit, as and when balance of payments deficits required such borrowing and bancor could be used to repay international debts. The advantage of such an adjustment mechanism was that it obviated the need for contractionary economic policies and instead, allowed for continuous expansion in world trade. This reflected lessons learned from earlier experiences where trade adjustment had inevitably resulted in domestic economic deflation and hardships for the general population. The British government also proposed that responsibility for trade adjustment be shared by the surplus country which would be levied a charge on surpluses as an incentive to correct balance of payments surpluses.

The Stabilization Fund

The US rejected the British proposal for two reasons. First it argued that the ICU, by issuing its own currency would undermine American sovereignty and be politically unacceptable. Second, that the proposal minimized the imperative of domestic economic adjustment and was excessively biased toward financing, which would inevitably be provided by the United States as the only country with sufficient credit resources. The United States objected to the near automaticity of borrowing from ICU and insisted that funding be both limited and conditioned on specific corrective measures. White, instead, proposed a stabilization fund. Under this plan, member countries could obtain limited credit for temporary balance of payments deficits but would be required to undertake economic adjustment for structural or chronic deficits. The American plan was more conservative than the British proposal. It was dictated by political considerations, primarily the belief that Congress would not countenance a blank check for deficit countries.

The differences between the British and the American positions ranged from the seemingly trivial to the serious. At one end, there was disagreement whether to name the proposed monetary institution the International Monetary Union (the British suggestion) or the Stabilization Fund (the American proposal). Ultimately they agreed on the International Monetary Fund. The issue may seem trivial but for White, the term "union" was politically unacceptable.[11] A more significant disagreement was whether trade adjustment should be imposed on the deficit or on the surplus country. As mentioned above, Britain proposed that the burden of adjustment be shared by the deficit and surplus countries. This was rejected by White, who declared that adjustment was a responsibility of the deficit country. The two positions reflected American and British national interests, since America expected to be a surplus country after the war and the British government knew that Britain would have to endure trade deficits for some time after the war as it rebuilt its economy. The British wished to avoid having to tailor their reconstruction program to accommodate balance of payments considerations and the Americans, for their part, did not wish to bankroll deficit countries indefinitely.

The final agreement, given the financial and political power of the US, was closer to the American proposals. The bilaterally negotiated agreement was then presented to, and accepted by, 44 countries at the Bretton-Woods Conference in July 1944 and led to the establishment of two separate institutions. The International Bank for Reconstruction and Development (IBRD or the World Bank) was designed to provide long-term financing for economic development and reconstruction projects. Complementing that, the International Monetary Fund (IMF or simply the Fund) was set up to provide trade adjustment financing for deficit countries to allow them to overcome temporary balance of payments difficulties.

The mechanism and amount the member countries were entitled to borrow from the IMF depended on their quota assessment. Each country, upon becoming a member, is assessed a quota payable to the Fund. The quota allocations, based on each member country's national income, trade and international reserves, are reassessed at regular intervals. Of the total assessed quota, 25 percent had to be paid in gold (after the late 1970s, in SDRs or any other useable currency) and the rest in their own currency. The quota was essentially their membership "fee" and also formed the basis of a system of weighted voting, where countries were given voting rights in proportion to their quota payments.[12] When any member experienced balance of payments difficulties it could borrow from either their "gold tranche" or their "credit tranche" under the following arrangement.

Gold Tranche: Members could borrow the equivalent of 25 percent of their total quota, or the amount of gold held with the IMF. Borrowing against the gold tranche was a members' right and not subject to any conditions.

Credit Tranche: Members could borrow in four equal tranche of 25 percent of their quota each time. However, borrowing was subject to conditions determined by the IMF and, in general, the stricter the conditions, the greater the level of borrowing. Conditions could include policy measures that a borrower had to implement in order to achieve trade balance. *Conditionality* formed the heart of IMF financial assistance.

Under the original agreement, any country could borrow up to 125 percent of their IMF quota but this was subsequently increased in the 1970s when other credit facilities were introduced to supplement the gold and the credit tranche. By 1979, a deficit country could borrow up to 467.5 percent of the quota.[13] Countries borrow from the IMF not only for balance of payments' reasons but also to assist with economic restructuring programs. In 1997, 58 countries had borrowed US$23 billion from the IMF to support macroeconomic and structural reforms. The amount borrowed was three times that which had been borrowed in 1996 but slightly below the figure lent out by IMF in 1995. To fund the lending programs, .the IMF has periodically adjusted members' quotas and at the 11th general review of quotas, in February 1998, the IMF proposed a total quota increase of about 45 percent, from US$199 billion to US$288 billion. The proposed US quota was about 17.5 percent of the total, whereas quota allocations for Japan and Germany were 6.3 and 6.1 percent, respectively. The smallest IMF member, the Republic of Palau, was given a quota allocation of 0.001 percent.

The established order centered around the rules of maintaining par values for exchange rates, a system of fixed exchange rates; currency convertibility to gold; and removal of exchange restrictions and controls for current account transactions. The agreement to maintain fixed exchange rate allowed for small movement within a narrow band of one percent on either side of the par value. To prevent exchange rates breaking out of the acceptable range, central banks were expected to intervene in currency markets to stabilize rates against market pressures. The process of currency realignment had to be initiated by the concerned country but with approval of the IMF. If currencies were devalued against the advice of the IMF, the errant country could potentially be expelled from the world body and or lose its borrowing privileges from the Fund, *unless* decided otherwise by the Fund. In 1948, when the French Franc was devalued despite objections from IMF, France was denied access to the resources of the Fund.[14]

Membership in the Fund implied a willingness to abide by the rules on exchange rate stability and unitary exchange rates. However, meaningful rule compliance was not achieved until about a decade after the establishment of the Fund. Even then, there were many exceptions. Many countries, especially in Latin America, maintained a system of multiple exchange rates, as revenue collection devices or as mechanisms restricting imports. Multiple exchange rates were used by cash-strapped developing countries to restrict the import of non-essential or non-preferred imports. In principle, the Fund was opposed to multiple exchange rates because of the potential for discrimination against certain products or products from certain region but tolerated it as unavoidable. The practice was phased out gradually but countries like Egypt continued with more than one exchange rate into the 1990s.

Currency convertibility and removal of exchange restrictions, too, were not realized immediately after the IMF began operations in March 1946. The agreement provided for a transition period of five years, ending February 1952, by which time all countries were expected to have achieved full currency convertibility. The actual transition, however, was much longer. The priority for the European countries and for Japan was economic reconstruction. This necessitated some exchange controls in the early stages to allow the prioritization of capital goods imports for reconstruction purposes. They were also protective of their relatively small foreign exchange reserves that could be further reduced if full convertibility was to be implemented at the end of the transitional period. The Fund promised to underwrite the transition to convertibility with its own resources, the paid up subscription of members. However, as W. M. Scammell wrote, "The promise that the Fund would meet part of the cost of convertibility was cold comfort to a nation like Britain which had experienced the gold drain and crisis attendant upon a premature experiment made under duress in the summer of 1947. The rest of the larger members had observed and learnt the lesson of that experiment and they listened politely to the Fund's homily but shook their heads."[15] The European countries accepted convertibility only in the late 1950s whereas Japan achieved this only in the 1960s.

When the Bretton-Woods regime was established, there were concerns that a shortage of international liquidity might jeopardize the reconstruction of the European countries and also induce severe deflation in the United States. These concerns were compounded by the communist threat.

The West European countries confronted the danger that if growth and reconstruction faltered, a bleak economic environment would provide fertile grounds for the spread of communist ideas. In this context of political and economic uncertainty, the United States played the crucial role as a source of international liquidity in the post-war period. The US provided international liquidity primarily through its preparedness to run balance of payments' deficits. As Eichengreen pointed out, "... it is difficult to envisage an alternative scenario in which the US balance of payments was zero but the world was not starved of liquidity."[16] Another source of international liquidity was the European Recovery Program, commonly known as the Marshall plan, which provided European countries with economic assistance, either as grant (92 percent of the total Marshall aid in 1946 was in the form of outright grant), or as long-term low interest loans.[17]

The Marshall plan was critical to the stability of the new monetary order. Indeed, the US government tried to link Marshall aid to compliance with the fixed exchange rate rules of the IMF. Ultimately however, this had to be dropped in the face of stiff European opposition.[18] The Marshall plan helped maintain high foreign demand for American products and hastened the process of European economic reconstruction and adoption of free and convertible currencies for current account purposes. In Asia, the outbreak of the Korean War in 1950 and the American special procurements program had a similar effect. Japan was the primary beneficiary of the special procurement plans of the US armed forces and this aided the process of Japanese recovery. Immediately after the war, the rest of the world worried about a potential dollar shortage and a liquidity crisis but as a result of the Marshall plan and the Special Procurements, the anticipated liquidity crisis failed to materialize. Indeed, in the period 1950–1956, the United States ran a modest balance of payments deficit of about US$1.5 billion per year. In the end, however, the main problem was not liquidity shortage but excess liquidity, especially after President Johnson initiated the Great Society program and escalated the Vietnam War effort. Excess liquidity and global inflation became the main sources of international financial instability.

In the 1960s, before the Great Society programs and the Vietnam war had produced excess international liquidity, the need for maintaining adequate liquidity was a major consideration.[19] Existing reserve assets were gold and increasingly, the American dollar. Although most countries agreed on the need for additional reserve instruments, there was disagreement on the nature of that instrument. On the one hand, France and West Germany argued for a reserve asset that was more like credit and which would eventually have to be repaid, with gold retained as the "heart" of the international monetary system. On the other hand, the United States and the United Kingdom preferred the creation of a genuine reserve asset that could be freely used in place of gold.[20] Both Britain and the US were experiencing balance of payments' deficits and advocated the creation of a new reserve asset that would eliminate the need for domestic economic adjustment, made all the more difficult by the demands of the welfare state. The Special Drawing Rights (SDRs) that was agreed to was a compromise solution and came into existence in August 1969, six years after the idea had first been mooted. Subsequently, to give the SDR a larger profile and importance, the IMF adopted it as its accounting unit but the role of SDRs in national reserves has remained small.

The Collapse of the Bretton-Woods Regime

Until the end of the 1950s, the Bretton-Woods system, according to Scammell, remained in abeyance, as many countries continued practices that violated the established rules.[21] It became a constraining regime only in the 1960s and by the late 1960s, there were enough pressure points to force its collapse. The backdrop to the eventual collapse of the Bretton-Woods system was the US balance of payments deficit through much of the 1950s and 1960s. In the 1950s, the deficit was functional in that it provided international liquidity and sustained trade expansion. In the 1960s, however, deficits generated excess international liquidity and the concern now was that surplus dollars would erode confidence in the dollar as reserve currency, if foreign dollar holdings exceeded US gold stocks and the US was unable to meet its international obligation (i.e. exchange foreign dollar holdings for gold). This was pointed out by Robert Triffen as a way of highlighting the potential dangers.

By 1965, foreign dollar holding exceeded gold reserves in the US and by the early 1970s, US liabilities exceeded gold stocks by 300 percent. Surplus dollars in foreign central banks, the so-called dollar overhang, fuelled speculation that the US government would be forced to devalue the dollar to reduce the prospect that foreign countries might cause a run on the dollar and deplete US gold holdings. Confidence in the American economy was shaken also when the US trade balance recorded its first deficit in 1968. The deterioration in the American trading position can be attributed to declining relative competitiveness of American industry. Whereas investments in new and modern factories and plants in Europe and Japan gave their industries a competitive edge, capital investment in the US failed to keep pace. The normal American practice of setting up overseas factories to consolidate and increase market share did not help either because the "decision to sell to a foreign market through branch plants rather than through exports often meant that capital was diverted from the expansion and modernization of domestic facilities."[22]

However, despite fears to the contrary, foreign central banks did not initiate a run on US gold reserves and were content to hold on to dollar as the reserve currency. Private holders of dollars were, however, less confident about the dollar especially after the devaluation of the sterling in November 1967. When the British government devalued the Sterling by 14 percent after chronic balance of payments deficits, this only heightened speculation that a dollar devaluation, too, was inevitable. After the devaluation of the pound, gold purchases in London shot up. Gold had been supplied to the London market by the seven central banks (Gold Pool) since 1966 and in the fourth quarter of 1967 alone, the United States lost US$953 million worth of gold deposits to the private markets.[23] Although the pressure eased after that, there remained a sense of uncertainty about the future of the dollar. Apart from the loss of gold from US reserves, the process was adding to inflationary pressures in other countries by increasing their levels of gold and dollar reserves. During 1970–1972 and the first three months of 1973, for example, official foreign holdings of US dollar claims increased by 346 percent.[24]

Moreover, as private holders of dollars switched to other forms of assets, central banks in these countries were obliged to purchase the surplus dollars to support the value of the dollar but in the process only added to domestic liquidity and to inflation, which reached double digit levels in 1973–1974.

Another source of instability in the international financial system was the speculative flow of capital across borders. The architects of the Bretton-Woods system had intended convertibility to apply to transactions on trade accounts but not on capital accounts, because freedom to import or export capital was incompatible with the fact that countries were required to periodically contract or expand their domestic economies to maintain fixed exchanges rates. For example, efforts to contract the domestic economy through higher interest rates could be easily undermined unless capital imports were restricted. However, capital flowed freely and rapidly across countries, and aided by advances in international communications, was quick to respond to real interest rate changes in the expectation of easy speculative gains.

Removal of controls and restrictions on capital accounts transactions allowed currency speculation to exacerbate pressures on a given currency. Corporations and speculators recognized the potential for easy profits by shifting capital from one country to another in anticipation of exchange rate changes. This flow of international capital undermined national economic management and allowed for the rapid dissemination of inflationary pressures throughout the system. From a purely national point of view, fixed exchange rates coupled with capital movements were becoming increasingly undesirable. A system of floating exchange rates seemed more promising because exchange rates would adjust rapidly without there ever being a perceived fundamental disequilibrium.

A final factor in the collapse of the Bretton-Woods system was the reluctance of major countries to implement measures to rectify payments imbalances. According to Margaret Garritsen de Vries, the IMF historian, the primary cause of the collapse of fixed exchange rate system was "without doubt ... the failure of the adjustment process."[25] That failure might be attributed to the ambiguity in the definition of "fundamental disequilibrium" in the IMF Articles of Agreement. This concept was left vague and there were no real pressures on surplus countries to make exchange rate adjustments.

The burden of adjustment was on the United States and there were two possible adjustment strategies: devaluation and deflation. First, the United States could have devalued its currency, that is, change the price of gold that had been fixed at US$35 per ounce. Devaluation of the dollar would have effectively reduced American obligations arising out of the balance of payments deficits but was ruled out as risky, given the position of the dollar as an international reserve currency. Any devaluation would have undermined confidence in the dollar. The nature of the monetary system, where the dollar was the key currency and all exchange rates were pegged to the dollar, made it difficult for the United States to devalue the dollar. Devaluation was also not politically acceptable because of its inflationary consequences. Deflation, of course, was also politically risky.

The international monetary system required the US to assume a passive position with regard to exchange rates and rely on speedy rate adjustments by other countries. Other countries, however, avoided this and the US smarted at its own inability to act and the refusal of others, especially Japan and West Germany, to revalue their currencies. Just as the US had decided that it was impossible or impractical to devalue the dollar, the European countries, too, were reluctant to accept currency revaluation. During the 1960s, a consensus had formed that fixed rates could not be tampered with. The reason was that such a step would be unpopular with exporters and have negative political fallout. For example, a 5 percent appreciation of the deutsche mark in March 1962 had sent shock waves through the export industry and "created within German industry a determination that it would not be repeated."[26]

The IMF agreement did allow for adjustments to par values but this happened on only a handful of occasions. The result of delays was to promote capital flows as speculators chased profits by moving currencies out of weak and into strong currencies. This added to adjustments pressures but, as Kenneth Dam wrote, national authorities responded to this by "new forms of capital controls, and, in some cases, by new controls on trade flows to attempt to stave off devaluation."[27] The net result of this was that where the monetary system had been designed to lubricate and facilitate trade expansion, trade was being sacrificed to stabilize a particular set of par values of currencies.

One reason why the US could not devalue its currency in the 1960s was because its overall trade balance was actually in surplus until 1968. Devaluation, under these circumstances, would have had the undesirable consequence, from the European and Japanese points of view, of further increasing the American trade surplus. This might have prompted retaliatory devaluation. According to Block, "Had a US devaluation in the early 1960s improved the US international trade position, it is likely that other countries would have devalued correspondingly to regain their earlier competitive position and to reverse any improvement in the US trade balance."[28] In 1971, however, the US current account registered a deficit for the first time in the postwar period and, on 15 August 1971, the US ended convertibility of the dollar. The American government also imposed a 10 percent surcharge on imports to force other countries to revalue their currencies.

The surcharge was a temporary measure until exchanges rates had been readjusted. This was a tremendous shock to the system because, "... not only had the United States formally suspended the dollar's convertibility ... [but] had also halted all other American measures for supporting the dollar in plain defiance of IMF rules."[29] It was a blow to the system but Odell argues that it did not spell the end of the monetary regime as the foundation was partially rebuilt shortly afterwards. Four months later the Smithsonian agreement did bring about a 8–9 percent depreciation of the dollar against other currencies and, consequently, the surcharge was removed. The Smithsonian agreement also widened the band within which currencies could fluctuate from 1–2.5 percent on either side of the par rates. This lasted until 1973, when a fully floating exchange rate system was adopted.

The Floating Exchange Rate System

By 1968, according to Gottfried Haberler and Thomas Willett, "The great majority of academic economists [were] in favor of flexibility of exchange rates."[30] A leading advocate of flexible exchange rates, Harry

Johnson, argued that the price of a currency, like all other prices, ought to be decided in the market place rather than by governmental fiat. Among the purported advantages were automatic adjustment to balance of payments imbalances, through the exchange rate mechanism which, like a sentinel on guard at a country's border, neutralized all external disturbances before they could impact on the domestic economy. Under fixed rate system, on the other hand, domestic economic activity, where necessary, had to be varied to defend the exchange rate. In principle, flexible exchange rates were assumed to possess the following specific advantages[31]:

1. Restore the effectiveness of monetary policy as a viable policy instrument for domestic economic objectives. Under fixed exchange rates, the sole function of monetary policy was to maintain par rates. Stable exchange rates were maintained by varying the level of money supply within a economy (a key element of monetary policy) depending on whether or not the exchange rate required defending or by altering interest rates to make the local currency more or less attractive to foreign investors and depending on whether the local currency required external support to sustain the par rates. As such, monetary policy under fixed exchange rates is available only as an instrument in securing external policy objectives but not very useful in securing domestic policy objectives. According to Milton Friedman, a system of flexible exchange rates, by contrast, would allow monetary policy to be used for domestic policy objective, such as controlling the level of inflation,[32] since the exchange rate would no longer be a concern for national governments;

2. Prevent a build-up of tension when different countries pursued different macroeconomic objectives. The US, for example, in the 1960s followed a policy of low unemployment and high inflation, whereas Germany had the opposite policy and yet had little control over imported inflation from the US, a result of profligate public sector spending in the US. Under fixed rates, for example, inflation in one country is readily transmitted to another. For example, assuming that Japan imported golf balls from the US at US$1 each and that prices increase to US$1.50. At a fixed exchange rate of ¥300 = $1,

the price of golf balls in Japan would increase automatically from ¥300 to ¥450. Flexible exchange rates, on the other hand, allow each country to pursue its own macroeconomic policy objective and insulate the economy from external disturbances. Under flexible rates, an increase in world prices would appreciate the domestic currency to compensate for foreign price increases. In the 1970s, because of its anti-inflationary policy bias, the German government was supportive of flexible rates, which, as Cooper observed, "... insulated West Germany from imported inflation ..."[33]

3. A third and final advantage, as already mentioned, is the automaticity of trade adjustments and the sharing of the burden by both the deficit and the surplus country. Also because of quick adjustment, sustained misalignment of currencies would be avoided and this would be a boon for liberal trade because currency misalignment and currency overvaluation (a tax on exporters) frequently is the cause of protectionist sentiments. According to Bergsten and Cline, the three periods of high protectionism in the US were also periods of an overvalued US dollar. They are as follows:

   a) late 1960s–1971. This was just before the collapse of Bretton-Woods, when the dollar was overvalued by about 20 percent. Many protectionist bills, like the Mills Bill were introduced in the Congress in 1971 and this was also the period of the textiles dispute between Japan and the United States, which resulted in restrictions on Japanese textiles exports;

   b) 1975–1976. The dollar was overvalued around 15 percent and this was also the period when the United States introduced import restrictions on Japanese steel, through the trigger price mechanism; and

   c) 1981–85. The dollar was overvalued by around 35 percent and this was the period when protectionism in the US reached its peak. Currency revaluation was finally achieved after the Plaza Accord of September 1985.[34]

In theory, currency overvaluation, or misalignment, should not occur under the flexible exchange rate regime. In practice, as indicated above, they did. A pronounced feature of the flexible exchange rate system was the tendency for exchange rates to overshoot their expected medium to long-run equilibrium points. Overshooting, both under and overvaluation, had its own specific problems. When currencies remain undervalued over a long period, there is a danger of competitive devaluation as other countries try to regain lost competitive advantage. On the other hand, sustained overvaluation of a currency is likely to worsen a country's trade balance by discouraging exports and promoting imports. This, in turn, may generate protectionist pressures. As pointed out above, it was no coincidence that the two periods of heightened protectionism in the United States, the mid-1970s, and the early to mid-1980s, were also periods of a significant overvaluation of the dollar and a deterioration of the balance of trade. In each of these two periods, the American response was to engineer a coordinated depreciation of the dollar to reduce the trade deficit and lower protectionist sentiments domestically. The results, however, were not as effective as anticipated and tended to support the view that exchange rate changes, by themselves, cannot restore trade balances.

This corrective to earlier expectations fits the particular instance of US–Japan trade imbalance. The United States relied on ex-change rate changes to reduce its trade deficit but without much success. An advisor to President Clinton, Robert Shapiro, vice president of the Progressive Policy Institute, admitted that the ability of currency realignments to restore trade balance was "much less than many economists once thought."[35] Critics argued that to balance trade it was essential also to reduce US fiscal deficits, but successive governments failed to deal with this issue, until the newly elected Clinton administration announced budget cutbacks in 1993.

The period of floating exchange rate also witnessed considerable, and erratic, fluctuation in rates. It had been anticipated that even with flexible exchange rates, the rates would reach equilibrium points fairly quickly and stabilize at that point for extended periods. This, however, proved not to be the case and exchange rate movements remained very volatile. The volatility and uncertainty appear to correlate with a slowdown in trade in the 1970s. The Bretton-Woods Commission, composed of former bankers and experts, in 1994, estimated that exchange rate instability had contributed to halving the long-term economic growth rate of

Table 3.1. Macroeconomic performance of US, Germany, and Japan.

	Unemployment Rate	Inflation Rate	GNP Growth Rate
Fixed Exchange Rates 1961–1971			
US	4.8	2.8	3.6
Germany	0.8	2.8	4.2
Japan	1.2	5.6	10.4
Flexible Exchange Rates 1973–1979			
US	6.6	8.6	2.3
Germany	3.8	4.6	2.3
Japan	1.9	9.8	3.5
1980–1987			
US	7.7	5.3	2.4
Germany	7.8	2.9	1.5
Japan	2.5	2.5	3.9

Source: Shinkai, Y., "Evaluation of the Bretton Woods Regime and the Floating Exchange Rate System," in Suzuki, Y., Junichi Miyake and Mitsuaki Okabe (eds.), *The Evolution of the International Monetary System: How Can Efficiency and Stability be Attained?*, University of Tokyo Press, Tokyo, 1990, p.120.

industrialized countries to about 2.5 percent, compared to the period when exchange rates were fixed.[36] Similar conclusions were reached by others.

It is simplistic to blame flexible exchange rates for the slowdown in GNP and trade growth. There were a number of reasons for the slowdown in GNP growth, including a quadrupling of oil prices in 1973. According to Blackhurst and Tumlir, the slowdown in world trade was also a reflection of domestic economic dislocation, such as inflation. The average rate of inflation in the seven major OECD countries in 1960–1965 was 2 percent but in the period 1970–1975 it was 7.9 percent. Inflation, they argued, affected national economic growth because it ultimately necessitated restrictive monetary and fiscal policies, leading to a recession.[37]

Moreover, the flexible exchange rate system did not operate true to its principles. Most major countries were reticent about accepting total and unconditional reliance on the market place for exchange rate determination. Policy makers, by and large, prefer the stability and certainty of relatively fixed exchange rates to market determination and have shown a willingness to intervene in foreign exchange markets to support desirable rates. Throughout the period of floating rates, state intervention in the market place was pervasive because most major states had a preconceived notion of what the exchange rate ought to be and intervened to realize that ideal. According to Kenneth Dam, "... the level of intervention since the commencement of generalized floating in 1973 has been as great and perhaps greater than during the par value period prior to 1971."[38]

According to Richard Cooper, there were good and legitimate reasons for why states intervened so extensively to control exchange rates. He wrote that, "For most countries, the exchange rate is the most important single price ... it is inconceivable that a government held responsible for managing its economy could keep its hands off this particular price."[39] Others, like Franco Modigliani suggested a reconsideration of fixed exchange rates saying that, "... I think that, in the long run, we ought to aim for a gradual return to a system of fixed exchanges like Bretton-Woods, but one purged of the major faults ..."[40]

Although a return to fixed exchange rates is unlikely, it is improbable that states will allow capital markets to freely determine exchange rates. At the same time, experience with state intervention had exposed the limitations of states' ability to influence exchange rates with their limited foreign reserves. The sums that states could deploy for market intervention were insignificant compared to total international capital flows. The relative ineffectiveness of autonomous intervention by states prompted moves toward developing a more orderly and coordinated process of state intervention in capital markets in the expectation that concerted intervention would enhance the effectiveness of states' ability to influence exchange rates.

Policy Cooperation and Monetary Stability

Currency instability and exchange rate pressures are largely the result of speculative capital flows, which have increased exponentially as a result of capital market deregulation and globalization of communication systems. The global financial revolution, excessive monetary instability, and pervasive misalignment of currency values led to new initiatives to preserve global monetary stability. These include macreconomic policy coordination by the G–7 countries to minimize global disruptions, and joint interventions in foreign exchange markets to defend currency values. The two precedents to exchange rate management were the Smithsonian Agreement of 1971 and the European Monetary System (EMS), established in 1979. The former was a multilateral arrangement that quickly collapsed and gave way to floating exchange rates.

The latter was the result of an agreement among the EU countries (excluding Britain) to maintain bilateral exchange rate stability of European currencies. The EMS was a reasonable success for more than a decade, during which time there were frequent exchange rate realignments but the narrow permitted margins of fluctuation gave the system a high degree of rigidity. European central banks intervened actively to defend weaker currencies from speculative assaults. In January 1993, for example, when speculators launched an onslaught on the French franc, the French and the German central banks intervened with about US$50 billion to prop up the French franc.[41] The system depended on the German mark as the key currency and proved viable as long as Germany itself emphasized monetary stability. However, confronted with the huge costs of reunification, Germany abandoned its commitment to the EMS and exchange rate stability in August 1993.[42]

The arena for more inclusive international economic cooperation and policy coordination has been the G–7 meeting of central bankers and finance ministers of the seven leading industrialized countries. The G–7 mechanism was institutionalized at the Tokyo summit of 1986 and meetings have been held three to four times each year. The record of policy coordination, however, is mixed although there are examples of success, such as the dollar devaluation following the Plaza Accord.

Policy coordination and negotiations were not intended to create a new set of universal rules. This was tried earlier in the 1970s by the Committee of Twenty (C20) but abandoned as a fruitless endeavor. Instead negotiations have aimed at macroeconomic policy coordination and management of exchange rate policies among the major states. Over time, policy coordination has become an institutionalized feature of the new monetary order. This has its advantages and disadvantages.

For example, compared to the low transactions cost of operating within a fixed exchange rate regime, policy coordination at periodic meetings is not as cost effective, especially when such negotiations involve more than two or three countries. By contrast, the single biggest advantage of policy coordination over fixed exchange rate system is that it removed the pressure on states to forego their employment and inflation goals. Under fixed exchange rates, employment objectives and domestic welfare were secondary to the objective of exchange rate stability and the collapse of the Bretton-Woods was largely the result of American refusal to accept this sacrifice.

In general, policy coordination had the advantages of being flexible whereas the fixed exchange rate regime imposed conditions that were hard to enforce in democratic polities. The stability that was reintroduced was however, without the inflexibility of the fixed exchange rate regime, which had become a burden to the smooth functioning of international monetary relations. Consequently, the floating exchange rate system gradually evolved to a more ordered system, characterized by coordinated and cooperative intervention to inject stability into exchange markets, away from unilateral intervention for mercantilist gains (dirty float) that prevailed in the early phase of floating rate system.

Exchange rate management as a legitimate issue on the international agenda can be traced to the summit meeting of the leaders of five leading industrialized countries in Rambouillet, France in 1975. On this occasion, leaders of the five industrial powers agreed that "monetary authorities will act to counter disorderly market conditions or erratic fluctuations in exchange rates."[43] The Rambouillet summit meeting was, to a large extent, inspired by monetary instability since the early 1970s. The lead role in convening the summit was played by the French president Giscard d'Estang and he justified the summit as useful in dealing with monetary disorder. In an interview, he stated that "What the world calls a crisis of capitalism is in fact a monetary crisis."[44] If President Giscard played an instrumental role in establishing the groundwork for the first summit, the idea had, first been broached by President Nixon's National Security Adviser Henry Kissinger in 1971. It is not surprising therefore that the summit meetings were likened to the nineteenth century Concert of Europe.[45] Just as the Concert of Europe recreated a stable and peaceful Europe, the annual summit meetings of the late twentieth century hoped to achieve similar results in crisis prone international economic and monetary relations.[46] The difference was that there was much less unity of purpose in the annual summit meetings and, consequently, these were not very effective in maintaining stability. The late 1970s continued to be marked by exchange rate volatility and disequilibrium.

It was only in the mid-1980s that policy coordination became more effective. Earlier attempts were relatively ineffective in maintaining equilibrium exchange rates and the dollar continued to be overvalued. Policy coordination required American support but the Reagan administration in the US, between 1980–1985, pursued a policy of laissez faire, or "capitalism in one country."[47] Even in early 1985, the strong dollar was being defended as a blessing, even though it was hurting domestic export industries. The success of policy coordination in the later period makes it possible to regard the flexible exchange rate system, after 1985, as an alternative regime, albeit much weaker than the Bretton-Woods regime, rather than one marked by a complete absence of rules.

The Plaza Accord was a significant new beginning in policy coordination. The Accord was the result of a meeting among the G–5 countries (US, Japan, Germany, England and France) in September 1985 in the Plaza Hotel, New York. The American role in the Plaza Accord was significant and illustrated its continued influence and dominance in international monetary relations. Prior to 1985, the US was less interested in correcting exchange rate disequilibrium because of the paramount interest in containing domestic inflation. It was feared that a devaluation of the dollar against other currencies would only exacerbate inflation in the US by making imports more costly. American interest in monetary stability also stemmed from the role of the American dollar as the international currency, for transaction, reserves and store of value. The continuation of a dollar standard required a stable dollar and it was in the American interest to maintain the dollar standard because it eased external constraints on American monetary policies. Thus, despite support for currency revaluation elsewhere, the United States failed to go along with this. In the mid-1980s, however, the US trade position had deteriorated drastically,[48] and it was in American interest to seek currency revaluation as a way of reducing the trade deficit that was prompting calls for protectionist legislation. The depreciation of the dollar that was achieved under the Plaza Accord had the added benefit of reducing, at one stroke, foreign claims on the US by decreasing the value of their dollar holdings.

Under the Bretton-Woods system, the American dollar was backed by gold, at the fixed rate of US$35 per ounce of gold. All other currencies were linked to the dollar by a fixed exchange rate and it was not surprising that the dollar was used as the international currency. However, even after the float and de-linking of dollar from gold, the dollar continued as the leading international currency. It was also in American interest to continue to have the dollar as the international currency (world money).

The Plaza Accord committed the US, Japan and Germany to intervene, in a coordinated manner, in foreign exchange markets to produce an appreciation of the yen and the deutsche mark. This was an example of successful policy coordination to counter rising protectionism in the US, resulting from a loss of American competitiveness caused by the appreciation of the dollar in the early 1980s. The Plaza Accord was followed by the Louvre Accord, signed in February 1987 at Louvre, France. This committed the G-7 countries (G-5 plus Canada and Italy) to achieving monetary stability around target zones.

The argument for target zones had been put forward by several scholars, such as by Williamson and Miller, by R. McKinnon, and by P. Kenen, for exchange rate stability through target zones and monetary policy coordination. John Williamson and Marcus Miller developed a specific proposal for international economic cooperation that extended beyond the targeting of exchange rates alone. They argued that policy coordination should include, apart from exchange rate coordination, macroeconomic policy coordination to achieve low inflation, high employment, rapid growth, and appropriate balance of payments outcomes. They cautioned, however, that focusing on these policy targets in the short term may defeat the purpose of policy coordination since some targets were either contradictory (low inflation and high employment) or produced results only with time lags (currency adjustment whenever current account is too large will lead to overshooting because currency adjustments are reflected in current account balances with time lags). They emphasized, therefore, that the policy targets should not be short-term targets but rather medium term targets. Williamson and Miller recommended that the targeted exchange rate should be the real effective exchange rate rather than the nominal rate with an acceptable range of 10 percent on either side of the target.[49]

At the time of the Louvre Accord, the target zones, reportedly, were set at between 1.77 to 1.87 marks and between 137 to 147 yen to the US dollar. Two years later, the target zones were believed to have been readjusted at between 1.6 to 1.9 marks and at between 120 to 140 yen to the dollar.[50] The establishment of target zones however, did not sanction intervention whenever rates reached the margins. The only obligation was to consult rather then to intervene in a prescribed manner.

The Louvre Accord did not produce the desired results immediately. Only the Japanese government followed up its commitment by announcing measures to stimulate domestic demand. Markets sensed a weakening of policy coordination and cooperation and the American dollar consequently continued to slide. Eventually, however, the US and German authorities followed through with appropriate policy measures to stabilize exchange rates and halt further depreciation of the dollar. Thus, after an initial backslide, the Louvre Accord strengthened policy coordination among the leading industrial countries.

As we have seen, the Plaza Accord initiated a period of coordinated exchange rate management and policy coordination. Commenting favorably on multilateral coordination, Nigel Lawson, British Chancellor of the Exchequer, stated that exchange rate management "... makes a great deal of sense. I can live with it for the foreseeable future. The more successful it is, then the more likely it is to be an enduring part of the scene."[51] A practical difficulty in exchange rate management is securing agreement on appropriate exchange rates. There is no consensus as to how to determine target rates and, in the past, analysts had come up with different equilibrium exchange rates.[52] The danger was that difficulty of objectively determining target zones might result in manipulation of the system to advantage particular countries.

Critics, including monetarists who favor a freely floating exchange rate, alleged that policy coordination, as symbolized in the Plaza and Louvre Accords, was no more than a misdirected focus on exchange rates to the neglect of broader macroeconomic policies. Milton Friedman, for example, argued that exchange rate volatility was simply the result of underlying macroeconomic imbalances, and that eliminating those imbalances would lead to a more stable exchange rate structure. Supporting government non-intervention in exchange rates and floating system, he argued, "Instability of exchange rates is a symptom of instability in the underlying economic structure. Elimination of this symptom by administrative pegging of exchange rates cures none of the underlying difficulties and only makes adjustment to them more painful."[53]

Similarly, according to Funabashi, the Louvre Accord was a quick-fix solution to the balance of payments problem of the United States rather than a determined attempt to tackle the real issue.[54] The argument was that exchange rates are simply a reflection of fundamental imbalances in macroeconomic policies and focusing on exchange rates as such merely concentrated attention on the symptoms rather than the basic problem. However, underlying macroeconomic imbalances have not been entirely neglected but, it is true that they have not received enough coordinated attention. Under the Louvre Accord, the United States agreed to reduce its fiscal 1988 budget deficit to 2.3 percent of GNP compared to the estimated level of 3.9 percent in fiscal 1987. The large American budget deficits meant high domestic interest rates, capital inflows, strong dollar and, consequently, poor export prospects and ballooning imports. Despite a commitment to reduce deficit spending, until 1993, little progress was made to cut the deficit by lowering spending and increasing tax revenue. Instead, the focus was exclusively on exchange rates and revaluation of the yen. In May 1994 and, again, in March 1995, for example, following a steady decline of the US dollar in exchange markets, central banks in 16 countries, including central banks in US, Japan and France, had to coordinate their dollar purchases so as to defend the dollar against further slippage. The American government, for its part, had opted to shift the burden of adjustment upon Japan. It hoped that a stronger yen would boost Japanese imports and reduce exports by eroding Japanese competitiveness.

Only the new Democratic government, in 1993, made a determined effort to cut spending and raise revenue. This was not because of external pressure but because of different principles and policy programs of the Democratic administration and a genuine belief that deficit spending was a drain on the economy. Despite inherent difficulties in reconciling divergent national objectives, exchange rate coordination and intervention, since the late 1980s, have not been abject failures.

Globalization and International and Monetary Reform

As mentioned above, the system of fixed exchange rate was abandoned in the 1970s and many countries, instead, decided to float their currencies and let markets determine exchange rates. Another important development has been the globalization of financial markets and capital mobility. This resulted from Bretton-Woods' inspired currency convertibility and removal of exchange controls, as well as improved communications technology. But the levels of capital mobility that resulted from these developments were not anticipated by the framers of the Bretton-Woods system. They had anticipated capital flows to correlate only with trade flows and in settlement of trade accounts. Deregulation and liberalization of capital markets have, however, unhinged the links between trade and finance and led to a situation where national financial liberalization has adversely affected prudential banking principles. International capital is beyond national jurisdiction and its flows are determined by differences in expected returns and even by market sentiments. Speculators shift large sums of capital across the globe in the hope that their calculation of risks and returns will bring quick and easy profits. Susan Strange called this "casino capitalism," where profits are made in speculative endeavors rather than in the real economy of production and trade. As a result of speculative capital flows, exchange rates have become more volatile and independent of economic fundamental and trade balances. An extreme example of exchange rate volatility was the sharp decline in the value of the Indonesian rupiah in 1997–1998, from around 2 500 to 17 000 rupiah to the American dollar.

Globalized financial and production systems may seem complementary but speculative capital flows have become a destabilizing factor in the real economy. This is because unlike producers, who work on a longer time horizon, speculative capital typically has a short-term outlook, seeking out high short-term real interest rates.[55] This inhibits productive investments and may result in lower growth rates and high unemployment which, in turn, could encourage protectionism and raise trade tensions in ways reminiscent of the inter-war period. To counter the potential negative impact of speculative capital flows, Will Hutton proposed a concerted approach by the US, Japan and Germany to create a "... new Bretton-Woods system of bracketed but flexible exchange rates, protected against excessive speculative currency flows by some form of turnover tax on financial transactions."[56]

In early 1998, even the IMF lent cautious support to controls on speculative capital flows to prevent currency instability. This was in the aftermath of the 1997 East Asian currency and debt crisis which, admittedly, cannot be blamed entirely on speculative capital flows but which had still contributed to the wave of panic that swept through Thailand, Malaysia, South Korea and Indonesia. When the crisis began in mid-1997, Prime Minister Mahathir of Malaysia blamed currency speculators, like George Soros, for undermining confidence in the Malaysian dollar, the Malaysian economy and the Malaysian political system in order to promote democratic forces in Malaysia. This was roundly criticized by western governments and by George Soros as an attempt to externalize the causes of the crisis, which, they insisted, lay with economic mismanagement and cronyism.

In order to deal with the currency crisis, the East Asian countries sought the financial help of the IMF and, in return, submitted to IMF conditionality and economic restructuring. The IMF demanded significant economic reforms in the affected countries on the assumption that underlying domestic economic conditions had produced the crisis. However, by April 1998, the IMF was distinctly more sympathetic to the view that currency speculation had contributed to the crisis and that it may be necessary, therefore, to introduce regulations to limit currency speculation and hot capital. Earlier, in January 1998, George Soros, in an address to the World Economic Forum, repeated his belief that market discipline required national and international regulatory measures. A few years earlier he had stated that the global economy had to be "... properly regulated, supervised, and directed."[57] To the extent that regulations would insulate currencies from speculative attacks, the growing support for regulation is an attempt to stabilize exchange rates without, however, going to the extreme of fixed exchange rates. There is no real likelihood of restoring the Bretton-Woods regime but, in the wake of the East Asian crisis, there is growing appreciation for strengthening the architecture of the international financial system so as to avoid future crises.

To understand the interest in systemic reform, it is useful to review the basic foundation of the Bretton-Woods system. The founders of the Bretton-Woods regime did not anticipate that national financial deregulation, mandated as desirable in the interest of financial openness, would contribute to the scale of international financial flows that it ultimately did, to the extent that international capital transactions vastly exceed total world trade. Compared to total world trade of US$5.2 trillion in 1990, daily world foreign exchange transactions, in 1992, averaged about US$1 trillion and the daily turnover in the major capital markets of London, New York and Tokyo was about US$300 billion, US$192 billion and US$128 billion, respectively.[58] The amount traded in capital markets exceeds, by far, exchange reserves of central banks and has complicated the task of governments trying to defend an exchange rate from speculative attacks.

The enormity of foreign exchange transactions, only a small portion of which is necessary for trade and investment purposes,[59] is facilitated by instantaneous global communication which has made it possible to shift capital, almost instantaneously, from one country to another to maximize returns. Markets have become sensitive to external events even in the absence of logical connections. For example, in early 1995, when the Mexican debt crisis resurfaced and the peso slumped, it affected currencies and stock markets in countries that, unlike Mexico, were in sound financial condition. Investors pulled money out of Brazil despite Brazilian reserves of US$43 billion, and East Asian currencies and stock markets were similarly affected despite the unparalleled success of East Asian economies. One consequence of deregulation and cross-border capital flows has been to confound the task of maintaining exchange rate stability. The scale of capital transactions vastly exceeds the capacity of any single institution or country to influence market conditions. Yet, the main objective of the founders of the post-war monetary regime was to create a stable monetary environment for trade growth and preempt predatory exchange rate policies.

The volatility of exchange rates in the post-Bretton-Woods period was not anticipated by early advocates of flexible exchange rates. But persisting volatility and financial crises have led to calls for a strengthened international financial architecture, because the existing system copes poorly with global capital markets. While there is no clear indication of the evolving shape of the financial system, according to Michel Camdessus, Managing Director of the International Monetary Fund, the revamped structure will have to ensure that the following three conditions are met:

1. greater transparency of international and national financial regulations;
2. controls on speculative capital movements; and
3. stronger international financial institution to exercise international surveillance.[60]

The first task is to ensure transparency of national and international banking regulations and to collect and disseminate relevant data and information to ensure that market decisions are informed and considered. This is necessary to sustain confidence in smooth and effective functioning of capital markets. The Latin American debt crisis was an important source of financial instability and although it led to a more active IMF role in debt management, the repeat of the Mexican crisis in 1995 and the East Asian crisis in 1997, revealed areas where the IMF could significantly improve its surveillance function and provide an early warning system. The events underscored the importance of establishing a code of conduct to ensure that member governments adhered to standards of transparency.

The IMF surveillance can be an important step in international financial stability. According to Manuel Guitian of the International Monetary Fund, surveillance "... must pinpoint the sources of instability and assign policy responsibilities for their correction to member countries. It is now necessary for all countries to keep their economies on an even keel for not just balances to obtain in each of them, but also to avoid the spillover of disruptions to other countries."[61]

Had the Mexican government been obliged to publish details of its reserve movements and short-term liabilities, financial markets and commercial banks would have been better informed about their exposure in Mexico. The Mexican government, too, might have been forced to take remedial action much earlier. One reason the debt crisis flared up again in 1995 was because there were no established mechanisms to study, identify, and prescribe correctives to potential problems. With better reporting and regulatory transparency, the free-fall of the Mexican peso against the US dollar might have been averted. Instead, the problem was hidden from view until it assumed crisis proportions. According to Mark Siegel of Putnam Investments, "The reason the marketplace was blind-sided in Mexico has everything to do with ... an absence of information about day-to-day and week-to-week short-term changes in current account and reserve levels."[62]

The 1995 Mexican crisis indicated that the lessons of the earlier debt crisis had not been learned by capital lending institutions. In the 1970s, commercial lenders to developing countries had failed to assess the net debt exposure of borrowing countries and their capacity to repay. This encouraged countries to borrow without due economic prudence and precipitated the debt crisis. The IMF, as a leading lending institution in the 1980s, should have exercised greater surveillance on borrowing countries, including Mexico, and acted sooner to prevent a recurrence of the Mexican debt crisis. If Mexico, in 1995, revealed the inadequacies of global surveillance system, the East Asian debt crisis in 1997 was further evidence of a need to devise crisis prevention strategies, not simply to empower the IMF to manage crisis and act as a lender of last resort.

Secondly, it is now increasingly being recognized that real exchange rate stability can only be maintained, as was true within the EMS, with capital controls. Without capital controls, it is unlikely that weak currency countries, within the EMS, could have participated in the exchange rate arrangement.[63] This, however, is not an easy option since any imposition of restraints and controls would adversely impinge on welfare and also because states do not necessarily agree on when stability is desirable or, in other words, when exchange rate movements have exceeded desirable targets. In March 1995, the American dollar slumped to record low levels against the Japanese yen and the German mark following a statement by a member of the Board of Governors of the US Federal Reserve Bank that the dollar-yen rate had not yet reached critical levels.[64] As the dollar slumped, central banks in Europe and Japan intervened, but with little success because markets sensed no certainty that Europe, Japan and the US were equally committed to halt the further decline in the value of the dollar. Consequently, in the first four months of 1995, the dollar declined about 20 percent against the yen and 10 percent against the German mark.

One radical solution to the instability of exchange rates is to recreate the classical international gold standard. Judy Shelton, for example, argued that a system of fixed exchange rates was inherently superior to flexible rates.[65] According to her, the gold-exchange standard of Bretton-Woods had built-in deficiencies in that it did not enforce sufficient discipline on national governments. She confidently predicted that the weakness that had plagued the gold-exchange standard could be overcome in the classical gold standard and fixed exchange rates.

A classical gold standard would, of course, have no need for the IMF and she suggested that the considerable resources of the IMF be distributed to the member countries so that they may pursue "currency stability with the kind of single-minded focus in keeping with the intent of the original Bretton-Woods agreement."[66] While acknowledging the difficulties involved in dismantling an established bureaucracy, she added that the exercise could be extremely rewarding, especially as the IMF reserves stood at around US$40 billion in pure gold. Shelton's analysis ignored the fact that the world had adapted to flexible exchange rates and that if excessive instability has hindered international trade, currency markets have developed new mechanisms, like currency futures and swaps, to deal with such instability.[67] Yet, even if the rigidity that Shelton advocated is unreal, there is still a need for more orderly international monetary relations.

In particular, the succession of debt crises has convinced many of the need to regulate speculative capital flows which have generated banking crises also excessive exchange rate movements, beyond levels that might be justified by the real economy. Concern has also been voiced that the "lack of discipline in exchange rates is pushing the world toward increased protectionism."[68] Suggestions for controlling speculative capital include a transactions tax, proposed by James Tobin in 1982. He argued that a relatively small transaction tax (small enough not to impact on trade transactions) would be sufficient to deter short-term speculative capital flows and eliminate the major source of exchange rate volatility.[69] For a transaction tax to be effective will require agreement of all countries. Without such an overarching agreement, any tax measure will only lead to the emergence of tax havens.

Another possibility would be to establish currency target zones and empower the IMF to police and maintain them. It is obvious that a centralized authority charged with managing rates within target ranges could significantly lower transactions costs. However, for the IMF to participate in capital market interventions to defend exchange rates will require a significant boost in funds through increase in members' quota. This may not be easy. The 9th quota review, completed in 1990 following lengthy negotiations, provided an increase in quota that was much less than what had been requested by the Fund.[70] This quota increase was related primarily to the IMF lending requirements to the East European countries and to the indebted developing countries. For the IMF to undertake the role of defending exchange rates, it will require a greater infusion of funds from the members. In late 1994, the IMF pushed member governments to approve a US$50 billion increase to international reserves through the Special Drawing Rights but this was rejected by the US, Germany and Britain as part of an empire-building campaign by Mr Camdessus and the IMF.

There remain other political impediments to a larger IMF role. It would diminish the lustre of the G–7 summits and diminish, also, the authority and responsibility of the respective central banks, especially at a time when central banks themselves have expanded their autonomy and influence.[71] Following the G–7 meeting in Naples in 1994, the joint communique in an obvious reference to the IMF hinted that "some supranational bodies might have outgrown their usefulness — and that it was time to start thinking about building new ones."[72] The IMF can hardly be termed a supranational institution and even the proposed changes would not transform it into a supranational institution, as long as the G–7 countries, themselves, remained the arbiter of appropriate exchange rates. The June 1995 G–7 summit meeting in Halifax, Canada, included discussions on international monetary reform and the future role of the IMF but, interesting enough, the leaders of the seven countries refused to invite the head of the IMF to their meeting.[73]

Leaving aside the rhetoric of confrontation, both the G–7 and the IMF have a potentially useful role. The G–7 process has become an important mechanism for policy coordination, even if its effectiveness is less than exemplary. It is unlikely that the G–7 countries will surrender their domestic political interests but even within the political constraints, the IMF can play a part in foreign exchange interventions in support of currencies and in prescribing appropriate policy choices. It was in this spirit that the IMF, in April 1995, weighed into the exchange rate crisis and urged US policy makers to increase short-term interest rates in order to strengthen the dollar, to complement the rate cut announced by the Bank of Japan. The managing director of the IMF, Michel Camdessus, also chided the US for fiscal irresponsibility and for not doing enough to reduce federal budget deficits. This was one of the first times that the IMF had so boldly proffered advice to the US. For the IMF to have a more systematic input into exchange rate policies, it will have to be fully integrated into the G–7 process. This presupposes that G–7 countries recognize that the IMF can look beyond limited national concerns to a broad global perspective. While the IMF cannot supplant the G–7 process, it can, apart from its lending activities, function both as an advisory agency, and as a reporting and surveillance authority to stabilize currencies.

Policy coordination, as noted above, is cumbersome and slow, and limited also by the fact that even the US, as noted by Peter Kenen, did not have large foreign currency reserves with which to intervene in currency markets.[74] The IMF, by contrast, has large foreign exchange reserves which can be used to defend currencies but its reserve position will also have to be supplemented significantly if it is to play a larger international monetary role. These issues were discussed in the late 1970s but no result was possible because member countries failed to agree on how to deal with potential exchange losses. However, with exchange rate management as a new issue in international monetary relations, it may be appropriate to explore ways of improving the efficacy of market interventions and of integrating the IMF into the process. Any large increase in the IMF's resource base will require an injection of funds from the United States but this is made difficult by a Congress that has refused to fulfill even existing financial obligations to the various multilateral institutions.

As an international institution, the fortunes of the IMF have fluctuated with developments within the international system. Following the decision to float major international currencies in the 1970s and the emergence of an international capital market, there was speculation as to whether the IMF had any role left to perform. A floating exchange rate system meant that there were no par values for the IMF to defend because, in theory at least, a floating rate system was expected to automatically correct sustained trade imbalances through the exchange mechanism. It seemed, therefore, that the IMF had lost its role as the lender of last resort.

Moreover, developments in international bond and capital markets also meant that countries could borrow in the major financial centers to cover payments difficulties and avoid IMF conditionality. If one function of the IMF was to encourage fiscal and monetary prudence, the new global reality made it extremely difficult for the IMF to influence national policies. Throughout the 1980s, for example, the US experienced both fiscal and balance of payments deficits but the easy availability of funds from other surplus countries, mainly Japan, meant that there was no urgency to rectify the twin deficit. In 1994, US fiscal deficit was in excess of US$200 billion and the shortfall was covered by a flow of funds from Japan and other countries. Large countries like the US could borrow funds on the open markets and escape strict IMF conditionality. This weakened the Fund's capacity to impose fiscal and monetary discipline on its members and weakened its role in managing the international financial system.

However, following the Latin American debt crisis of 1982, the IMF began to carve out a new role for itself in assisting developing countries undertake structural adjustment and in providing adjustment loans. Yet, given its increasingly close involvement with the developing countries, it appeared to have lost a distinctive identity. It was seen as behaving like the World Bank because, as noted by Jacques Polak, both institutions were providing "... similar types of credit on similar terms to the same group of countries.[75] The IMF had found a role to play but it still had no distinctive identity. It was perceived more as an "aid" agency rather than a "monetary" institution. Ironically, it was also not well-liked by the developing countries because of its intrusive policy directions and micro-level interventions. For example, in one instance, the IMF ventured so far as to stipulate the appropriate urban property taxes for a borrowing country.[76] The IMF has been criticized also for neglecting the poor in the developing countries and for pursuing economic rationalism with little sensitivity to social consequences.

In the late 1980s, the IMF was also at the forefront of western efforts to assist the former communist economies make a transition to market-based economic systems. To most observers, the IMF looked like an aid agency, and yet, Michel Camdessus, the Managing Director of the Fund defiantly protested that, "We shall not get out of the aid business because we are not in it."[77] Even so, there is growing support for the IMF to return more to its original mandate of exchange rate management.

According to the Bretton-Woods Commission, the responsibility for monetary coordination should be devolved to the IMF. On the 50th anniversary of the Bretton-Woods agreement, the Commission met to explore ways of strengthening monetary order and the Chairman of the Commission, Paul Volcker, declared that the G–7 could not be entrusted with the task of managing and coordinating the monetary system. He recommended that this should be left to the IMF.[78]

Similar views were also expressed by the Managing Director of the IMF and by Jacques Attali, former advisor to President Mitterand of

France and, later, Chairman of the European Bank for Reconstruction and Development.[79] Apart from political acceptability of a larger IMF role, the proposal itself made eminent common sense. Centralized direction and control, or intervention in foreign exchange markets, by the IMF to maintain exchange rates within target zones, determined by the G–7, is necessarily more efficient than coordinating such intervention among a large number of central bankers.

The difficulty for the IMF is that it is composed of the member nations and lacks autonomy. It has little capacity to dictate policies to members, unless when countries require the IMF assistance for balance of payments reasons. For the IMF to be an effective world central bank, it has to have autonomy and independence but it may take a while before the member states are prepared to contemplate this possibility. Should the IMF move toward becoming an international central banker, it will be a small step away from the possibility of issuing an international currency. Richard Cooper advocated the adoption of a common currency since the "... most effective way to eradicate exchange rate uncertainty is to eradicate exchange rates ... ."[80] The idea of an international currency, obviating even the need for exchange rates, can only be a long-term proposition but the European Union, with its agreement on a common European currency, has shown that it is not unthinkable. For the foreseeable future, exchange rate management and policy coordination are the more promising options.

Conclusion

The post-war Bretton-Woods agreement has produced a system of relatively rigid and fixed exchange rates. Its collapse in the early 1970s led to a flexible exchange rate structure, but one which was also volatile. To control volatility, the advanced industrial countries agreed upon policy coordination and intervention to stabilize exchange rates. The new arrangement, unlike the Bretton-Woods regime, promised a combination of flexibility and stability based on periodic policy coordination. To these changes in monetary relations, it is necessary now to add the impact of financial globalization.

The international flow of capital and emergence of a "borderless economy" have, undoubtedly, complicated the task of economic management. Capital moves freely and quickly between states and industrial production also is organized on a global scale that weakens the extent of national control. Participation in the global economy is certainly advantageous to countries but demands also a sound institutional base and regulatory transparency in order to ensure confidence in national markets. When the IMF was established, it was meant largely to ensure compliance with the fixed exchange rate structure, but the new conditions demand that the IMF become more active in other areas as well.

The international community and the G–8 countries (which now includes Russia) will have to decide upon the future of the IMF but it is desirable for the IMF to exercise a more thorough surveillance function within the global economy. A useful beginning might be to include the IMF as a full and equal member of the G–8 process and expand the G–8 to G–9. At present, the IMF integration into the G–8 process is limited because it is excluded from discussions that are considered sensitive by the G–8 countries.

References

1. Eichengreen, B., *Elusive Stability: Essays in the History of International Finance, 1919–1939*, Cambridge University Press, Cambridge, 1990, pp. 19–20.
2. See Blackhurst, R. and Jan Tumlir, *Trade Relations Under Flexible Exchange Rates, GATT Studies in International Trade, No. 8, General Agreement on Tariffs and Trade, Geneva*, 1980, pp. 55ff. We do not intend, however, to prejudge a system of flexible exchange rates and advocates of exchange rate flexibility insist that, other things being equal, markets will settle on a stable equilibrium exchange rate.
3. Ford, A. G., "International Financial Policy and the Gold Standard, 1870–1914," in Mathias, P. and Sidney Pollard (eds.), *The Cambridge Economic History of Europe*, Vol. 8, Cambridge University Press, Cambridge, 1989, p. 199.

4. Drummond, I. M., *The Gold Standard and the International Monetary System, 1900–1939*, Macmillan Education Ltd., Basingstoke, 1987, p. 15.

5. As we shall see below, the US, in the post-war period, also avoided policies to overcome its balance of payments deficits because other countries were willing to accumulate dollar reserves.

6. Crabbe, L., "The International Gold Standard and US Monetary Policy from World War I to the New Deal," *Federal Reserve Bulletin*, Vol. 75, No. 6, June 1989, p. 426.

7. Block, F. L., *The Origins of International Economic Disorder: A Study of United States International Monetary Policy from World War II to the Present*, University of California Press, Berkeley and Los Angeles, 1977, p. 20.

8. Moggridge, D. E., "The Gold Standard and National Financial Policies, 1919–1939," in Mathias, P. and Sidney Pollard (eds.), *The Cambridge Economic History of Europe*, Vol. 8, Cambridge University Press, Cambridge, 1989, p. 306.

9. Cited in Odell, J. S., *US International Monetary Policy: Markets, Power, and Ideas as Sources of Change*, Princeton University Press, New Jersey, 1982, p. 80–81. This is a very broad definition that includes rule-based, interventionist regimes, such as fixed exchange rate regimes and market based, non-interventionist regimes, such as flexible exchange rate regimes.

10. For details of the two plans, see Dam, K. W., *The Rules of the Game: Reform and Evolution in the International Monetary System*, The University of Chicago Press, Chicago and London, 1982, pp. 77–83.

11. Van Dormael, A., *Bretton-Woods: Birth of a Monetary System*, The Macmillan Press Ltd., London and Basingstoke, 1978, p. 110.

12. Each member is assigned a total of 250 votes plus an additional vote for each SDR 100 000 of quota. Quota increase requires an 85 percent majority of the total voting power. The quotas of ten largest IMF members at the end of 1990 were:

USA	SDR 26 526.8
Germany	8 241.5

Japan	8 241.5
France	7 414.6
UK	7 414.6
Saudi Arabia	5 130.6
Italy	4 590.7
Canada	4 320.3
Netherlands	3 444.2
China	3 385.2

13. Cohen in Krasner, 1983, p. 328.
14. Scammell, W. M., *International Monetary Policy: Bretton-Woods and After*, The Macmillan Press Ltd., London and Basingstoke, 1975, p. 149. This denial of resources was largely symbolic because as a recipient of Marshall Plan aid, France, like all other recipients of Marshall assistance, had no access to Fund resources.
15. Scammell, W. M., *International Monetary Policy: Bretton-Woods and After*, The Macmillan Press Ltd., London and Basingstoke, 1975, p. 135.
16. Eichengreen, B., *Elusive Stability: Essays in the History of International Finance, 1919–1939*, Cambridge University Press; New York, 1990, p. 298.
17. The Marshall Plan is generally regarded as a successful example of economic aid. It provided crucial financial assistance to the European countries to finance their import requirements and is considered an important factor in the rapid economic growth rate of the recipient countries which grew by an average of 5.3 percent in real terms, between 1948 and 1953. See Kostrzewa, W., Peter Nunnenkamp and Holger Schmieding, "A Marshall Plan for Middle and Eastern Europe," *The World Economy*, Vol. 13, No. 1, March 1990, p. 28.
18. Milward, A. S., *The Reconstruction of Western Europe, 1945–1951*, Methuen and Co. Ltd., London, 1984, pp. 114ff.
19. In reality, instead of a liquidity crisis, there was a surplus of international liquidity through the 1960s.
20. de Vries, M. G., *The IMF in a Changing World, 1945–1985*, International Monetary Fund, Washington, DC, 1986, p. 78.

21. Scammell, W. M., *International Monetary Policy: Bretton-Woods and After*, The Macmillan Press Ltd., London and Basingstoke, 1975.

22. Block, F. L., *The Origins if International Economic Disorder: A Study of United States International Monetary Policy from World War II to the Present*, University of California Press, Berkeley and Los Angeles, California, 1977, p. 146.

23. Odell, J. S., *US International Monetary Policy: Market, Power, and Ideas as Sources of Change*, Princeton University Press, Princeton, 1982, pp. 174–175.

24. Yeager, L. B., "Opportunities and Implications of a Return to Fixed Exchange Rates — Is Gold an Answer for International Adjustments?" in Agmon, T., Robert G. Hawkins and Richard M. Levich (eds.), *The Future of International Monetary System*, Lexington Books, D.C. Heath and Co., Lexington, 1984, p. 28.

25. Cited in Katz, S. I., "Balance of Payments Adjustments, 1945 to 1986: The IMF Experience," in *Atlantic Economic Journal*, Vol. 17, No. 4, December 1989, p. 71.

26. Katz, S. I., "Balance of Payments Adjustment, 1945 to 1986: The IMF Experience," *Atlantic Economic Journal*, Vol. 17, No. 4, December 1989, p. 72.

27. Dam, K. W., *The Rules of the Game: Reform and Evolution in the International Monetary System*, The University of Chicago Press, Chicago and London, 1982, p. 177.

28. Block, F. L., *The Origins of International Economic Disorder: A Study of United States International Monetary Policy from World War II to the Present*, University of California Press, Berkeley and Los Angeles, California, 1977, p. 161.

29. Odell, J. S., *US International Monetary Policy: Markets, Power, and Ideas as Sources of Change*, Princeton University Press, Princeton, 1982, p. 167.

30. Cited in Odell, J. S., *US International Monetary Policy: Markets, Power and Ideas as Sources of Change*, Princeton University Press, Princeton, 1982, p. 181.

31. See Crockett, A., *et al.*, *Strengthening the International IMF*, Occasional Paper No. 50, 1987.

32. See The Economist (London), 9 January 1988, p. 70.

33. Cooper, R. N., "Flexible Exchange Rates, 1973–1980: How Bad Have They Really Been?" in Cooper, R. N., Peter Kenen *et al.*, *The International Monetary System Under Flexible Exchange Rates: Global, Regional, and National*, Ballinger Publishing Company, Cambridge, 1982, p. 11.

34. See Salvatore, D., *The New Protectionist Threat to World Welfare*, North-Holland, NY, 1987, Chapter one.

35. *The Australian*, 10 March 1993, p. 37. According to H. Jager, currency depreciation may be necessary but "not under all circumstances a sufficient requirement for a trade deficit reduction," See Jager, H., "The Global Exchange Rate System in Transition," *The Economist* (Netherlands), Vol. 139, No. 4, 1991, p. 477.

36. "G–7 Reshapes Bretton Woods," *The Banker*, October 1994, p. 38.

37. Blackhurst, R. and Jan Tumlir, *Trade Relations Under Flexible Exchange Rates, GATT Studies in International Trade*, No. 8, General Agreement on Tariffs and Trade, Geneva, 1980, p. 13.

38. Dam, K. W., *The Rules of the Game: Reform and Evolution in the International Monetary System*, The University of Chicago Press, Chicago and London, 1982, p. 197.

39. Cooper, R. N., "Recent History of World Monetary Problems," in Agmon, T. Robert G. Hawkins and Richard M. Levich (eds.), *The Future of the International Monetary System*, Lexington Books, D.C. Heath and Co., Lexington, 1985, p. 16.

40. Modigliani, F., "Comment," in Agmon, T., Robert G Hawkins and Richard M. Levich (eds.), *The Future of the International Monetary System*, Lexington Books, D.C. Heath and Co., Lexington, 1984, p. 52. For a discussion of the flaws of fixed exchange rates, see Cooper, R., "The Gold Standard: Historical Facts and Future Prospects," *Brookings Papers on Economic Activity*, No. 1, 1982.

41. Shelton, J., *Money Meltdown: Restoring Order to the Global Currency System*, The Free Press, New York, 1994, p. 6.

42. See Shelton, J., *Money Meltdown: Restoring Order to the Global Currency System*, The Free Press, New York, 1994, pp. 196–211.

43. Dam, K. W., *The Rules of the Game: Reform and Evolution in the International Monetary System*, The University of Chicago Press, Chicago and London, 1982, p. 197.

44. See Putnam, R. D. and Nicholas Bayne, *Hanging Together: The Seven-Power Summits*, Heinemann Educational Books Ltd., London, 1984, p. 16.

45. Henry Kissinger's Ph.D. dissertation had been a study of the Concert of European which remade European stability after the Napoleonic Wars of the early nineteenth century. Many scholars have suggested that Kissinger's public life betrays a strong fondness for the nineteenth century structure of peace and, as such, it may be possible to argue that policy coordination in monetary matters was a sort of 'monetary concert' fashioned after the Concert of Europe.

46. See Kirton, John J., "Introduction: The Significance of Seven-Power Summit," in Hajnal, Peter I. (ed.), *The Seven Power Summit: Documents from the Summits of Industrialized Countries 1975–1989*, Kraus International Publications, New York, 1989, pp. xxii–xxiii.

47. The phrase, suggesting a complete reliance on the market place, is a modification of the Leninist slogan of 'socialism in one country.' See Funabashi Y., *Managing the Dollar: From the Plaza to the Louvre*, 2nd ed., Institute for International Economics, Washington, DC, 1989, p. 66.

48. Until 1984, US current account was either in surplus or almost balanced but in 1984, the US current account deficit was 1.5 percent of GNP. This increased to 2.0 percent of GNP in 1985, to 2.5 percent in 1986 and to 2.7 percent in 1987. See Shinkai, Y., "Evaluation of the Bretton Woods Regime and the Floating Exchange Rate System," in Suzuki, Y., Junichi Miyake and Mitsuaki Okabe (eds.), *The Evolution of the International Monetary System: How Can Efficiency and Stability be Attained?*, University of Tokyo Press, Tokyo, 1990, p. 132.

49. Williamson, J. and Marcus H. Miller, *Targets and Indicators: A Blueprint for the International Coordination of Economic Policy*, Institute for International Economics, Washington, DC, September 1987, p. 12.

50. Richter, R., "The Louvre Accord: From the Viewpoint of the New Institutional Economics," in Furubotn, E. G. and Rudolf Richter (eds.), *The New Institutional Economics*, J. C. B. Mohr, Tubingen, 1991, p. 279 and p. 284, respectively.

51. Richter, R., "The Louvre Accord: From the Viewpoint of the New Institutional Economics," in Furubotn, E. G. and Rudolf Richter (eds.), *The New Institutional Economics*, J. C. B. Mohr, Tubingen, 1991, p. 280.

52. For example, Williamson (1987) proposed a nominal equilibrium exchange rate of Y140–145 = $1, whereas Krause (1986) suggested a rate of Y100 = $1, and Krugman (1988) a rate of Y100–150 = $1. See, Shinkai, Y., "Evaluation of the Bretton Woods Regime and the Floating Exchange Rate System," in Suzuki, Y., Junichi Miyake and Mitsuaki Okabe (eds.), *The Evolution of the International Monetary System: How Can Efficiency and Stability be Attained?*, University of Tokyo Press, Tokyo, 1990, p. 144.

53. Cited in Meier, G. M., *Problems of a World Monetary Order*, 2nd ed., Oxford University Press, New York, 1982, p. 281.

54. Funabashi, Y., *Managing the Dollar: From the Plaza to the Louvre*, Institute for International Economics, Washington, DC, 1988.

55. Hutton, W., "Relaunching Western Economies: The Case for Regulating Financial Markets," *Foreign Affairs*, Vol. 75, No. 6, November/December 1996.

56. Hutton, W., "Relaunching Western Economies: The Case for Regulating Financial Markets," *Foreign Affairs*, Vol. 75, No. 6, November/December 1996, p. 12.

57. Javetski, B. and William Glasgall, "Borderless Finance Fuel for Growth," in Neelankavil, James P. and Yong Zhang (eds.), *Global Business: Contemporary Issues, Problems and Challenges*, McGraw-Hill, Inc., College Custom Series, New York, 1996, p. 177.

58. Walter, A., *World Power and World Money*, Revised edition, Harvester Wheatsheaf, Hertfordshire, 1993, p. 197.

59. It is estimated that more than 80 percent of foreign exchange transactions in New York, Tokyo, and London are for speculative gains. See

Wachtel, Howard M., "Taming Global Money," *Challenge*, January–February 1995, p. 36.

60. See Press Conference of Michel Camdessus on 14 April 1998, IMF Headquarters, Washington.

61. Guitian, M., "The IMF as a Monetary Institution: The Challenge Ahead," *Finance and Development*, Vol. 31, No. 3, September 1994, p. 39.

62. Hirsh, M., "All Shook Up," *Newsweek*, 23 January 1995, p. 10.

63. See Marston, Richard C., "Exchange Rate Policy Reconsidered," in Feldstein, M. (ed.), *International Economic Cooperation*, The University of Chicago Press, Chicago, 1988, p. 117.

64. *The Straits Times*, 4 March 1995, p. 1.

65. Shelton, J., *Money Meltdown: Restoring Order to the Global Currency System*, The Free Press, New York, 1994.

66. Shelton, J., *Money Meltdown: Restoring Order to the Global Currency System*, The Free Press, New York, 1994, p. 335.

67. Norton, R., "Back to Bretton Woods," *Fortune*, 27 June 1994, p. 108.

68. Attali, J., "The Costs of Changing the International Monetary System," in Feldstein, M. (ed.), *International Economic Cooperation*, The University of Chicago Press, Chicago, 1988, p. 148.

69. See Cooper, Richard N., "What Future for the International Monetary System?" in Suzuki, Y., Junichi Miyake and Mitsuaki Okabe (eds.), *The Evolution of the International Monetary System: How Can Efficiency and Stability be Attained*, University of Tokyo Press, Tokyo, 1990, p. 291. Any transaction tax would have to be globally coordinated to prevent the emergence of tax havens. The difficulty of global coordination makes this suggestion impractical.

70. Roncesvalles, O. and Andrew Tweedie, "Augmenting the IMF's Resources," *Finance and Development*, December 1991, p. 26.

71. Governments have in recent years granted central banks greater autonomy, from political interference to control domestic inflation, and the relative success of anti-inflationary policies pursued by central banks means that government will find it difficult to tamper with the existing arrangement.

72. "G–7 Reshapes Bretton-Woods," *The Banker*, October 1994, pp. 37–38.

73. "IMF Chief's Plans Include greater Role for Himself," *The Asian Wall Street Journal*, 12 June 1995, p. 1

74. Kenen, P., "The Use of IMF Credit," in *The International Monetary Fund in a Multipolar World: Pulling Together*, Transaction Books, New Brunswick, 1989, p. 87.

75. Polak, Jacques J., "Strengthening the Role of the IMF in the International Monetary System," in *The International Monetary Fund in a Multipolar World: Pulling Together*, Transaction Books, New Brunswick, 1989, p. 50.

76. See Cooper, Richard N., "External Adjustment: The Proper Role for the IMF," *Challenge*, May–June 1993, p. 55.

77. "G–7 Reshapes Bretton-Woods," *The Banker*, October 1994, p. 42.

78. "G–7 Reshapes Bretton-Woods," *The Banker*, October 1994, p. 37. See also Ryrie, Sir William, "Where do We Go From Here?" *Euromoney*, September 1994, p. 59.

79. Attali, J., "The Costs of Changing the International Monetary System," in Feldstein, M. (ed.), *International Economic Cooperation*, The University of Chicago Press, Chicago, 1988, p. 150.

80. Cooper, Richard N., "What Future for the International Monetary System?" in Suzuki, Y., Junichi Miyake and Mitsuaki Okabe (eds.), *The Evolution of the International Monetary System: How Can Efficiency and Stability be Attained?* University of Tokyo Press, Tokyo, 1990, p. 295.

Chapter Four

PROTECTIONISM, REGIONALISM AND THE GLOBAL ECONOMY

Countries resort to trade protectionism for a variety of reasons. For instance, protectionist measures may constitute part of a sanctions package against a foreign country. Used in this way, trade becomes an instrument in the pursuit of foreign policy objectives. Governments may also introduce protection in order to ensure the viability of industries that are considered strategic or essential to the national interest. Usually however, protectionism is in response to demands from a weak sector of the economy for relief from imports. When industries are unable to compete against imports, the choices are to undertake structural adjustment, accept a decline in market share, or secure protection from imports. Not surprisingly, the last option is more attractive and less painful. For governments, providing protection to an industry is a quick and easy way to save a declining industry and jobs but it is not necessarily a cheap response to structural decline.

Of course, consumers, as beneficiaries of liberal trade, may also lobby governments, but the reality is that effective lobbying demands a high level of organizational unity and determination. This gives manufacturers a decided advantage because, being few, they are in a better position to achieve unity of purpose and mount a concerted campaign for protection. Consumer interests, by contrast, are difficult to organize not only because of the size factor but also because the cost of lobbying to each individual consumer may be greater than the potential benefit from free trade. Moreover, consumers have divided loyalties. As employees in affected industries, safeguarding employment is, naturally, a higher priority than cheaper imports.

The nature and form of protectionism has continued to evolve with changing economic conditions. In the nineteenth century, for example, protectionism usually meant the unilateral imposition of tariffs and quota restrictions on imports. Under the GATT system, quotas, on most products, were phased out and tariffs reduced but governments found other novel ways of offering protection to domestic industries. In the 1980s, protection for an industry was also bilaterally negotiated. This led to such unlikely measures as "voluntary" export restriction by the exporting country. Voluntary export restraint (VER) agreements, typically, included quantitative limitations on permitted exports and to that extent, operated similarly to quota restrictions. In principle, therefore, a VER and its variants, like voluntary import targets, were in breach of GATT injunctions against quantitative quota restrictions. Nevertheless, countries relied on these measures because of their simplicity and effectiveness. In the US, resort to such neo-protectionist instruments was propelled by a perception of unfair trade practices by its trading partners.

Another challenge to global free trade was posed by strategic trade theorists, who argued that it was possible to improve on free trade outcomes by selective state intervention and trade management. Strategic trade theorists suggested that in certain instances, states could offer subsidies to domestic industries in order to eliminate foreign competition and capture production and trade in that sector.

In broad terms, neo-protectionists advocated a denial of domestic markets to "unfair" foreign traders in the interest of protecting weak industries or industries deemed strategically important. They did not rely on theoretical precepts to influence policy makers and their success was the result of the democratic distemper of interest group activities. By contrast, proponents of strategic trade argued that government subsidies to domestic industries could boost international competitiveness and lead to the capture of foreign markets and, thereby, prove beneficial to the domestic economy. They rely on theoretical innovations to suggest a path for promoting growth industries or industries at the cutting edge of technology.

GATT multilateralism was threatened also by the spread of regionalism. The drive toward regional trading agreements was premised, partly, on a belief that smaller groups were easier to manage and, therefore, a better alternative to the GATT's "failed" multilateralism. Lester Thurow de-clared that the cumulative effect of these new developments was the destruction of the GATT and its replacement with a new trade regime underwritten by a united Europe.[1]

In this chapter, I will look at each of these challenges that threatened to reduce the GATT to an irrelevant international institution and explain how and why the United States, which had created liberal institutions after the Second World War, had increasingly turned to various forms of protectionism.

Protectionism and Neoprotectionism

The rise of neo-protectionism in the United States, in the 1970s and 1980s, was, at least partly, a reaction to perceptions of Japan as an unfair trader. Critics argued that Japan exploited open markets in America and elsewhere, to boost its economy while denying other countries reciprocal access to its own markets. In the early post-war period, the US had tolerated this as necessary to facilitate Japanese economic reconstruction but the mood turned sour when Japanese protectionism persisted and could no longer be justified on grounds of economic necessity.[2]

The result of an unequal trade relationship was evident in Japan's growing trade surpluses against the US and the rest of the world. In the United States, trade with Japan was portrayed as a zero-sum game, with gains for Japan coming at the expense of the American economy and industries. It mattered little whether there was evidence to support the conclusion that Japan's so-called predatory practices were behind American economic decline. The perception, by itself, was sufficient to fuel protectionism.

Table 4.1. Japan's international trade.

Year	Trade balance against world	Trade balance against US
1981	US$8 740 b	US$13 312 b
1985	US$46 099 b	US$39 485 b
1988	US$77 563 b	US$47 597 b
1991	US$77 788 b	US$38 221 b
1993	US$120 241 b	US$50 168 b

Notes: * = 1980

Source: *Japan 1995: An International Comparison*, Keizai Koho Center, Tokyo, 1995, pp. 34–36.

Neo-protectionists in the US concentrated on Japan because of its low levels of manufactured imports compared to other industrialized countries. In 1983, Japan's import of manufactured goods as a percentage of GNP was only 2.7 percent compared to 5.2 percent for the US and 13.4 percent for West Germany. By 1988, Japan's import of manufactured goods as a percentage of GNP had increased to 3.2 percent but was still much less than the corresponding German figure of 15 percent.[3]

The trading imbalance in key industrial sectors of the economy also rankled public opinion and angered law makers. For example, it seemed inexplicable and unfair that, in 1979, Japan exported more than 3 million cars against total imports of only about 64 000 units. It was not unreasonable to assume that low levels of Japanese car imports were due to protectionist policies. It followed that if Japan failed to demonstrate market openness, through real improvements in trade balance, then retaliation was justified. Reciprocal retaliation, therefore, became the means to force Japan to abide by the GATT regulations.[4] The automobile dispute between Japan and the US, was ultimately resolved when Japan agreed in 1981 to voluntarily restrict car exports to the United States.

Neo-protectionists gained legitimacy by insisting that American trading difficulties were largely a product of unfair foreign trading practices by others, especially Japan. When the United States concluded VER agreements with several countries on steel exports, a spokesperson for the US

Trade Representative stated, "We are responding to unfair trade in the US; defending yourself against unfair trade is not, in our opinion, protectionism."[5] Neo-protectionism was presented simply as a reciprocal denial of export opportunity to countries that restricted the import of American products or as a means to open up foreign markets through guaranteed minimum market share for US products. This was the principle that underpinned US-Japan agreement on semiconductors and the US government, in 1995, also insisted that Japan accept this framework to resolve the dispute on auto parts exports to Japan.

The blame for resurgence of protectionism cannot be attributed entirely to Japan. A simpler explanation is that these reflected a slowdown in global economic activity and a scramble to secure market shares through political means. Free trade is easy to advocate when economic conditions are favorable but economic stagflation,[6] following the oil crisis of 1973, led to a questioning of liberal trade principles. The delicate consensus on free trade was displaced with visible frustration, in the US, over rising imports, especially of Japanese electronics and automobiles. This provided fertile soil for protectionists to gain prominence. Just as the hegemon, in ascendancy after the Second World War, had instigated a "global" move toward free trade, the "diminished giant" now seemed ready to move toward protectionism in order to safeguard its industries.

Others, like William Cline, for example, argued also that if foreign markets were closed, the American market was not much better. According to him, "[I]t is a sobering fact that the available empirical evidence on non-tariff barriers ... does show that the portion of the market covered by non-tariff barriers in the United States is comparable to or wider than in other major countries ... [B]y now, Japan's tariffs and overt non-tariff NTBs [non-tariff barriers] in industry are as low as, or lower than, those of the United States."[7] The obsession with alleged foreign trade barriers was also dismissed as diverting attention away from the more important domestic factors responsible for the continuing US trade malaise, including lack of fiscal discipline and sluggish investment growth.[8]

According to Enrico Sassoon, the growth of new protectionism or neo-protectionism could be traced to the following factors[9]:

1. increased competition from Japan and the newly industrializing countries and the concomitant impulse to protect declining labor intensive industries;
2. reduced labor mobility across industrial sectors due to social preferences and conservative labor unions. This rendered structural adjustment more difficult;
3. the recession and slowdown in economic growth, which encouraged protectionist policies to benefit weaker industries;
4. rapid appreciation of the American dollar in the early 1980s which boosted imports and reduced exports and resulted in demands to protect the domestic market. The demand for protection, however, did not disappear even after the revaluation of currencies in the mid 1980s.

Liberal economists, like Sassoon, were more apt to attribute the growth of neo-protectionism to problems of US industrial restructuring and exchange rate imbalances rather than to foreign factors. The imbalance in exchange rates, it was pointed out, was the result of American monetary and fiscal policies, in particular, the failure to control federal budget deficits. The deficits increased through the 1980s as the Reagan administration invested heavily in the defense sector to enhance American military capabilities. Given a relatively low savings rate domestically, the fiscal expansion was financed by overseas capital, which was attracted into the US by high real interest rates.[10] The foreign demand for American dollars artificially inflated its price relative to other currencies with the net effect of impeding American exports and stimulating imports.

The appeal of protection is that it can bring disproportionately large gains to a small group of producers, while dispersing costs to the wider community of consumers. For example, restrictions on textile import under the Multifibres Agreement cost American consumers US$11 billion in 1987 while the gain to producers was only US$4 billion. Similarly, the 1981 US-Japan voluntary export restraint (VER) agreement, which limited Japanese automobile exports to the US, cost US consumers US$5.8 billion in 1984 whereas the gain to US car manufacturers was only US$2.6 billion.[11] In neither instance did consumers act to defend their interests. This may have been because of the inherent difficulty of organizing a large group for collective action and also because the welfare losses to individuals, from protectionism, might be smaller than the cost of organizing in defense of free trade.

The alternative to protection is structural adjustment to shifting international realities and competitiveness. In negotiations to establish an international monetary regime after the Second World War, the US had insisted that the burden of adjustment had to be the responsibility of countries in trade deficit. British negotiators wanted a sharing of the responsibility but the US rejected this, expecting to be a surplus country after the War. Later, as it became a deficit country, the US conveniently shifted the burden of adjustment upon the surplus country. During the acrimonious textiles dispute between Japan and the US in the late 1960s and early 1970s, the American Secretary of State William Rogers stated that, "We believe that any country in chronic surplus as Japan is, has an obligation to take necessary measures — increasing imports, eliminating export incentives, stimulating capital outflow and revaluating its exchange rate — to bring its global balance of payments into equilibrium."[12]

The reason countries tend to avoid adjustment is that it is not a painless process. It is not easy, for example, to phase out established industries or to provide alternative employment opportunities for displaced workers. It is easier and less painful, in human terms, to avoid adjustment by insulating the economy from externally generated forces of change. This was an important factor behind the growth of protectionism in the US. Industries that had previously championed free trade, such as the automobile industry, now actively lobbied politicians for relief from foreign competitors. Political leaders, dependent on electoral support, found such pressures hard to ignore. Fear of the Japanese industrial juggernaut also prompted strategic and defence-related concerns for US industrial strength. Thus, according to Paul Seabury, "As the only genuine guarantor of security for both itself and the Free World as a whole, the United States simply cannot afford to allow its industrial base to wither away ... The American industrial base constitutes the strategic core of Free World defenses."[13]

It was against this backdrop that economic nationalism returned to influence American public policy. Neo-protectionism differed from the protectionism of the pre-war period in that it was often negotiated rather than unilaterally imposed and the instruments employed by neo-protectionist, too, were different. Reciprocity was the catch-cry of neo-protectionists and it attracted support even from free traders, who mistakenly, saw them as possible allies in fighting protectionism rather than for what they, according to Bhagwati, really were: closet protectionists. Moreover, because neo-protectionism targeted particular countries and the measures were either unilaterally imposed or bilaterally negotiated, these stood in violation of the basic principle of trade multilateralism. Below, we look first at the bilateral focus in international trade and follow that with a review of neo-protectionist measures.

Bilateralism in International Trade

Neo-protectionism violated the principles of non-discrimination and multi-lateralism. Curzon and Price lamented that the trading system was being changed from one based on law and applied without discrimination to one based on power, applied selectively.[14] Exemplary of the use of national power, rather than established GATT procedures, to realize trade objectives was Section 301 of the US Trade and Tariff Act of 1974 and its later amendment in 1988 known as Super 301. Section 301 of the 1974 Trade Act was designed to enforce GATT-conferred trade rights to the US and retaliate against foreign countries found guilty of violating the GATT principles. In this, Section 301 was GATT-consistent because it required the US to, initially, use dispute settlement mechanisms of the GATT. Amendments in 1988, and the introduction of Super 301 gave teeth to the Section 301 legislation. In Super 301, the US government, having determined that the GATT's dispute resolution mechanism was cumbersome, arrogated to itself the right to retaliate unilaterally against foreign countries. It also required the United States Trade Representative (USTR) to prepare an inventory of foreign barriers, establish a deadline for their removal, and retaliate if there was no progress.[15] Super 301 was clearly GATT-unfriendly because it permitted the United States to act as both judge and jury in deciding whether other countries pursued unfair trading practices.

In June 1989, the US identified six trade barriers maintained by India (investments and insurance), Japan (satellites, supercomputers and forest products), and Brazil (import licensing) and threatened retaliation under Super 301 unless they changed their trading practices. Again in 1992, the US cited EU agricultural policies as bestowing unfair advantages to European exports and threatened retaliation. In both instances, the target countries reached a compromise agreement, which obviated the need to implement retaliatory measures.

In the absence of objective definitions of what constituted unfair trade, it was easy to define as unfair anything that could be conceived as deleterious to American interests or as contributing to the US trade deficit. A persistent trade deficit in a particular area could be labelled as unfair.

Increasingly, neo-protectionism and reciprocity became linked to the new evaluative criterion of actual results. US Senator Robert Dole argued that, "Reciprocity should be assessed not by what agreements promise but by actual results — by changes in the balance of trade and investment between ourselves and our majority economic partners."[16] Illustrative of this development, the US government, in its dealings with Japan adopted the position that alleged market openings in Japan were superficial since they had not produced the tangible result of reducing bilateral trading imbalance. For instance, in 1993, President Bill Clinton stated that, "If you look at the history of American trade relationships, the one that never seems to change very much is the one with Japan."[17] The conclusion reached by most Americans, and President Clinton, was that the Japanese market continued to be closed and that Japanese exporters were benefiting from unfair advantages provided by the Japanese government. To make for a fairer trade, Rudiger Dornbusch stated that, "Japan must increase imports of manufactured goods from the United States at an average rate of at least 15 percent per year, with adjustments for inflation in each country."[18]

A possible redeeming feature of trade bilateralism was the assertion that all additional liberalization outcomes would be multilateralized. US Trade Representative Carla Hill stressed that she would use Super 301 legislation to open foreign markets in a non-discriminatory manner.[19] The results in some cases belied the rhetoric. In March 1988, the Japanese government agreed to allow the US firms to bid for construction projects in Japan but this concession was not extended to European countries. Even if the result were to lead to multilateral liberalization of international trade, the use of such devises, according to Curzon and Price, was "Ramboesque" and in violation of the spirit of the GATT. They also argued that, "The problem is, if the United States can achieve 90 percent of its trade policy objectives with a combination of Section 301 investigations and bilateral free trade agreements, there will be precious little for the GATT and the Uruguay Round to do, except perhaps negotiate on a bilateral basis with the European Community."[20] However, even some supporters of the GATT regarded Super 301 as a necessary jolt to the cumbersome GATT mechanism.[21]

Neo-Protectionist Instruments

Neo-protectionist measures that were adopted include voluntary export restraint agreements, trigger price mechanisms and orderly marketing agreements. As mentioned before, a distinctive feature of neo-protectionism was that it was often a negotiated outcome. Insofar as it was negotiated, neo-protectionism had the potential for benefiting both the exporting firms and the import competing firms. For example, voluntary export restraint (VER) agreements were, "... supposed to allow domestic industry to generate profits as well as to allow an exporter to reap scarcity rents."[22]

In the early 1980s, Japan and the United States negotiated a VER agreement on automobiles. This was justified as necessary to provide breathing space for American manufacturers so that they could shift their production away from large cars to more fuel-efficient cars, in line with changing demand patterns. It was signed in 1981 and provided for a reduction of Japanese exports, from 1.82 million units in 1980, to 1.68 million units in the first year of the agreement. It should be pointed out that there was nothing "voluntary" about a voluntary export restraint agreement. The choice for the exporting country often could be reduced to either negotiated VER or the unilateral imposition of import restrictions by the importing country. In this binary choice, VERs were a preferred alternative for the exporting country for the following two reasons:

1. In a negotiated outcome, the exporting country retained some influence in deciding the volume of exports. For example, in the case of VER in automobiles between Japan and the US, there was a considerable gap between initial American demands and the Japanese offer. The final agreed level of permissible exports was a compromise that was more acceptable to the Japanese government and car manufacturers;

2. Unlike tariff protection, where economic rent accrues to the importing country, VERs allowed manufacturers in the exporting country to appropriate a part of the economic rent. VERs were thus profitable because they allowed the exporter to demand a premium on the actual price. For example, following the US–Japan VER agreement, the retail price of a Japanese car in 1984 was 14.4 percent more than what it would have been without the trade restriction.[23]

From the perspective of the United States, VERs and other trade restrictive practices were preferred because of the following three reasons:

1. VERs were effective as a support to depressed industries and a more efficient form of protection than the available GATT escape clause;
2. It allowed them to adhere to the pretence that the GATT rules had not been violated and that their support for free trade remained unaffected. This was so because it did not entail any formal resort to trade restriction through tariff etc;
3. The US could use its superior power position to secure a better outcome in a bilateral negotiation than in a multilateral GATT forum with equal voting rights.

Bhagwati expressed concern that voluntary export restraint could also become the basis for "voluntary import expansion."[24] This could be the result if American pressure to open foreign markets imposed a commitment to buy from the United States and guarantee a specific share of the market to American exporters. In 1993, during the visit to the US by Japanese Prime Minister Miyazawa, there was considerable pressure for

Japan to agree to a system of guaranteed market shares for American exports but the Japanese government rejected this as inconsistent with liberal trade. There were instances, however, such as in semiconductors trade, where this approach was used to expand American exports to Japan. The first semiconductor pact between Japan and the United States covered the period 1986–1991 while the second pact covered the period 1991–1996. Under the agreement, Japan promised American semiconductor manufacturers a 20 percent share of the Japanese domestic market. This after the US government declared it unreasonable that US manufacturers should have only a miniscule share of Japanese market compared to their domination of other foreign markets. To fulfill the terms of the agreement, the Japanese government had to bear upon major electronics manufacturers to increase the import of chips from the United States.[25] The 20 percent market share was achieved in 1993 after extraordinary purchases by Japanese firms.

Other commonly employed neo-protectionist measures were antidumping and countervailing duty actions. Such actions were initiated as retaliation against unfair foreign competition but were themselves arbitrary and unfair. Again, the United States was among the most frequent user of anti-dumping action, together with the EC, Canada and Australia. In the US, the Commerce Department is responsible for investigating allegations of dumping and, since 1980, it handed down findings of dumping on all but 5 percent of cases, penalizing more than 3000 foreign companies. The process is completely arbitrary. A determination of "fair price" was made after comparisons with an arbitrarily chosen group of countries and the Commerce Department also used an arbitrary profit margin of 8 percent, even though the average profit rate for US companies was only around 6 percent, below the figure chosen by the Commerce Department as to what constituted normal profit. In Japan, in the early 1980s, the after tax return on sales for the average manufacturing company was only about 1–2 percent.[26] Using the American definition of dumping, Lester Thurow pointed out that 17 out of the 20 largest US industrial firms could be accused of dumping.[27]

Using such dubious tactics, the Commerce Department handed down many controversial decisions. For example, China was found guilty of dumping manhole covers after comparisons with production prices in Belgium, Canada, France and Japan showed Chinese prices to be too low.[28] Much more pathetic was the case of Japanese TV exports to the US where the Commerce Department decided to include TV sets donated to charity as sales at $0.00. This lowered the Japanese company's average selling price in the US and raised its dumping margin.[29] Such arbitrariness only eroded the gains made by the GATT since the end of the Second World War.

Strategic Trade Theory

The classical and neoclassical argument that the incentives for trade can be found either in different levels of technological development between countries (Ricardo/classicalists) or in differences in factor endowments (Heckscher-Ohlin-Samuelson/neoclassicalists) assumed perfect competition and constant returns to scale.[30] Strategic trade theory, also known as new international economics or new trade theory, contested these assumptions and suggested that trade could arise also from imperfect competition and increasing returns to scale.[31] Strategic trade theorists did not necessarily disclaim free trade arguments but added the caveat that under certain circumstances, deviations from free trade could enhance national welfare. This attacked the core of free trade principle and the conviction that free trade was the optimum trade policy from the viewpoint of national welfare. As discussed below, strategic trade theory has evolved from an early emphasis on increasing returns to scale to a greater emphasis on external economies.

The term "strategic" in strategic trade meant several things. It suggested that long-term considerations and gains may require some short-term sacrifices such as the granting of initial subsidies to ensure profitability of firms and trading opportunities that might, otherwise, be lost to foreign competitors. It also implied that international trade could be a zero-sum game where the gain of one country came largely at the expense of another. In this, strategic trade theory was similar to earlier principles of mercantilism.

Strategic trade theorists argued that in industries characterized by increasing returns[32] and imperfect competition (or oligopolistic competition), firms might be able to extract higher returns if new entrants were deterred or forced to vacate the production space. Recognizing the possibility that oligopolistic firms could internalize excess rent, strategic trade theory proposed that governments might step in with policies to shift the advantage away from foreign to domestic firms. Using this insight, Paul Krugman suggested that, "A country can raise its national income at other countries' expense if it can somehow ensure that the lucky firm that gets to earn excess returns is domestic rather than foreign."[33] Similarly, according to Lester Thurow, "Economic analysis shows that there are gains to be made with strategic trade policies, especially in industries with increasing returns ... ."[34]

Moreover, strategic trade theorists, predominantly Americans, argued that where potential gains were high, states could intervene to ensure success of domestic firms even if the advantage of the first-mover was lost to foreign competitors. If a foreign firm, without state subsidy, entered the market first, the home government could still force it out of the market by offering subsidy payments to domestic firms. If however, a foreign firm entered the market with subsidies, the home government could offer countervailing subsidies to domestic firms, not only to punish foreign governments and producers but to capture the industry for domestic firms. The latter possibility attracted the most attention because of the belief that American firms were being driven away from profitable sectors by subsidized foreign production.

As with neo-protectionism, the main empirical referent of strategic trade theory was Japan. In his survey of Japanese industrial policy and its impact, Gregory Noble observed that, "... there is no doubt that the new theorizing on international economics [i.e. strategic trade theory] has been inspired in part by Japan's success ... ."[35] We might also add examples of other East Asian economies, Korea and Taiwan in particular, that realized similarly "miraculous" economic development in the postwar period by adopting the Japanese model.

Industrial policy implies that a state not only intervenes in the economy to compensate for market failure, but assumes also a more proactive role in targeting and promoting specific industries as potential winners.

Chalmers Johnson attributed Japanese economic success to the Ministry of International Trade and Industry (MITI), which used protection, subsidies and various other measures to nurture the competitiveness of particular industries. There is, of course, no consensus that industrial policy and industrial targeting is a sufficient or a valid explanation for Japanese economic success, given that the Japanese government also committed numerous mistakes, such as promoting a domestic aluminium industry or funding research for fifth generation computers. Presenting the opposing viewpoint, Gary Saxonhouse argued that Japan's rapid economic growth was largely the result of market conditions and good macro-economic policies, such as policies to encourage domestic savings and investment, rather than sectoral targeting.

Nonetheless, proponents of industrial policy argued that the US government should learn from, and emulate, the Japanese experience to avoid falling behind in the industrial race. Alternatively, since the Japan government was already assumed to be providing special assistance to particular sectors of the economy, proponent of industrial policy advocated retaliatory trade policies and industrial targeting. Lester Thurow prescribed retaliation to create a "level playing field" for American firms and to safeguard American interests. He suggested that, "The United States ... announce that it will duplicate any policies put in place in the rest of the world. Foreign industrial policies in wealthy countries will be matched dollar for dollar. Any subsidy going to Airbus Industries in Europe will be matched by an equivalent subsidy to the American airframe manufacturing industry."[36] The assumption was that the terrain upon which American and foreign firms were engaged in competition was tilted in favor of foreign firms and that the American government, therefore, had to step in to provide a level playing field that did not disadvantage American producers.

For Robert Reich, a strong advocate of strategic trade and Secretary of Labor in the Clinton administration, defending free trade was no longer a viable option for the United States. The real issue, he asserted, was how the US should manage its international trade. He argued that because other nations pursued strategic trade, the US should do likewise to avoid being left behind in the competitive race. According to Reich, "If other nations are being more strategic about their trade policies than we are, to our detriment, then it is reasonable to conclude that we must change our ways."[37]

Robert Reich recommended a dual strategy for the US to regain competitive advantage. First, he suggested that the government spend more on education and on developing skills in the work force. The need was obvious because a modern economy depended on trained and well-equipped workforce and only the public sector was in a position to invest in human resource development. The second strategy related to industrial policy. He observed that the United States already had an industrial policy but one that was run from the Defence Department. While acknowledging the commercial spinoffs of military technology, he suggested that the American "... investment strategy should be to take the nation's research and development efforts out from under Pentagon and its sister agencies, and turn them over to civilian agencies whose explicit goal is to spur the nation's commercial competitiveness."[38]

Proponents of free trade, understandably, found little to recommend in strategic trade. One criticism of strategic trade theory was that a policy of state intervention on a sectoral basis would be dysfunctional and leave the state captive to special interest groups. This, the critics asserted, would naturally erode the state's capacity to behave in a strategic manner. Others argued that the nature of government-business relationship in the US was very different from countries like Japan and which reduced the capacity of the American government to behave strategically.

The intense interest that was generated when strategic trade theories were first advanced has subsided and indeed, appears to have been relegated to the background. Even proponents were willing to recant and as Klaus Stegemann mentioned, "... a more sober assessment is beginning to take hold. Indeed, the authors of the theories of strategic trade policy are anxious to put some distance between themselves and those who recommend an activist trade policy or industrial policy."[39] The reasons for this reversal of fortune can be found in the tenuous and flawed assumptions behind strategic trade theory and the potential for misuse of the theory by protectionists groups for their selfish, rather than strategic, gains. According to Stegemann:

"A combination of reasons seems to have been responsible: the realization that the apparent policy implications of models of strategic trade policy are highly sensitive to changes in the special assumptions of these models; the difficulty of identifying real-world situations in which the special assumptions apply; the recognition that the costs of implementing strategic trade policies might easily exceed the benefits; even if appropriate 'target' industries could be identified; and the apprehension that economic theory was becoming a supplier of intellectual ammunition for powerful forces that favor protection of particular sectors for the 'wrong' reasons."[40]

The main problem with a strategic trade policy was the potential for retaliation and initiation of a spiralling increase in subsidy expenditures, detrimental to both countries. This was the outcome in the case of agricultural subsidies in the US and the EC. The escalating costs of subsidy payments in the EC and US are illustrated in the table below.

The escalating US farm subsidy payment bill was, to a considerable extent, predicated on the earlier EC policy of subsidizing agricultural production and exports under the Common Agricultural Policy. The Common Agricultural Policy (CAP) was part of the 1958 Treaty of Rome which led

Table 4.2.   Agricultural subsidy payments.

	1980	1980	1980	1980
US	US$2.7 b (100)	US$7.4b (274)	US$17.7 b (656)	US$25.8 b (956)
EC	ECU11.3 b (100)	ECU18.3 b (161)	ECU20.0 b (195)	ECU22.1 b (196)

Notes: The figures in parentheses are index numbers, with 1970 = 100. [The exchange rate between the ECU and the US dollar is about 1ECU = US$0.80.]
Source: *Nihon to Uruguay Round* [Japan and the Uruguay Round], Ministry of Foreign Affairs, Tokyo, Japan, 1988, p. 34.

to the formation of the Common Market. Under the CAP, target prices were established for agricultural commodities and while the primary objective was to stabilize farm incomes, it resulted in large-scale over-production, given the attractiveness of the target prices. The surplus domestic stock was released in the export market and progressively, EC farm producers encroached into traditional US markets for agricultural goods. At the same time, because of high American support prices for grain during the early 1980s, potential exports were diverted into in-creasing government stocks. As a consequence of the European push and inappropriate farm policies in the US, American agricultural exports declined from US$43 billion in 1980 to US$26 billion in 1986, before recovering to US$37.6 billion in 1988, helped by the Export Enhancement Program of 1985. The costliness of the subsidy war, at a time of escalating fiscal deficits and budgetary constraints, was one factor that prompted American interest in placing agriculture trade on the agenda of the Uruguay Round of trade negotiations in the hope of reducing levels of farm subsidy. The EC, for its part, had been aware and concerned about the costliness of the CAP and as early as 1968 the Mansholt Plan pointed to the negative results of maintaining high target prices for agricultural goods. The progressive worsening of fiscal conditions led to reforms beginning in 1984 and in 1988, additional reform measures were accepted, including ceilings on the annual growth rate of agricultural appropriations, greater reliance on market forces, and penalties for production in excess of specified targets.[41]

Each, for its own reasons, had realized the folly of a subsidies war but it was not just the US and the EC that were affected. It also had a detrimental impact on smaller, and non-subsidized, agriculture producing countries, like the Cairns Group,[42] which were disadvantaged in com-peting with subsidized exports originating in the US and the EC.

Krugman eventually acknowledged that retaliation would erode any strategic advantage that a country might acquire through subsidized pro-duction but continued to maintain that where the potential gains were large, the risks might be worth taking.[43] He also conceded that strategic trade theory only supplemented, but did not necessarily supplant the more traditional arguments in favor of free trade.

Another weakness of the strategic trade theory was that the payoff matrix might not be known to national decision makers in advance, in which case it would be very difficult to quantify the potential gains or the necessary subsidy levels. A final criticism was that subsidized industries would remain inefficient producers and dependent on continuation of subsidies.

In light of criticisms, strategic trade theorists subsequently shifted grounds. As we saw above, critics attacked strategic trade as unworkable on logical and theoretical grounds and strategic trade theorists themselves failed to provide convincing evidence that strategic trade theory, in its original formulation which emphasized increasing returns to scale, could be a useful guide to policy makers. Paul Krugman admitted as much when he stated that tests on strategic trade policy suggested that "... the best policies are usually very low tariff or subsidy rates, say 10–20 percent. The gains from deviating from free trade, furthermore, are very small ... If no effort to quantify the strategic trade policy argument has produced a strong case for taking it seriously, we can take it as likely that there is not much in it."[44]

Without abandoning completely the case for state intervention in the economy, Paul Krugman modified his original argument to suggest that industrial policy was viable only in industries with real external economies and spillover effects. He illustrated this by saying that when a strong semiconductor industry led to a more productive aircraft and computer industry (external economies), it might be worthwhile supporting the semiconductor industry.[45] By the mid-1990s, however, Krugman appeared to have abandoned strategic trade theory altogether. In *Competitiveness: A Dangerous Obsession*, he argued that proponents of managed trade were guilty of ignoring the fact that growth in living standards was achieved not by out-competing other countries but through domestic productivity. He went on to add the note of caution that obsession with international competitiveness was misplaced because it contained a real risk of "... trade conflict, perhaps even ... world trade war."[46] Krugman may have seen the light but he did not convince the committed advocates of managed trade who criticized him for "... running away from the implications of his own [initial] findings."[47]

Apart from a lively and intense theoretical debate, strategic trade theory did not overwhelm policy directions in the US. Indeed, neither strategic trade nor neo-protectionism completely undermined the GATT-based liberal trade regime but the dangers were clearly recognized by the leading economic powers. It was to avert further erosion of the rule-based multilateral regime that the GATT members decided to initiate the Uruguay Round of trade negotiations, in the expectation that the process of negotiations would, at least, put a cap on the protectionist sentiments.

Protectionism in a Global Economy

The emergence of a global economy has altered the nature of inter-state trade and the calculus of protectionism. For instance, President Clinton, in 1993, threatened retaliation against the European Airbus for unfair trading, but was forced to reconsider when it became clear that actions against Airbus would hurt American firms, since half the production of Airbus was subcontracted to US firms.[48]

Historically, every period of liberal trade has relied on certain sectors of the economy to push for progressive liberalization. In the early post-war period, the US auto industry was, for example, an advocate of liberal trade. In the contemporary period, global corporations are both the main beneficiaries of globalization and proponents of liberalization. The output of global corporations are, typically, global products with components and parts sourced from many different countries. Consequently, as global corporations become dominant players, it will become increasingly difficult to distinguish a foreign import and a domestic product. Protectionism, however, requires an ability to specifically target imports in order to benefit domestic products. It stands to reason, therefore, that under globalization, protectionist arguments will be harder to sustain.

Global corporations are important new players in the international political economy but globalization is, by no means, a complete reality and protectionist policies will continue to find favor in some sectors of the economy which are less globalized. It is optimistic to presume that protectionism or the threat of it, have been purged from the international

economic system. In the contemporary period, proponents of protectionism have teamed up with opponents of globalization to push for
their own definition of the national interest. Opposition to liberal trade,
according to Michael Hart, now comes from a collection of populist and
national interests such as unions, human rights and environmental
activists.[49] Opposition to globalization comes from defenders of existing
social values and national political sovereignty. If free trade is the engine
of globalization, it is dismissed simply as a moral doctrine and one
that is less desirable than the alternative values of social stability and
harmony. For David Morris,[50] the social cost of globalization is too high
and if the march of globalization can be impeded only be preventing
further economic liberalization, it is easy to see that champions of
protection to sectors of the economy should find natural allies in the
opponents of a global economy.

It is ironic that despite the fact that free trade benefits consumers,
one of the leading consumer activists, Ralph Nader, was at the forefront
of opponents to the Uruguay Round agreement. He argued that further
liberalization of the US economy would lead to unemployment and
reduced labor standards. More seriously, he charged, that globalization
was a conspiracy led by the corporate sector [essentially the global cor-
porations] to diminish US sovereignty and undermine American
democracy.[51] His campaigns were directed not only at the American
government but governments everywhere, on grounds that the Uruguay
Round was the first step toward an erosion of national sovereignty.

The scare tactics to prevent American ratification of the Uruguay
Round Agreement was a repeat of the earlier campaign mounted against
the International Trade Organization after the Second World War. The
only difference was that this time, few were convinced that the WTO was
a supranational institution that would usurp national sovereignty by
stealth.

Amid progressive globalization, the reaction of governments cannot be
expected to be uniformly enthusiastic. As mentioned in Chapter one,
globalization tends to expose weaknesses in national economic structures,
as happened most recently in the Asian economic crises of 1997–1998.
There may be a backlash to globalization in some countries and an

attempt to de-couple national economies from global forces with the objective of preserving national economic autonomy. Following the Asian crisis, there were some concerns that there may be attempts to roll-back liberal reforms and disengage from global market reforms. This however, did not eventuate. IMF structural adjustment loans prevented a backslide but even in Malaysia, which refused to submit to IMF conditionality, there was no lasting departure from relatively liberal policies. Indeed, these is clean appreciation of the fact that recovery from the crisis will depend on access to global markets and resources.

We cannot be sanguine that the demon of protectionism has been exorcised, but even in the 1970s and 1980s, the resurgence of protectionism had failed to overwhelm support for freer trade. Indeed, many countries also introduced policies to liberalize and deregulate their national economies. Thus, unlike in 1880s and 1890s, when reciprocitarians undermined the free trade regime, Andrea Boltho emphasized that reciprocitarians failed to achieve that outcome in the late 1980s. Boltho said this divergent outcome might be attributed to higher levels of institutionalization of liberal trade and to the presence of regionalism. The view on regionalism is not uniform (see below) but according to Boltho, "The protectionism of the 1970s and 1980s may have been limited in part because it was unable to attack intra-regional trade head-on. Infringing multilateral treaties seems a much more hazardous enterprise for countries nowadays than reneging on bilateral agreements was in the 1880s or 1890s."[52]

Finally, issue linkage has emerged as a controversial feature of international economic relations. The link between trade and investment is not particularly controversial but that cannot be said about attempts to link trade with human rights or international labor standards. Globalization has enabled countries to link into a global strategy and benefit from trade development. Developed countries have, however, tried to link it with political objectives such as human rights. Left to themselves, corporations and businesses, of course, will make their trade, production and marketing decisions purely on market principles rather than political considerations. Thus, as Xiaohua Yang argues, "The needs of the global economy ... are always under some tension from the needs of national and foreign policy objectives."[53]

Alternatively, governments may embrace economic globalization and seek to profit from global opportunities. The policy structure could be geared more to ensuring liberal trade practices so that corporations can pursue a strategy of flexible production and rapid response to changing conditions.

Regionalism

In 1995, the WTO Secretariat produced a report on international trade and argued that while it was unlikely that the world would slide into protectionism as in the 1930s, there remained the threat of regionalism and the "... fracturing of the global economy into inward-looking and potentially antagonistic trading blocs."[54] The WTO Director-General, Renato Ruggiero, while acknowledging that there was no natural contradiction between multilateralism and regionalism, expressed concerns that of the 80 regional associations examined by the GATT/WTO by 1995, only six were found consistent with GATT rules.[55]

In contrast to the above, opponents of globalization are more likely to support regional association. For example, James Goldsmith argued that globalization will lead to a rapid race to the bottom as gains in the standard of living in advanced countries are whittled down to the level of the cheapest competitor, in the interest of remaining internationally competitive. He suggested that it is better therefore to oppose globalization across a diverse range of countries in favor of aggregation of more similar countries. He wrote that, "We must reject the concept of global free trade and replace it with regional free trade. This does not mean closing off regions from trading with the rest of the world. It means allowing each region to decide whether and when to enter into bilateral agreements with other regions for mutual economic benefit."[56]

Regionalism refers to the establishment of preferential economic arrangements among a small group of countries, usually within a particular geographical region. In the post-war period, despite the presence of a "universal" trade regime, such preferential trading arrangements have proliferated. The early justification of regionalism often was that regional associations were stepping stones towards effective and real multilateralism, rather than alternatives to multilateral institutions.

The many forms of regionalism include free trade agreements, customs union, and common markets. Free trade agreements refer to the abolition of trade restrictions between the constituent countries while each constituent member retains the right to establish its own structure of restrictions against all other countries. A customs union refers to abolition of trade restrictions internally and the maintenance of a common external trade policy. A common market is the highest form of union and involves members in a customs union which, at the same time, guarantees free factor (labor and capital) mobility.

The GATT did not forbid regional associations provided that the level of protection against outsiders was no higher than before (Article 24). trade purists and defenders of the principle of multilateralism reject regionalism as undesirable. Jagdish Bhagwati, for example, argued that regional institutions are neither easily universalized nor necessarily more effective, because of relatively small membership, in reaching trade liberalization agreements. Using the example of European integration, he pointed out that Project 1992 (see below) only got underway in 1992, more than three decades after the establishment of the EC.[57] In general, however, any assessment of regionalism must distinguish between closed and open regionalism and while closed regionalism may indeed be deleterious to world trade, open regionalism need not belong in the same category.

Regional trade blocs are also frowned upon because of their trade diversionary potential, which would be a violation of the principle of non-discrimination. Empirical evidence does suggest that viable trading blocs do trade more intensively with members than with non members, or that there is indeed a trade diversionary effect. This, however, may be due to entirely natural results, such as geographical proximity and lower transportation costs. Likewise, if members enjoyed higher growth in production and trade than the rest of the world, intra-group trade would normally be expected to grow more rapidly than trade with other countries. In an empirical test, Fieleke controlled for these factors to determine whether EC had resulted in trade diversion. Using 1948 as an arbitrary baseline, he defined "neutral" trade as trade free of government preferences, and actual 1948 trade between the EC member

Table 4.3.   European community trade (%).

	Actual intra-EC trade	Neutral intra-EC trade
1948	27.4	27.4
1950	34.7	31.3
1955	36.7	30.1
1960	39.8	35.4
1965	47.6	36.6
1970	51.9	36.3
1975	51.4	35.0
1980	52.4	34.8
1985	53.5	30.3
1990	59.2	35.7

Source: Fieleke, N. S., "One Trading World, or Many: The Issue of Regional Trading Blocs," *New England Economic Review* (Federal Reserve Bank of Boston), May/June 1992, p. 12.

countries was assumed to reflect neutral trade. For succeeding years, neutral trade is that which would have resulted if the share of intra-EC trade in total EC trade increased or decreased by the same percentage as the EC share of world trade. The results are reproduced in the table below.

Based on the evidence above, Fieleke concluded that, "In fact, the share of intra-EU trade in the EU total has risen faster than the EU share of world trade, with the result that, by 1990, the share of EU trade taking place within the group was 23.5 percentage points greater than that if that trade had increased neutrally, or free of any growing bias toward doing business within the group $(59.2 - 35.7 = 23.5)$."[58]

The EU is also criticized as excessively protectionist, not only in terms of tariff protection but also in its usage of anti-dumping measures, for instance, to restrict imports into the European market. Criticisms notwithstanding, EU member countries have pressed ahead with greater regional integration. In 1992, the Union moved toward the creation of a Single European Market (SEM). The establishment of SEM had been agreed to by the members of the European Community in the Single European Act adopted in 1987. The SEM guaranteed free exchange of goods, persons, services and capital, and created the largest single market in the world. Insofar as the global significance of the SEM was concerned, there was some apprehension, particularly in the US and Japan, that the new Europe after 1 January 1993 would create a "Fortress Europe," despite assurances that Europe would remain committed to global liberal trade.

Another group of scholars, who might be labelled free trade realists,[59] are inclined to see regionalism as a supplement to and, indeed, as a catalyst for multilateral trade liberalization, partly on the assumption that free trade agreements between a small group of countries are eventually universalized through an ever increasing circle of membership, as with the European Union, whose membership increased from 6 in 1952 to 15 in 1995, and likely to increase further with the incorporation of former socialist European countries. These scholars regard regionalism as either a benign development or positively beneficial to multilateral free trade. Among the realists, we might include Lester Thurow, Rudiger Dornbusch, and Paul Krugman, who portray regionalism as an alternative to multilateralism that is unwieldy and unsuited to contemporary conditions.

A third group of scholars is inclined to see the resurgence of regionalism as a response to the emergence of a global economy or, more appropriately, regional economies. They see regionalization, rather than globalization, as the dominant contemporary trend. For this group, globalization is more appropriately defined as regionalization, with true globalization a project for the future. Production processes, therefore, are not truly globalized but regionalized. Speculative capital flows may be global, but foreign trade and direct foreign investment tend more to be regionally concentrated. Indeed, if we consider trade flows for certain regions, we find that intra-Asia trade was 42 percent of total trade in 1989 and the corresponding figures for North America and the European Union were 35 percent and 58 percent, respectively.[60]

Whether globalization or regionalization captures the true essence of the emerging reality, it is clear that regionalism, or regional association, has proliferated. Regionalism might be seen either as the appropriate response to regionalization, or an initial, if partial, response to globalization, given that global integration is much more difficult than regional integration. Moreover, regional association may also bring greater influence within a global economy. Indeed, some proposals for regional associations, like the East Asian Economic Caucus (EAEC), were premised on the assumption that such a grouping would add to the influence of Asian economies vis-a-vis Europe or North America.

Among the many regional associations that exist, the most successful is the European Union. The European Union began with ambitious objectives after the Second World War to create economic integration and political unity in order to lay the foundations of peace on the European continent. No other regional association has been inspired by such an ambitious goal. Most have a stated objective of maximizing economic welfare through freer trade. Examples of this include the North American Free Trade Agreement (NAFTA), which was signed in mid-December 1992, and established in 1994. It created the largest and richest trading bloc with a population of 370 million, a combined GDP of US$6.4 trillion, and total internal trade of US$267 billion. The agreement was approved by the US Congress in late November 1993, clearing the way for progressive tariff reduction from January 1994, and for the creation of the largest free trade zone in 15 years. The passage of the NAFTA bill by the American Congress was heralded as an important signal of American commitment to free trade and its rejection would have been interpreted as a protectionist response to protect the American economy from cheap Mexican imports. At the very least, it swept away the fears that the US would turn inwards. NAFTA strengthened American moral authority to press for global trade liberalization and, indeed, NAFTA was intended, in part, to act as a catalyst for the stalled GATT talks.[61]

It is unlikely that NAFTA will become a closed trading bloc of the existing members. One significant difference between NAFTA and EC, for example, was in their intra-regional trade patterns which made it unlikely that NAFTA would pursue closed regionalism. Although 60 percent of EC trade was intra-regional, the comparative figure for NAFTA was only 20 percent and in particular, the US was more export-dependent on both the EC and on the Pacific Rim economies (Japan, Southeast

Asia, and Australia) than on its other two NAFTA partners.[62] To enable future expansion, NAFTA incorporated an accession clause which made membership available to others on the condition of significant trade liberalization. In a way, perhaps, NAFTA could be useful in locking in more of the former South American countries into a more liberal and export-oriented industrialization (EOI) pattern, and away from their earlier policies of import substitution industrialization (ISI) with its many economic distortions.

In East Asia, Malaysian Prime Minister Mahathir has vigorously advocated a grouping consisting only of the East Asian countries and centered on Japan. The proposal, however, has not received much support in other Asian countries or in Japan. The bulk of Japan's trade is with countries outside the proposed EAEC and it made no practical sense for Japan to promote an East Asian regional concept. American hostility to the EAEC was, probably, another reason why Japan refused to embrace the concept. Instead, the Association of Southeast Asian Nations (ASEAN) agreed to set up its own free trade area to be known as AFTA, the ASEAN Free Trade Area.

By contrast to EAEC, the idea of open regionalism and an Asia Pacific Economic Community (APEC), proposed and initiated by the Australian government, attracted a more favorable response. At least, there was no vehement opposition to it. The initial US reaction was lukewarm but not overtly hostile. APEC member countries held their first ministerial meeting in November 1989 but there was no major breakthrough until 1993. That year, the US government took the initiative to invite APEC members to a leaders' summit in Seattle in November. The purpose was to counter concerns that NAFTA would divert trade away from the Asian countries and make access to the North American market more uncertain, as well as to allay fears that the US was retrenching its commitments in Asia and to underscore that the US could not be excluded from any regional grouping in the Pacific region. Since receiving a critical boost of momentum in 1993, APEC leaders have agreed to achieve free trade by the year 2020.

There remain, however, many unanswered questions about the future viability of APEC. One unresolved issue is whether open regionalism and its benefits should be extended to non-APEC member countries as well, on a WTO-consistent MFN basis. The United States, for example, is not enthusiastic about extending free access to its markets without some form of reciprocal liberalization. Such uncertainties and ambiguities have not helped APEC develop a strong sense of purpose and unity. Nor is APEC served well by the decision not to institutionalize APEC. The practice of a rotating annual leader has meant also that APEC has not been able to rely on a strong leader to push it through its infancy. This handicap was most clearly evident in the Asian financial crisis of 1997–1998. The crisis was an opportunity for APEC to take the initiative in managing the crisis but it remained, instead, well in the background and unable to put forward constructive proposals.

APEC has yet to prove its worth but the proliferation of regional associations led the WTO, in February 1996, to establish a Committee on Regional Trade Agreements to examine agreements, consider the systemic implications of regional initiatives for the multilateral trading system, and make recommendation to the General Council of the WTO. To date, while the WTO has been unable to affirm the consistency of most regional agreements with multilateralism, it has voiced strong support for the principle of open regionalism. Open regionalism may be consistent with the multilateralism of the GATT, if it is understood as open regionalism based on the MFN principle but this is not necessarily the consensus within APEC.

Conclusion

As discussed in this chapter, strategic trade theory, neo-protectionism, and regionalism all seriously challenged the theory and practice of free trade in the post-war period. The United States was guilty of a large number of protectionist measures, but it was not alone in this. The official US view was that it was only defending itself from unfair trade practices of countries like Japan. Not everyone, of course, accepted the view that Japanese economic prosperity was largely achieved at American expense. According to Charles Wolf, the differential performance of American and Japanese economy was due to macroeconomic imbalances, higher savings and investment rates in Japan, and to better labor and management practices in Japan.[63]

Similarly, according to Gary Saxonhouse, the peculiar Japanese trade structure was the inevitable outcome of its lack of natural resources and raw material. This meant that Japanese imports would always be skewed in favor of primary and secondary products over manufactured imports. None of this could, however, dent the perception of closed markets.

The prevailing domestic mood in the US was one of anger and frustration and proved a ready breeding ground for modern protectionists. The problem was that while arguments in favor of neoprotectionism and strategic trade may be theoretically deficient and flawed, policy makers were frequently under pressure to be seen as doing something. Even if strategic trade was not the answer to underlying problems, the immediate political imperative was enough, in some cases, for policy makers to deviate from liberal trade principles.

However, while protectionism was a serious challenge to liberal trade in the 1970s and 1980s, it would be remiss not to point out that in this same period, many countries, developing and otherwise, dismantled existing protectionist measures and adopted a more liberal foreign trade policy. Countries like Japan[64] and Australia were at the front of a conscious push to become more internationally competitive through open trade policies. Moreover, while the sentiment for retaliatory protectionism was strong, the US administration did not give in completely to the forces of protectionism.

References

1. Thurow, L., Head to Head: The Coming Economic Battle Among Japan, Europe, and America, William Morrow and Company, Inc., New York, 1992, p. 75.
2. One British scholar argued that open American markets were the biggest factors in Japan's rapid economic progress and the concommitant American decline. See Nester, William R., *Japan's Growing Power Over East Asia and the World Economy*, The Macmillan Press Ltd., Basingstoke and London, 1990, pp. 42–43.

3. Lawrence, R. Z., "The Reluctant Giant: Will Japan Take Its Role on the World Stage?" *The Brookings Review*, Vol. 9, No. 3, Summer 1991, p. 38.

4. Of course, every regime must contain some negative sanction to ensure compliance but it was a source of some concern that the United States chose to bypass the GATT in resolving trade disputes.

5. Cited in Baldwin, R. E., "The New Protectionism: A National Response to Shifts in National Economic Power," in Baldwin, R. E., *Trade Policy in a Changing World Economy*, Harvester-Wheatsheaf, London, 1988, p. 216.

6. This term was coined in the 1970s to depict the anomalous situation of high inflation and high unemployment. In neoclassical economics, the Phillips curve suggests an inverse relationship between unemployment and inflation which made it highly unlikely that the two could coexist together. This, however, ignored the possibility that, in the short term, the Phillips curve could shift to the right of the unemployment and inflation axis, leading to higher inflation and unemployment. For a graphic representation of this, see, for example, Dornbusch, R. and Stanley Fischer, *Macroeconomics*, 3rd ed., McGraw-Hill International Student Edition, Singapore, 1985, pp. 432–433.

7. Cited in Lieberman, S., *The Economic and Political Roots of New Protectionism*, Rowman and Littlefield Publishers, New Jersey, 1999, p. 161.

8. The Japanese, on their part, condemned it as crude Japan-bashing and a misplaced attempt to make Japan the scapegoat for real problems within the US.

9. Sassoon, E., "Protectionism and International Trade Negotiations During the 1980s," in Grilli, E. and Enrico Sassoon (eds.), *The New Protectionist Wave*, New York University Press, New York, 1990, pp. 11–12.

10. The high interest rates induced by domestic capital shortage and budget deficits in the US was one important factor that to a sharp increase in the debt financing burden of the developing countries and the debt crisis of the 1980s. We will explore this in a later chapter.

11. *Economic Report of the President*, US Government Printing Office, Washington, DC, February 1991, pp. 240–241.
12. See Destler, I. M., Haruhiro Fukui and Hideo Sato, *The Textile Wrangle: Conflict in Japan-America Relations, 1969–1971*, Cornell University Press, Ithaca, 1979, p. 296.
13. Cited in Bhagwati, J., "Protectionism: Old Wine in New Bottles," in Salvatore, D. (ed.), *The New Protectionist Threat to World Welfare*, North-Holland, New York, 1987, p. 38.
14. Curzon, G. and Victoria Curzon Price, "The GATT Regime: Issues and Prospects," in Rode, R. (ed.), *GATT and Conflict Management: A Transatlantic Strategy for a Stronger Regime*, Westview Press, Boulder, Co., 1990, p. 10.
15. For details see Bhagwati, J., "Aggressive Unilateralism: An Overview," in Bhagwati, J. and Hugh T. Patrick (eds.), *Aggressive Unilateralism: America's 301 Trade Policy and the World Trading System*, The University of Michigan Press, Ann Arbor, 1990.
16. See Dell, E., 1987, p. 246.
17. *The Straits Times* (Singapore), 25 March 1993, p. 1.
18. See Salvatore, 1991, p. 45.
19. See Bhagwati, J., "Aggressive Unilateralism: An Overview," in Bhagwati, J. and Hugh T. Patrick (eds.), *Aggressive Unilateralism: America's 301 Trade Policy and the World Trading System*, The University of Michigan Press, Ann Arbor, 1990, p. 35.
20. Curzon, G. and Victoria Curzon Price, "The GATT Regime: Issues and Prospects," in Rode, R. (ed.), *GATT and Conflict Management: A Transatlantic Strategy for a Stronger Regime*, Westview Press, Boulder, Co., 1990, p. 12.
21. Hudec, R. E., "Thinking about the New Section 301: Beyond Good and Evil," in Bhagwati, J. and Hugh T. Patrick (eds.), *Aggressive Unilateralism: America's 301 Trade Policy and the World Trading System*, The University of Michigan Press, Ann Arbor, 1990, p. 115.
22. Aggarwal, V. K., Robert O. Keohane and David B. Yoffie, "The Dynamics of Negotiated Protectionism," *American Political Science Review*, Vol. 81, No. 2, June 1987, p. 347.

23. Kawaharada, S., "Shin jidai o Mukaeru jidosha kaigai jigyo," *Tekko Kai*, Vol. 35, No. 9, 1989, p. 13.

24. Pearson, C. and James Riedel, "United States Trade Policy: From Multilateralism to Bilateralism," in Grilli, E. and Enrico Sassoon (eds.), *The New Protectionist Wave*, New York University Press, New York, 1990, p. 110.

25. Lieberman, S., *The Economic and Political Roots of New Protectionism*, Rowman & Littlefield Publishers, New Jersey, 1988, p. 164.

26. Abegglen, J. C. and George Stalk, Jr., *Kaisha: The Japanese Corporation*, Charles E. Tuttle Company, Tokyo, Japan, 1988, p. 149.

27. Thurow, L., Head to Head: The Coming Economic Battle Among Japan, Europe and America, William Morrow and Company, Inc., New York, 1992, p. 236.

28. Dodwell, D., "Increasing Use of Anti-dumping Actions Bodes Ill for World Trade," *The Straits Times,* 24 December 1992, p. 17.

29. Oppenheim, P., *Trade Wars: Japan Versus the West*, Weidenfeld and Nicolson, London, 1992, p. 21.

30. This implies that costs are constant regardless of the number of units produced and therefore, returns, or profits, are also constant.

31. This implies that costs are a function of production volume and that costs decline as production levels increase producing higher returns, or profits, as production volume increases.

32. Neoclassical economics assumes diminishing returns whereas it is now commonly understood that high technology products, for instance, are characterized by increasing returns Brian Arthus explained that "To produce a new pharmaceutical drug, computer spreadsheet program, or passenger jet, perhaps hundreds of millions of pound must be spent on research and development. Once in production, however, incremental copies are comparatively cheap. The average cost of producing high technology items falls off as more of them are made." See Arthur, W. Brian, "Pandora's Marketplace," *New Scientist Supplement,* 6 February 1993, p. 6.

33. Krugman, P. R., "Is Free Trade Passe?" *The Journal of Economic Perspectives*, Vol. 1, No. 2, Fall 1987, p. 135. On the theory and

practice of free trade, see also Milner, H. V. and David B. Yoffie, "Between Free Trade and Protectionism: Strategic Trade Policy and the Theory of Corporate Trade Demands," *International Organization*, Vol. 43, No. 2, Spring 1989.

34. Thurow, L., Head to Head: The Coming Economic Battle Among Japan, Europe, and America, William Morrow and Company, Inc., New York, 1992, p. 295.

35. Noble, G. W., "The Japanese Industrial Policy Debate," in Haggard, S. and Chung-in Moon (eds.), *Pacific Dynamics: The International Politics of Industrial Change*, CIS-Inha University, Westview Press, Boulder, Co., 1989, p. 57.

36. Thurow, L., Head to Head: The Coming Economic Battle Among Japan, Europe, and America, William Morrow and Company, Inc., New York, 1992, p. 296.

37. Reich, R. B., "We Need a Strategic Trade Policy," *Challenge*, July–August 1990, p. 42.

38. Reich, R. B., "The Economics of Illusion and the Illusion of Economics," *Foreign Affairs*, Vol. 66, No. 3, 1987/1988, p. 527.

39. Stegemann, K., "Policy Rivalry Among Industrial States: What Can We Learn from Models of Strategic Trade Policy?" *International Organization*, Vol. 43, No. 1, Winter 1989, p. 79.

40. Stegemann, K., "Policy Rivalry Among Industrial States: What Can We Learn from Models of Strategic Trade Policy?" *International Organization*, Vol. 43, No. 1, Winter 1989, p. 90.

41. Rosenblatt, J. *et al.*, The Common Agricultural Policy of the European Community: Principles and Consequences, The International Monetary Fund, Occasional Paper No. 62, Washington, D.C., November 1988, p. 21.

42. The Cairns Group comprises Argentina, Australia, Brazil, Canada, Chile, Colombia, Fiji, Hungary, Indonesia, Malaysia, New Zealand, the Philippines, Thailand, and Uruguay.

43. Krugman, P. R., "Is Free Trade Passe?" *The Journal of Economic Perspective*, Vol. 1, No. 2, Fall 1987, p. 142.

44. Krugman, P., "Does the New Trade Theory Require New Trade Policy?" *The World Economy*, Vol. 15, No. 4, July 1992, p. 435.

45. Krugman, P., "Does the New Trade Theory Require a New Trade Policy?" *The World Economy*, Vol. 15, No. 4, July 1992, p. 435.

46. Krugman, P., "Competitiveness: A Dangerous Obsession," *Foreign Affairs*, Vol. 73, No. 2, March/April 1994, p. 41.

47. Prestowitz, Clyde V. Jr., "Playing to Win," *Foreign Affairs*, Vol. 73, No. 4, July/August 1994, p. 186.

48. See de la Mothe, J. and Gilles Paquet, "Evolution and Inter-Creation: The Government-Business-Society Nexus," in de la Mothe, J. and Gilles Paquet (eds.), *Evolutionary Economics and the New International Political Economy*, Pinter, 1996, p. 16.

49. Hart, M., "WTO and the Political Economy of Globalization," *Journal of World Trade*, Vol. 31, No. 5, October 1997, p. 78.

50. Morris, D., "Free Trade: The Great Destroyer," in Mander, J. and Edward Goldsmith (eds.), *The Case Against the Global Economy: And for a Turn Toward the Local*, Sierra Club Books, San Fancisco, 1996.

51. Nader, R. and Lori Wallach, "GATT, NAFTA and the Subversion of the Democratic Process," in Mander, J. and Edward Goldsmith (eds.), *The Case Against the Global Economy: And for a Turn Toward the Local*, Sierra Club Books, San Francisco, 1996.

52. Boltho, A., "The Return of Free Trade," *International Affairs*, Vol. 72, No. 2, April 1996, p. 256.

53. Yang, X., "Globalization of the Automobile Industry: The United States, Japan, and the People's Republic of China," Praeger Publishers, Westport, 1995, p. 188.

54. See *WTO Focus*, No. 5, October/November 1995, p. 2.

55. Ruggiero, R., "Growing Complexity in International Economic Relations Demands Broadening and Deepening of the Multilateral Trade System," *WTO Focus*, No. 6, October/November 1995, p. 13.

56. Goldsmith, J., "The Winners and the Losers," in Mander, J. and Edward Goldsmith (eds.), The *Case Against the Global Economy: And for a Turn Toward the Local*, Sierra Club Books, San Francisco, 1996, p. 178.

57. Bhagwati, J. N., "Regionalism Versus Multilateralism," *The World Economy*, Vol. 15, No. 5, September 1992, p. 550.

58. Fieleke, Norman S., "One Trading World, or Many: The Issue of Regional Trading Blocs," *New England Economic Review* (Federal Reserve Bank of Boston), May/June 1992, p. 11.

59. The labels are used only for their heuristic value and are not intended to privilege one over the other.

60. Busch, Marc L. and Helen V. Milner, "The Future of the International Trading System: International Firms, Regionalism, and Domestic Politics," in Stubbs, R. and Geoffrey R. D. Underhill (eds.), *Political Economy and the Changing Global Order*, The Macmillan Press Ltd., London, 1994, p. 261.

61. Aho, C. M. and Sylvia Ostry, "Regional Trading Blocs: Pragmatic or Problematic Policy?" in Brock, W. E. and Robert D. Hormats (eds.), *The Global Economy: America's Role in the Decade Ahead*, W.W. Norton & Co., New York, 1990, p. 159.

62. Nihon Keizai Shinbun, Sunday, 23 August 1992, p. 3.

63. Cited in Auer, James E., "The Imperative U.S.-Japanese Bond," *Orbis*, Winter 1995.

64. Revisionists will, of course, argue that Japanese market opening measures were half-hearted and a cynical ploy to reassure other countries that it was committed to free trade.

Chapter Five

THE TRANSITION ECONOMIES: RUSSIA AND CHINA

The collapse of centrally planned economies in Eastern Europe and the Soviet Union in late 1980s ended the bifurcation of the world economy into two competing economic systems and created an opportunity to globalize the liberal trade regime. Indeed, as of 1995, GATT/WTO had established around 30 working parties to consider applications for membership. In this chapter, I will examine the transition from command to market-oriented economies in China and Russia; their drive to secure membership in the World Trade Organization and the implications of their membership for the World Trade Organization.

Globalizing the WTO Membership

During the Cold War, socialist economies had only limited access to the GATT and to western markets.[1] After all, as one US trade official explained, "How can you have a centrally planned economy, in which all the decisions are made by the state, in an organization whose fundamental principle is market economy?"[2] The GATT required transparency of national trade regulations and decentralized decision-making, whereas command economies had trade rules that were opaque and arbitrary, and a centralized decision-making structure. Central authorities pre-determined the level of trade by government fiat and decisions could also be altered arbitrarily or applied selectively with no recourse for a trading partner to verify nondiscrimination in trade practices. Denied access to the GATT, the socialist countries formed their own economic grouping, the Council for Mutual Economic Assistance (known either as CMEA or Comecon). This completed the political and economic bifurcation of the international system.

Nonetheless, some command economies, such as Poland and Romania, were given conditional GATT membership.[3] The benefits of participating in a liberal trading regime were selectively extended to entice some East European countries away from the Soviet Union and weaken the socialist bloc. Yugoslavia, the first East European country to join in 1966 was given the easiest entry conditions and allowed to join as if it had a market-type economy. Its only commitments were in the realm of tariff reduction. In the case of Poland, however, the GATT imposed a requirement that it expand annual imports by 7 percent to compensate "... for a similar annual increase in exports anticipated out of Poland's participation in the GATT."[4] This was done to ensure that in the absence of an operating and effective market, Polish imports would increase at least as fast as the projected increase in exports. Hungary's accession also was conditioned on a similar commitment. Romania benefited from being accorded the status of a developing country and was only required to give vague commitments to increase imports.

In the 1980s, economic difficulties forced East European countries to initiate economic reforms. The process of reform culminated in the dissolution of the CMEA in June 1991. Reform was an admission that central planning in complex and large economies could not anticipate and respond to the needs of the people.[5] Poland led the reform movement in East Europe with the objective of establishing a market-based economy within a short span of two to three years. The architect of the Polish model was Professor Jeffrey Sachs of Harvard University. It was based on three main elements: economic liberalization; macroeconomic stabilization; and privatization.[6] Economic liberalization referred to administrative and other reforms to introduce market competition. Macroeconomic stabilization was intended to created a stable and functioning monetary system and privatization was designed to transfer ownership of state corporations to the private sector. Because of the rapid pace of transition from command to a market economy, the Polish model is variously described in terms of a "big bang," "shock therapy" or going "cold turkey." The rapidity of change was justified as necessary to prevent a subversion of the reform agenda, despite the anticipated short-term economic difficulties.

Once reforms were underway, Poland and Hungary applied for a renegotiation of the terms under which the GATT membership had been extended. Poland, for example, requested the re-negotiation of its Protocol of Accession in 1989, indicating its willingness to make tariff concessions in exchange for the elimination of the special provisions. These led to the establishment in 1991 of working parties to consider the Polish and Hungarian request.[7] More important, given relative size and influence, is the question of Russian and Chinese accession to the WTO, the successor to the GATT. The main criterion for this will no doubt be economic transformation but progress toward political liberalization may also influence the final decision.

Economic Transition in China and Russia

The "big bang" approach, adopted by Poland and, later, by Russia, was a derivative of neoclassical economics. It assumed that it was better to unshackle the market from state regulations and to revive profit/ utility maximizing behavior as quickly and as thoroughly as possible. By contrast, the "gradualist" approach, adopted by China, assumed that any transition from state to market mechanisms and to new rules of behavior had to be gradual or risk general chaos and instability. If the progenitor of the big bang approach was neoclassical economics, then the antecedents of the gradualist model can be traced to institutional economics. The main insight of the institutional approach is that economic performance is dependent on institutional efficiency to lower transactions costs. For transitional economies, institutionalism advocated a gradual, rather than drastic and quick, overhaul in order to avoid the possibility of institutional vacuum and attendant chaos. The possibility of institutional vacuum was based on a reasoning that institutions take time to develop and that new structures cannot be instantly rebuilt over the ashes of a previous system.

Each school claimed superior outcomes for its model of transition but these claims have yet to be verified. It should be emphasized also that divergent Russian and Chinese reform experience, cannot be interpreted as evidence of the merits or demerits of either the gradualist or the radical approach. It is easy to fall into this logical trap but the reality is that the initial conditions in each of the two countries were so different as to make it meaningless to make a comparative assessment. While underperforming, the Chinese economy was not, at the time of the reforms, in fundamental macroeconomic imbalance as was the Russian economy. Nor did Chinese reformers have to contend with political vacuum and instability, except for a brief period in 1989, whereas the Russian reform agenda was adversely affected by the collapse of political authority and effective governance.

The impetus to reform, as mentioned above, was poor economic performance in China, the Soviet Union and elsewhere. In China, erratic economic policies under Mao Zedong had created serious economic difficulties and the post-Mao leadership was anxious to discard campaign-driven economic policies. Similarly, the Stalinist model of centralized planning had produced, in the Soviet Union, a rigid economy that was incapable of providing even for some of the basic needs of the people. Economic under-performance and constraints to economic growth forced the leadership in Russia and China to respond to the challenge of economic reform.

Starting in the late 1970s, Chinese leaders introduced greater reliance on market mechanism and decentralized decision making. The Chinese government introduced reforms at a measured pace. The reform process centered around the promotion of entrepreneurial activity rather than privatization of state-owned enterprises. By reintroducing profit incentives, the reformers hoped to encourage private initiatives and entrepreneurship. The state sector continued to operate but with a reduced share of total industrial output. In allowing public sector enterprises to coexist with private sector firms, the Chinese government followed the Taiwanese model.[8] The table below gives the share of industrial output by type of enterprises.

Table 5.1.   Percentage share of industrial output by ownership.

	State	Collective	Private
1980	76.0	23.5	0.5
1981	74.8	24.6	0.6
1982	74.4	24.8	0.7
1983	73.4	25.7	0.9
1984	69.1	29.7	1.2
1985	64.9	32.1	3.1
1986	62.3	33.5	4.2
1987	59.7	34.6	5.7
1988	56.8	36.2	7.1
1989	56.1	35.7	8.3
1990	54.5	35.7	9.8

Source: Knell, M. and Wenyan Yang, "Lessons from China on Strategy for the Socialist Economies in Transition," in Knell, M. and Christine Rider (eds.), *Socialist Economies in Transition: Appraisals of the Market Mechanism,* Edward Elgar, Aldershot, 1992, p. 220. [taken from Statistical Yearbook of China]

The Chinese government also did not commit itself to any firm schedule for completion of reforms. Indeed, there was no plan to guide the restructuring process, only an evolutionary dialectic between what was considered desirable and what was practically achievable. The initial measures involved removing state monopoly over industry. This encouraged local entrepreneurs to establish small-scale firms.

The amount of entrepreneurial investment was significant and by 1990, as indicated in the table above, nonstate firms were producing nearly half of total industrial output.[9] By the late 1990s, state-owned enterprises (SOEs) were contributing less than 30 percent to the country's industrial output.[10] However, by avoiding large-scale privatization, unemployment was kept to a minimum and state enterprises, assisted by state subsidies, continued to employ excess workers and act as a social safety net. Although such subsidies distorted the industrial structure, they also provided a safety net without which reforms may not have been so readily accepted. Even so, by allowing state enterprises to withhold part of their profits instead of remitting it all to the state, efficiency and productivity improvement was encouraged. However, profit retention and declining profitability of the state-owned enterprises, as a result of pressures from the nonstable sector, had an adverse impact on state revenue. Yet, subsidy payments continued to make enormous demands on the state budgets. This resulted in growing fiscal deficits which, in 1992, amounted to 4.7 percent of GNP, compared to a surplus of 0.3 percent in 1978.[11]

The state-owned enterprises are an unmistakable drag on the Chinese economy. In the late 1990s, there were approximately 340 000 state-owned enterprises employing more than 110 million workers. Nearly half of these are loss-making ventures and in 1996, approximately 6 200 SOEs declared bankruptcy. The inefficiencies within the SOEs pose a challenge for the state-owned commercial banks which have considerable loan exposure to the SOEs. The four state-owned commercial banks, with 90 percent of China's bank assets, are estimated to have about US$200 billion in bad debt and are technically insolvent.[12] Cognizant of the dangers for the banking industry and mindful of the need to control subsidies and fiscal deficits, the government, in September 1997, announced plans to turn around the SOEs by around the end of the century. The plan includes mergers to form more internationally competitive and viable units as well as privatization. If the plans are implemented, unemployment can be expected to increase dramatically from the existing official estimate of 4 percent.[13] Unless mechanisms are devised to deal with the growing numbers of unemployed, the restructuring schedule could fuel social instability and jeopardise the reforms. Yet, reforms are imperative because commercial banks cannot be expected to carry the burden of the SOEs indefinitely into the future, even with the plans, announced by the government in late February 1998, to recapitalize the debt-ridden banks through a bond issue of US$48 billion.

Despite burgeoning economic difficulties, China's economic transition is regarded as a success. This is evidenced by impressive increases in export levels and GNP growth. In 1992, the Chinese economy grew by

13 percent. Between 1978 and 1990, real per capita GNP growth was 7.2 percent a year and export growth was 10 percent a year.[14] The high export growth reflected the success of reforms to enhance the country's level of international competitiveness and efficiency.

Critical to the success of reforms is the flow of foreign investment into China. Foreign investment has been led by overseas Chinese, not only for reasons of ethnic identity, but also to take advantage of a developing regional division of labor. The level of investment reflects investor confidence that the new openness is not a transient phenomenon. Between 1979 and 1992, the authorized level of total direct foreign investment in China was US$109.8 billion, of which US$34.5 billion had actually been invested. Approximately 70 percent of total foreign investment was from Hong Kong, Macao, Taiwan and the ASEAN countries.[15]

In Russia, economic reforms were initiated by Gorbachev and were, initially, gradual and piecemeal. The program however, was unable to stem the crisis within the Soviet economy, and indeed by early 1991, according to Grigorii Khanin, the state of the economy had deteriorated into a catastrophe. In the first quarter of 1991, for example, Soviet national income declined by an estimated 15–16 percent in real terms.[16] There is no clear and simple explanation for the failure and Anders Aslund identified nine stumbling blocks in the process of transition, such as the neglect of democratic processes, unfound belief in gradualism, inability to conceptualize the market, and excessive confidence in the capabilities of the state apparatus.[17] The importance of democratization to legitimize economic reform was also recognized by Jude Wanniski, who explained that, "The economic structure must change continually to keep pace with changing times in a competitive world economy; an optimum democratic structure provides the foundation for such change, enabling the people to exert their wisdom in guiding the direction and contour of economic change."[18] Essentially, the argument was that democratic decision making processes are better suited to coping with change.

It did not help either that the Soviet central government was plagued by political instability and contending forces within the country. While Gorbachev struggled to preserve the Union and pursue reforms, other centrifugal forces were working in the opposite direction. Gorbachev's tragedy was that while he introduced reforms, he seemed incapable of making a fundamental break with the old system. As Carl Linden argued, "Gorbachev was not radical enough. He failed to follow a public that began to press for a break with, not a reform of, the communist autocracy."[19] His equivocation alienated both defenders of the old system and proponents of a new order. He was eventually swept away by the more reformist and elected Boris Yeltsin but before that also had to contend with a coup attempt in August 1991 led by officers in the Soviet military who sought to strengthen central authority. The coup was a desperate move to preempt a new treaty limiting the powers of the central government in favor of a more devolved structure of governance. The coup leaders, however, failed to isolate and suppress the opposition, and the ensuing struggle ended disastrously for them and for the Soviet Union. It hastened the dissolution of the Soviet Union, and the 15 constituent republics, in quick succession, declared independence. A loose confederation was, however, agreed upon on 8 December 1991 and, consequently, on 26 December, the Soviet Union was replaced by the Confederation of Independent States (CIS). Thereafter the reform process in Russia, the largest republic in the CIS, received a tremendous boost under the leadership of its reformist President Boris Yeltsin.

In suggesting the options available to Russia, analysts and policy makers gravitated to the Polish model. This was notwithstanding the relative success of the Chinese experience. Among the few who have favored the Chinese model, Amitai Etzioni advocated gradual transition simply because economic transformation was not a mechanical process that could be made to work like clockwork.[20] Similarly, McMillan and Naughton criticized the big bang strategy for weaknesses similar to that inherent in central planning. They argued that its success depended on the availability of reliable and comprehensive information on the economy, and on the ability of big bang planners to do better than former economic planners.[21] Critics of the gradualist reform model, however, argued that the absence of a plan made it impossible for other countries to replicate the Chinese model. Advocates of radical reform also feared that momentum for change might be lost if the process was too gradual.

Inside Russia, the radical option was reflected in the Shatalin 500 Day Plan, named after Stanislav Shatalin under whose direction Yegor Gaidar and Aleksandr Shokhlin, advisers to Boris Yeltsin, drafted the plan. The plan entailed a sequence of reform measures that would enable the transition to a market-dominant economy within 500 days, beginning on 1 October 1990. The plan can be roughly summarized as below.[22]

0–100 Days: Privatization of small business and macroeconomic stabilization. Establish the legislative foundations for privatization, taxation, banking etc.

100–250 Days: Large-scale privatization of housing and agricultural land.

250–400 Days: Continuation of privatization, anti-monopoly activities and full price liberalization.

400–500 Days: Beginning of economic upswing, major public investment program to combat unemployment.

Not surprisingly, the actual reform strategy did not adhere to the plan as envisaged. The main features of the reform agenda were privatization of state-owned enterprises, price liberalization, and economic stabilization. Because public enterprises were inefficient and managed to survive only with generous state subsidies, it was obvious to reformers that privatization had to be a key component of the restructuring program. The faith in privatization as a solution to economic problems stemmed from the view that public companies, weaned off governmental subsidies and support, would be forced to accept financial discipline and that exposure to market conditions would force them to achieve allocative efficiency.[23] The approach to privatization was a key difference between the Russian and Chinese models. Defenders of the gradualist model argued that privatization had to be sequential and slow because market valuations could not be ascertained and rapid privatization at less than fair values would only lead to inequities over the longer term.[24]

Privatization in Russia was to cover state enterprises other than state farms and it was stated that roughly 20–25 percent of state property would be privatized in 1992. Privatization of state-owned enterprises could be initiated by workers and employees. The privatization plan announced by President Yeltsin in December 1991 established four categories of privatization criteria. The sector where privatization was obligatory included retail and wholesale trade, unprofitable enterprises and construction materials enterprises. Those that could be privatized with permission of the Russian government included defense industry and research, air transport, pharmaceutical, and fuel and power industry. Those enterprises that could be privatized with consent of local authorities included taxis, municipal services and hotels. The final category included enterprises that could not be privatized and included natural resources, historic and cultural facilities, highways, and power stations.[25] Major privatization began in August 1992 with the distribution of 10 000 rouble vouchers to every individual to buy into state corporations.

Price liberalization proceeded on the belief that unless true relative prices were established, progress on other fronts would continue to be distorted by inaccurate prices. Price decontrol was begun in early January 1992 and the immediate result was high levels of price increases. In the month of January alone, consumer prices increased by 250 percent but the inflationary spiral subsided in later months after the initial surge. The problem with price liberalization was that, in the absence of an open import regime, there was very little effective control on price rises to ensure that prices did not overshoot international market prices. Excessively high prices not only affected individual consumers, but also consumers of secondary inputs. This may have forced otherwise viable firms into bankruptcy, because with high input costs and no recourse to cheaper imported inputs they were no longer profitable.

Unlike the transition in China, which was assisted by a large inflow of foreign direct assistance, the Russian economy received little foreign capital input. The importance of such assistance had increased following downward revision of estimated Soviet gold reserves which were now regarded as inadequate to finance the transition process.[26] According to David Roche of Morgan Stanley International, Russia's total financial needs, including infrastructure, social welfare and balance of payments assistance, were between US$76 to US$167 billion a year.[27] Jeffrey Sachs extrapolated that since western countries had provided Eastern European countries — with a population base of 125 million — with approximately US$57 billion between the summer of 1989 and May 1990, Russian requirements were likely to be in excess of US$100 billion.[28]

Compared to Russian needs, promised financial assistance was insignificant. Not only was official assistance slow in coming but private sector capital flows, too, did not materialize because of continued political and economic instability in Russia. This was in sharp contrast to China and, Jeffrey Sachs, the leading Western proponent of shock therapy, blamed setbacks in the Russian reform process to Western insincerity and poor strategy of aid disbursement. For example, he pointed out that the West had failed to provide even the aid that had been promised. In 1992, US$24 billion had been promised but only US$10 billion was actually delivered and in 1993, US$28 billion was promised and only US$5 billion delivered.[29] Foreign assistance remained limited for a number of reasons.

The United States was burdened by its own fiscal accounts deficits and an improbable source for large-scale financial assistance. Germany, too, was in no position to extend significant aid to Russia considering that the reunification of East and West Germany had already cost the Bonn government more than US$100 billion. Japan, a capital surplus country, was reasonably well placed to provide financial assistance, but was unwilling to assist the Russian economic transition. Jeffrey Sachs observed that the Japanese government played an essentially harmful role in the process of Russian transition,[30] by withholding substantial aid until a resolution of the territorial dispute and return of the four northern islands, Habomai, Shikotan, Kunashiri and Etorofu, occupied by the Soviet Union after the Second World War.[31]

The Japanese government relented in April 1993 and declared that it would no longer link aid to Russia with the territorial issue. This turn-around followed a French proposal to convene a special summit to discuss aid to Russia, which the Japanese government feared would sideline the Tokyo summit of the seven industrialized countries in July 1993. The Japanese government finessed over its embarrassment by distinguishing between the territorial dispute, which was a *bilateral* issue, and aid to Russia which was a *multilateral* policy to encourage Russian economic reforms and in the interest of world peace and democracy. In April 1993, both the United States and Japan announced separate aid packages to Russia. The G–7 finance ministers also agreed on a major aid package totalling about US$45 billion.

Sachs also criticized the Western strategy of disbursing aid through the IMF which acted like a cautious banker rather than as coordinators of Western aid. His recommendation was for a radical restructuring of the IMF and the World Bank to make these institutions more responsive to Russian needs. One IMF official, however, dismissed Sach's criticisms as misdirected and suggested that the real problem afflicting the Russian economy was a general inability of the political system to fend off sectional interests and their demands for welfare and transfer payments. These, he claimed, had rendered the task of balancing the state budget much more difficult and, consequently, resulted in poor macroeconomic stabilization.[32]

In the area of stabilization policy and budget reform, apart from reducing budget deficits, the plan involved a float of the Russian rouble and currency convertibility from 1 January 1992. Major emphasis was on reducing budget deficits and controlling inflation. The importance of combating inflation was emphasized on grounds that reform would not succeed if inflation was not kept in check because inflation sapped work incentives and social support for reform.[33] Western aid agencies similarly emphasized the importance of reducing inflation levels and, in 1992, when Russia joined the IMF, it secured loans of US$24 billion, conditioned on drastic cutbacks in budget deficit and strict adherence to fiscal austerity.

On paper, at least, the Russian government appeared to comply with fiscal austerity needs. In the first half of 1992, budget deficit was reduced to only 5 percent of GNP, compared to 20 percent in the previous year. Similarly, in 1995, the government adopted an austere budget in order to secure additional IMF funding. While no one expected reforms and fiscal austerity to produce an immediate turnaround of the Russian economy, what eventuated was a curious mix of negative growth rates and high inflation.

It is possible to give several explanations for Russia's tortured transition experience. It might be argued, for example, that the nature of the

Table 5.2.   **Russian economic indicators.**

	1992	1993	1994	1995	1996
Real GDP growth	−14.5%	−8.7%	−12.6%	−4.0%	−2.8%
Inflation	1, 353%	699.8%	302%	190.1%	47.8%

Source: *World Economic Outlook*, May 1997, International Monetary Fund, Washington, DC.

privatization process itself hindered efficiency gains. The sale of state enterprises to workers, through the voucher system, meant that inefficiencies were retained because the new class of worker–owners were unlikely to sacrifice jobs for the sake of efficiency. It might have made a difference if there had been a functioning secondary capital market where worker-owners could sell their shares for an immediate capital gain. However institutions like the stock market, had not developed fully and in the absence of the profit motive, efficiencies too could not be generated.[34] Hostility to the government's program for economic reform came also from managers of state enterprises who feared that privatization would divest them of their privileged position. Another contributing factor may have been poor implementation of stated reform policies. The simultaneous occurrence of rampant inflation amidst negative growth rates suggest that budget cuts and fiscal austerity were more contrived than real. It was obvious, according to Jeffrey Hough, that "The Gaidar government followed a loose-money policy from the beginning, but put most of the deficit off-budget to create the impression of a balanced budget."[35] This might be explained by the fact that the political system was pulling in different directions. For example, a conservative parliament forced President Yeltsin to include antireformers in the government,[36] and it did not help that the Russian Central Bank, under the jurisdiction of the Russian Parliament, was also not very enthusiastic about the pace of economic reform.

The power struggle between the president and the parliament was also a major obstacle to the reform process. The ability of the government to push ahead with reforms was constrained by the parliament. Not surprisingly, the central government found it increasingly difficult to implement its preferred policies. In early 1993, William Pfaff correctly observed that, "Real power, ability to change Russia, is available to neither of them [the Parliament or the President]. Moscow no longer is in command of the rest of the country."[37] The difficulties for the Russian government were complicated by the victory of the communists and the nationalists in the parliamentary elections held in December 1995. In the lead-up to the presidential elections in June 1996, President Yeltsin dismissed his reform-minded Deputy Prime Minister Anatoly Chubais and promised expanded public sector spending to secure electoral victory. This threatened the integrity of reform but the rhetoric of expanded fiscal spending, however, was not matched by policy programs and Russia stayed the line with IMF reforms securing, in return, a three-year IMF loan for US$10.2 billion.

By the mid-1990s, Russia was also beginning to benefit from increased capital inflows, encouraged by high interest rates and a stable rouble. In 1995, capital inflows amounted to US$1.5 billion, roughly half of which was FDI capital. Russia's export position also improved compared to the early 1990s. The reality of the Russian export position was that in the first six months of 1992, exports actually declined by 35 percent due mainly to decline in exports to the former COMECON countries. Richard Cooper argued that the Russian government should adopt commercial and exchange rate policies designed to generate exports. An appropriate commercial policy, according to Cooper, would encourage not simply exports but also imports since cheaper imported inputs could lower production costs and increase export competitiveness.[38] An attractive exchange rate for the rouble will certainly help lay the foundation for export led recovery and, in July 1992, the rouble rate was unified and allowed to float. By October 1992, the exchange rate had jumped to 310 roubles to the dollar after opening at 125 roubles to the dollar.[39] Exchange rate and trade policy reforms had, by the mid-1990s, improved the export outlook for Russia with good growth in the export of manufactured goods to the European Union.

To assist trade recovery, the 17 western nations of Coordinating Committee for Multilateral Export Controls (COCOM), in June 1990, relaxed export controls on sophisticated military and dual-use technology to the communist countries. The COCOM had been established in 1949 but its continuation had become an anomaly given western commitment to assist the reform process in the communist countries. COCOM was finally terminated in 1994,[40] and this opened up the possibility of significant technology transfer which may, in turn, enhance productivity of Russian industries and their export prospects. The restrictions that remain seriously impede Russian capacity to generate export revenue. While export stagnation is partly the result of poor quality and uncompetitive industries, there are sectors, such as space technology, where Russian technology is highly sophisticated and competitive.

After six years of economic decline, 1997 was the first year of economic growth in Russia. The transition to a market dominant system has been significant and the European Bank for Reconstruction and Development estimated that roughly 70 percent of the Russian GDP in 1997 was accounted for by the private sector. In 1998, the privatization program was earmarked for further acceleration, as well as several other reform measures, including liberalization of foreign trade, better legal and institutional framework, and a sound banking system. Stanley Fischer, Deputy Managing Director of the IMF, confidently predicted that in the new millenium, if reform policies were implemented as planned, output growth in Russia will be around 6 percent, fiscal deficit will be halved to around 3–4 percent of GDP, and significantly reduced inflation rates.[41]

Chinese and Russian Membership in WTO

Admission into the WTO requires a two-thirds majority of existing members. In June 1986, the People's Republic of China applied to resume its GATT membership after the Kuomintang government in Taiwan withdrew from the GATT in 1950 following the communist revolution in China in 1949. With the formal application, the GATT set up a working party in 1987 to negotiate the terms of membership. Negotiations were suspended after the suppression of the democracy movement in China in June 1989 but resumed in December 1989. The Soviet Union was granted observer status in the GATT in May 1990 and in June 1993, Russia applied for formal membership.

In order to strengthen its membership application, the Chinese government has progressively reduced the level of state intervention and expanded the scope of market forces in the economy. The state monopoly and privilege in foreign trade was ended and in 1987, 22 ministries/departments and 77 other associations, enterprises and organizations were given the right to engage in foreign trade.[42] To entrench market oriented economic reform, the Party, in February 1993, decided to write these into the 1982 Constitution and remove the clause in Article 15 which stated that the "country will practise a planned economy on the basis of a socialist public ownership."[43] A further step to liberalize the economy was the abolition of a dual currency system in January 1994, which had disadvantaged foreign investors who had to purchase the Chinese yuan at an artificially high rate.

On the merits of the Chinese application, McKenzie argued that, "The refusal of China's application would be close to an admission that the GATT is not capable of dealing effectively with economies other than those of western industrial democracies. Moreover, the disruptive threat of the Chinese economy is greater outside the GATT than within it."[44] The dominant Western perception, however, was that a market economy was incompatible with socialist political structures.

Western reluctance to extend the GATT membership to China relate, in part, to lack of transparency in Chinese trade rules. There remain lingering doubts about openness of the Chinese market, despite import liberalization programs that have been adopted and which did have the desired effect of reducing China's growing trade surplus from US$9 billion in 1991 to US$4.4 billion in 1992.[45] To allay western doubts and strengthen its membership application, the Chinese government submitted a report on new developments in its foreign trade and associated reforms to the GATT working party on China's membership but in February 1992, the working party, noting the improvements, still withheld recommending Chinese membership.[46]

The June 1989 Tienanmen incident was a major setback to China's membership of the GATT, as the West attempted to link trade privileges to improvements in human rights conditions within China. The United States was at the forefront of demands for Chinese political reforms and in 1993, linked its own extension of MFN status to China beyond 1994 to human rights improvements. In late May 1994, however, the United States government backed down and delinked trade and political considerations.

The Chinese government worked strenuously to have the GATT approve its membership in 1994 so that it could join the World Trade Organization as a founding member from January 1995. Instead, western governments again rejected the application on grounds that economic and legal reforms were inadequate to protect property and intellectual property rights. The GATT members were concerned, for example, that Chinese trade rules still lacked transparency and uniformity, with different rules applying at different Chinese ports.[47]

Expansion of WTO membership will have significant impact on international trade patterns, both positive in terms of welfare gains, and negative in terms of regime management. In what follows, these positive and negative implications for WTO and for the new members will be discussed.

On the positive side, WTO inclusiveness will enhance its status and prestige and transform it from a discriminatory to a universal institution. It would also add to the Gatt's role and influence given that China is a large economy and a major trading country. Economically, per capita Chinese GNP may be small but in purchasing power, it is a behemoth. According to Liew, if China maintained its growth pattern, its total output in purchasing power will exceed that of the US in the early part of the new century and if Chinese living standards reached current Taiwanese levels, the Chinese economy will be larger than the combined economy of the OECD countries.[48] In 1978, total Chinese trade was approximately US$92 billion but by 1993, this had increased to around US$196 billion, making it the 11th largest trading country in the world.[49] In 1997, following the reversion of Hong Kong from British rule, China further enhanced its trading status as one of the world's five largest trading nations.

In the mid-1980s, the Soviet Union ranked sixth in merchandise exports and seventh in merchandise imports, and its trade with the West was substantial.[50] Since the start of economic restructuring, however, Russian foreign trade suffered drastically as a result of economic and political upheavals, domestically and in Eastern Europe. With disruptions to trade with the East European countries, Russian trade as a percentage of GDP declined dramatically, from US$164 billion in 1990 to US$96 billion in 1991.[51] Trade expansion will have to be an important component in the success of economic transition and this trade expansion will have to be based on reorienting trade in favor of the advanced economies of Europe and North America. To facilitate trade, Russia has progressively liberalized its payments for current account transactions, accepting obligations under Article 8 of the IMF's Articles of Agreement in June 1996.[52]

Given the potential trade significance of Russia, China, and the transition economies, it is important to integrate them into a rule-based global trade system rather than leave them unencumbered by rules of international trade. It will improve the transparency of their trade regulations and restrictions and, moreover, subject them to internationally recognized dispute resolution standards. Greater transparency and tariffication of trade restriction will facilitate access to Chinese markets and the importance of this cannot be belittled. Increased exports have the potential also to add significantly to western welfare and employment levels.

Yet, at another level, membership expansion can also frustrate regime management. It is a well-known assumption of group theory that cooperation and policy coordination are easier in small groups than in larger ones. Chinese and Russian membership will expose WTO to problems of increased magnitude. The inclusion of two large, and potentially influential, members can be expected to further complicate the already difficult task of manufacturing consensus.[53]

The dilemma for the WTO was not unlike that faced by the European Community in terms of its membership expansion. At the end of 1992, the 12-member EC had, before it, eight membership applications that would, if approved, widen membership to 20 countries. In a report prepared in June 1992, the European Commission highlighted the negative consequences of size expansion in the following manner:

"The Community is attractive because it is seen to be effective; to proceed to enlargement in a way which reduces its effectiveness would be an error ... In that perspective [of a union of 20 or 30 members], how can we ensure that 'more' does not lead to 'less'?"[54] The report recommended a gradual pace of expansion, although it must be acknowledged that European caution on size expansion is the result of several other factors as well, such as the potential diminution of influence of existing European members.

The anticipated management difficulties are not insurmountable because new members will inevitably be socialized into the norms and principles of liberal trade and economics. And because rules are universal and non-discriminatory, they are consequently more readily extended to and accepted by late entrants. According to Ruggie, "All other things being equal, an arrangement based on generalized organizing principles should be more elastic than one based on particularistic interests and situational exigencies."[55]

For both China and Russia, the advantage of WTO membership is beyond question. It will liberalize their export environment and provide a positive boost to industrial productivity and export revenue. Russia, in particular, could benefit from export derived injection of foreign capital given that western financial assistance has been tardy and insufficient. In the case of China, an important advantage would be that it would obviate the need for separate trade treaties with other countries and secure a stable export environment.[56] The significance of this is easy to appreciate when we consider the phenomenal growth of Chinese exports since the late 1970s. In 1982, for example, total Chinese exports were only about US$22 billion whereas by 1993, this had increased to around US$92 billion. Moreover, in the absence of WTO membership, China has had to negotiate MFN access to other countries on a bilateral basis. Such agreements tend to be steeped in uncertainty, can be easily revoked, or extended only on conditional terms. The US, for example, granted MFN status to China in 1980 and has renewed it on an annual basis but on numerous occasions, had threatened to revoke it, expressing dissatisfaction with the government's human rights record.

Conclusion

The collapse of Communism was a unique opportunity to globalize liberal trade. This chapter discussed the process of economic reform in Russia and China and considered the problems and prospects of achieving a global political economy. In Russia, economic reforms centered around the issue of privatization. By mid-1993, half of all shops and small businesses had been privatized and the Russian Deputy Prime Minister, Anatoli Chubais, declared that complete privatization of small businesses was likely by the end of the year. Privatization, however, did not have the desired result of increasing efficiency within factories. One reason for this was that privatization, in many cases, resulted in workers acquiring control over the former state enterprises. Employees and workers in control over a production unit were, however, more concerned with maintaining existing employment levels and job security than with pursuing efficiency and rationalization. The situation could have been different if a secondary capital market had developed quickly enough to entice workers to sell their shares to outsiders for capital gains, but not only did this not happen but, there exist other problems why outsiders may not want to invest prior to clear confidence about property rights and their ability to pursue rationalization of firms without being concerned that potential large scale unemployment may force the state to intervene and curtail their property rights. Based on these conditions, Roman Frydman and Andrzej Rapaczynski stated that, "So far, the Russian program has resulted in a large degree of decentralization of economic decision making, which is certainly not equivalent to the introduction of a governance structure characteristic of modern capitalistic economies."[57]

The parlous state of the Russian economy was eloquent testimony of the ease with which existing structures can be destroyed and of the difficulties in replacing them with new structures and institutions. The Shatalin Program had optimistically proposed a timeline of 500 days when it might have been more meaningful to speak of a 500-week period of economic reform.[58] The necessary institutions and rules, such as property rights and a secondary capital market, that underpin an efficient market take time to establish themselves. Continuing political turmoil did not make the task any easier.

In contrast to the Russian experience, structural reforms in China, although less spectacular, have produced rapid economic growth and prosperity. Economic growth in China and contraction in Russia might be, and has been, used to compare and contrast the relative merits of gradualism and radical change but such a comparison, according to Sachs and Woo, is problematic. They asserted that outcomes diverged not because gradualism was superior to radicalism but because the two economies introduced reforms at different stages of economic development. Whereas China benefited from the "advantages of backwardness," Russian reforms suffered because of an overdeveloped industrial structure that emphasized heavy industry, an extensive social welfare system, and a pervasive system of subsidized employment that rendered structural adjustment more difficult.[59] Sachs and Woo also suggest that estimates of Chinese economic growth, 13 percent in 1992 and 1993, were exaggerated and erroneously painted a picture of successful reform.

However, even if the indicators of economic growth were not truly representative, there is no denying that the Chinese economy outperformed the Russian economy. Reforms have created the conditions for economic take-off, but it is still uncertain whether the reforms are far-reaching enough to satisfy the GATT members to extend membership to China. Chinese membership of WTO is vexed also because of other factors, such as human rights considerations, Chinese insistence on joining the GATT and WTO as a developing country, and resuming its membership rather than join anew. Resuming membership as a developing country will mean that China will not be required to reciprocate with equivalent tariff concessions. In contrast, the United States and other western governments insist on attaching conditions on Chinese membership for fear of being swamped with cheap Chinese exports and insist also on reciprocity. These complications make it unlikely that there will be an early decision on the Chinese application, although it was reported that the settlement of a copyright dispute in 1995 involved a *quid-pro-quo* from the United States not to block Chinese admission into WTO.

However, as of mid-1999 China, along with Taiwan, remained outside the WTO, with the West unwilling to approve its membership application. The stumbling blocks have been the unfinished nature of Chinese reforms, as will as its insistence on joining WTO as a developing country. Quite apart from these real concerns, Western reluctance to approve Chinese membership has also been influenced by human rights consideration.

References

1. This was not simply the result of an exclusionary policy but also the result of deliberate policy choices of the East European economies.
2. Haus, Leah A., *Globalizing the GATT: The Soviet Unions's Successor States, Eastern Europe, and the International Trading System*, The Brookings Institution, Washington, DC, 1992, p. 11.
3. Some of the East European countries are already members of the GATT. Czechoslovakia is an original member state, Yugoslavia and Poland became members in the late 1960s (1966 and 1967 respectively), while Romania and Hungary became members in 1971 and 1973 respectively. The Soviet Union acquired observer status in May 1990. China was an original member of the GATT but withdrew in 1949 after the Communist revolution.
4. McKenzie, P. D., "China's Application to the GATT: State Trading and the Problem of Market Access," *Journal of World Trade*, Vol. 24, No. 5, October 1990, p. 141.
5. The collapse of Communism was neither foreseen nor is there any consensus on what caused it. Explanations range from the inability of central planners to manage a complex economy; the failure of Communism to satisfy the self-recognition needs of individuals (Francis Fukuyama); the arms race and its deleterious consequences; to economic stagnation caused by the non-substitutability of capital for labor. The last factor explains the collapse of command economies in terms of extremely low returns on capital investments. See Easterly, W. and Stanley Fischer, "What We Can Learn from the Soviet Collapse," *Finance and Development*, Vol. 31, No. 4, December 1994.
6. Sachs, J., "The Economic Transformation of Eastern Europe: The Case of Poland," *Economics of Planning*, Vol. 25, No. 1, 1992, p. 6.
7. *GATT Activities 1991: An Annual Review of the Work of the GATT*, General Agreement on Tariffs and Trade, Geneva, July 1992, p. 102.

8. Dorn, James A., "Economic Liberty and Democracy in East Asia," *Orbis*, Vol. 37, No. 4, Fall 1993, pp. 611–612.

9. McMillan, J. and Barry Naughton, "How to Reform a Planned Economy: Lessons from China," *Oxford Review of Economic Policy*, Vol. 8, No. 1, Spring 1992, p. 133.

10. "Painful but Inevitable Restructuring," *Asiamoney*, Vol. 8, No. 10, December 1997/January 1998, p. 40.

11. Liew, Leong H., "Chinese Reform Strategy: A Unity of Opposites," mimeo, February 1998.

12. See *The Australian,* 2 March 1998, p. 8.

13. Other sources put urban unemployment at higher than 15 percent. See "A Balancing Act on the Road to Reform," *Asiamoney*, Vol. 8, No. 10, December 1997/January 1998, p. 16.

14. McMillan, J. and Barry Naughton, "How to Reform a Planned Economy: Lessons from China," *Oxford Review of Economic Policy*, Vol. 8, No. 1, 1992, p. 131.

15. Bohnet, A., Zhong Hong and Frank Muller, "China's Open-Door Policy and Its Significance for Transformation of the Economic System," *Intereconomics*, Vol. 28, No. 4, July/August 1993, p. 193.

16. Khanin, G., "The Soviet Economy — From Crisis to Catastrophe," in Aslund, A. (ed.), *The Post-Soviet Economy: Soviet and Western Perspectives*, Pinter Publishers, London, 1992, p. 13. According to Khanin (p. 10), an economic crisis is usually perceived as a temporary state of affairs whereas an economic catastrophe represents "... chaos in the economy, when it becomes impossible to provide for the most elemental needs of the population."

17. Aslund, A., "A Critique of the Soviet Reform Plan," in Aslund, A. (ed.), *The Post-Soviet Economy: Soviet and Western Perspectives*, Pinter Publishers, London, 1992, p. 168.

18. Wanniski, J., "The Future of Russian Capitalism," *Foreign Affairs*, Vol. 71, No. 2, Spring 1992, p. 18.

19. Linden, C., "Yeltsin and the Russian Republic's Rebirth in a Time of Troubles, " in Linden, C. and Jan S. Prybyla (eds.), *Russia and China on the Eve of a New Millennium*, Transactions Publishers, New Jersey, 1997, p. 118.

20. See Etzioni, A., "How is Russia Bearing Up?" *Challenge*, May/June 1992.
21. McMillan, J. and Barry Naughton, "How to Reform a Planned Economy: Lessons from China," *Oxford Review of Economic Policy*, Vol. 8, No. 1, Spring 1992, p. 140.
22. Fischer, S., "Stabilization and Economic Reform in Russia," *Brookings Papers on Economic Activity*, Brookings Institution, Washington, DC, 1992, pp. 86–87. See also, Bleaney, M., "Economy: Economic Reform," in Spring, D. W. (ed.), *The Impact of Gorbachev: The First Phase, 1985–1990*, Pinter Publishers, London and New York, 1991, p. 31.
23. For a discussion of privatization in Western countries see Hemming, R. and Ali M. Mansoor, *Privatization and Public Enterprises*, Occasional Paper No. 56, International Monetary Fund, Washington, DC, January 1988.
24. Tsang, Shu ki, "Against 'Big Bang' in Economic Transition: Normative and Positive Arguments," *Cambridge Journal of Economics*, Vol. 20, No. 2, March 1996, p. 185.
25. Noren, J. H., "The Russian Economic Reform: Progress and Prospects," *Soviet Economy*, Vol. 8, No. 1, January–March 1992, p. 12.
26. Khanin, G., "The Soviet Economy — From Crisis to Catastrophe," in Aslund, A. (ed.), *The Post-Soviet Economy: Soviet and Western Perspectives*, Pinter Publishers, London, 1992, p. 12. Khanin estimated Soviet gold reserves, in 1990, at a maximum of 500 tons instead of CIA estimates of 2000 tons.
27. *Economist* (London), Vol. 324, No. 7766, 4 July 1992, p. 18.
28. Sachs, J., "The Grand Bargain," in Anslund, A. (ed.), *The Post-Soviet Economy: Soviet and Western Perspective*, Pinter Publishers, London, 1992, p. 210.
29. Sachs, J., "West May Be Losing Critical Chance to Help Advance Russian Reforms," *The Straits Times*, 28 January 1994, p. 35.
30. Sachs, J., "Strengthening Western Support for Russia," *International Economic Insights*, Vol. 4, No. 1, July/February 1993, p. 11.
31. During the height of the Cold War, the Japanese claim had received strong support from the US and encouraged by this, the government

adopted a maximalist position and demanded the return of all four islands before concluding any peace treaty with the Soviet Union. However, once the Cold War was over, American support evaporated quickly and the Japanese government found itself isolated but unable to abandon the long-held policy without 'losing face.' The Russian government, too, refused to negotiate a face-saving settlement for fear of reviving irredentist claims by other countries. In 1992, Russian President Boris Yeltsin cancelled, at short notice, a scheduled visit to Japan, concerned that Japan would simply exploit the occasion to press for the return of the islands.

32. Ernesto Hernandez–Cata., "Russia and the IMF: The Political Economy of Macro-Stabilization," IMF Paper of Policy Analysis and Assessment, PPAA/94/20, September 1994.

33. Noren, J. H., "The Russian Economic Reform: Progress and Prospects," *Soviet Economy*, Vol. 8, No. 1, January–March 1992, p. 14.

34. The institutional problem is very complex but of course, institutions cannot be created overnight. Nonetheless, fully functioning institutions are essential to efficient market-based transactions. According to McKinnon, reform and privatization also required an efficient taxation structure but which had not been established before privatization commenced. He argued that since privatization inevitably reduced the tax base and revenue flow to the government, this could affect budgetary conditions and lead to fiscal and monetary instability that could jeopardize the entire reform process, unless there were other means of collecting revenue. Emphasizing the importance of an efficient tax structure, McKinnon argued that "An internal revenue service must be rebuilt — or I should say built from scratch — at the outset of the liberalization. If this is not done, then the liberalization itself will tend to greatly undermine the public finances." See, Harberger, A. C. Michael R Darby *et al.*, "Central and Eastern Europe in Transition," *Contemporary Policy Issues*, Vol. 10, No. 1, January 1992, p. 12. By 1994, the situation had improved considerably. Sixty new stock exchanges had become operational and approximately 70 percent of large state-owned enterprises had been privatized. See *Euromoney*, June 1994, p. 115.

35. Hough, J., "On the Road to Paradise Again? Keeping Hopes for Russia Realistic," *The Brookings Review*, Vol. 11, No. 1, Winter 1993, p. 15.

36. Yegor Gaidar himself was forced out of office by the conservative opponents of President Yeltsin. Following the April 1993 referendum, however, which produced results supportive of continued reform some of the conservative forces within the government were forced out but the conservative Vice-President Alexander Rutskoi continues to defy Yeltsin and shows no indication of resigning.

37. Pfaff, W., "Up to Russians to Solve Problems," *The Straits Times* (Singapore), 23 March 1993, p. 26.

38. Cooper, R. N., "Opening the Soviet Economy," in Peck, Merton J. and Thomas J. Richardson (eds.), *What is to be Done? Proposals for the Soviet Transition to the Market*, Yale University Press, New Haven and London, 1991, pp. 122 and 124.

39. See "Eastern Europe," *Economic Trends in Eastern Europe*, Vol. 1, No. 3, 1992, p. 134.

40. COCOM is to be replaced with a new body to restrict technology exports to 'rogue' states, in general. See, for example, Crocker, Thomas E., "An Export Control Plan Saddam Will Love," *The Asian Wall Street Journal*, 24 January 1994, p. 6.

41. Fischer, S., "The Russian Economy at the Start of 1998," Address at the 1998 US-Russian Investment Symposium at Harvard University, 9 January 1998 (http://www.imf.org/external/np/speeches/1998/010998.HTM).

42. Balassa, B. and Michael P. Claudon, "Reflections on Perestroika and the Foreign Economic Ties of the Soviet Union," in Krauss., M. and Liebowitz, R. D. (eds.), *Perestroika and East-West Economic Relations: Prospects for the 1990s*, New York University Press, New York, 1990, p. 114.

43. *The Australian*, 17 February 1993, p. 12.

44. McKenzie, P. D., "China's Application to the GATT: State Trading and the Problem of Market Access," *Journal of World Trade*, Vol. 24, No. 5, October 1990, p. 150.

45. *The Straits Times* (Singapore), 13 March 1993, p. 34. This is based on Chinese statistics which excludes re-exports from Hong Kong. Naturally, American figures which include re-exports from Hong Kong suggests that the American deficit is much larger. According to Economist Intelligence Unit estimates, Chinese trade, in 1993, had turned into a defict of approximately US$12 billion. See The Economist Intelligence Unit, *Country Report: China, Mongolia*, 1st quarter 1994, p. 4.

46. Feinerman, J. V., "The Quest for GATT Membership," *The China Business Review*, Vol. 19, No. 3, May–June 1992.

47. "China and the GATT: Reaching an Impasse," *The Economist*, 6 August 1994.

48. Liew, Leong, *The Chinese Economy in Transition: From Plan to Market*, Edward Elgar, Cheltenham, 1997, p. 143.

49. The Director General of the GATT, Peter Sutherland, during a visit to China in May 1992, stated that keeping China out of the GATT and the proposed World Trade Organization would cast doubts about the universality of the WTO. See *China Daily*, 12 May 1994, p. 2.

50. Kennedy, K. C., "The Accession of the Soviet Union to GATT," *Journal of World Trade Law*, Vol. 21, No. 2, April 1987, p. 24.

51. *Russian Economic Reform: Crossing the Threshold of Structural Change*, A World Bank Country Study, The World Bank, Washington DC, 1992, p. 295.

52. *Word Economic Outlook*, May 1997, International Monetary Fund, Washington DC., 1997, p. 94.

53. Formal GATT rules require only a majority approval for policies and decisions but in reality the GATT had adopted the universal rule which gives each country, however big or small, a veto power in the decision making process.

54. See Wijkman, Per Magnus, "The Existing Bloc Expanded? The European Community, EFTA, and Eastern Europe," in Bergsten, C. Fred and Marcus Noland (eds.), *Pacific Dynamism and the International Economic System*, Institute for International Economics, Washington, 1993, p. 141.

55. Ruggie, J. G., "Multilateralism: The Anatomy of an Institution," *International Organization*, Vol. 46, No. 3, Summer 1992, p. 594.
56. This is one of the reasons why the People's Republic of China has been anxious to secure membership to the General Agreement on Tariffs and Trade since the early 1980s. The bulk of Chinese trade is with the other members of the GATT and membership into this multilateral trade body, with its own established rules and procedures, will enable Beijing to end the 90 bilateral trade agreements that it had negotiated and which have to be periodically negotiated and which may be unilaterally terminated. See Feinerman, J. V., "The Quest for GATT Membership," *The China Business Review*, Vol. 19, No. 3, May–June 1992.
57. Frydman, R. and Andrzej Rapaczynski, "Privatization in Eastern Europe: Is the State Withering Away?" *Finance and Development*, Vol. 30, No. 2, June 1993, p. 13.
58. Kudrov, V., "Soviet Union: Programmes of Economic Reform," in Saunders, Christopher T. (ed.), *Economics and Politics of Transition*, The Macmillan Press Ltd., Houndmills, 1992, p. 346.
59. Sachs, J. and Wing Thye Woo, "Structural Factors in the Economic Reforms of China, Eastern Europe, and the Former Soviet Union," *Economic Policy*, No. 18, April 1994, p. 104.

Chapter Six

INTERNATIONAL DEBT CRISES

Since the early 1980s, stability of the international banking and financial system has been rocked by three developing country debt and financial crises. These crises adversely affected global growth, and, of course, developmental prospects for many developing countries. In each of the three crises, the IMF played a pivotal role in providing financial assistance for structural adjustment measures to stabilize the affected economies. As a result of its involvement, the IMF successfully carved out a niche for itself in the international financial system. Ever since the collapse of the fixed exchange rate system in the early 1970s until the Latin American debt crisis in 1982, the IMF had confronted a crisis of relevance. Its primary function had been to monitor and maintain the fixed rate system but once that fundamental principle had been set aside, there were serious doubts as to whether the IMF had any residual purpose or relevance.

The flexible rate system contained no role for the IMF and the IMF was also not given any positive function in the system of coordinated market intervention and policy coordination. That task was assumed by the G–7 (Group of Seven) meeting of industrialized countries. The IMF had seemingly outlived its mandate but through its role in managing the debt crises, it secured a new lease of life. The crises involved debt servicing difficulties encountered by the developing countries, which if left unmanaged, could lead to large-scale collapse of western banking institutions and, ultimately, to global monetary chaos.

These were also crises that threatened economic development and growth in developing countries. The debt crisis set back the developmental objectives of many countries and the 1980s is, frequently, described as a decade lost to development. Growth in developed OECD countries was also affected where, according to William Cline, the first debt crisis reduced exports by US$14 billion between 1981 and 1982, equivalent to the loss of approximately 350 000 jobs.[1] Still, the immediate response of the international community, and of the IMF, when the Latin American debt crisis began in 1982, focused on preserving the western banking system and the stability of international monetary relations. In this chapter, I will discuss the three crises in terms of the specific causes and international management strategies.

The Latin American Debt Crisis

The Latin American debt crisis began on Friday, 13 August 1982. On that inauspicious day, the Mexican Finance Minister Jesus Silva–Herzog met with Paul Volcker of the US Federal Reserve Bank and bluntly admitted Mexico's inability to meet scheduled debt repayments. The crisis spread to other developing countries, in Latin America and Africa, but not, however, to the East Asian economies. The difficulty in debt servicing (meeting interest payments on accumulated debt) was brought on by several factors, including higher interest rates, collapse of commodity prices, poor policy choices of debtor countries, and failings within the international banking community. These combined to undermine the capacity of debtor countries to service their debt obligations. The potential for widespread debt default, in turn, threatened the viability of the international banking community that had, through the 1970s, increased its exposure in the developing countries. The debt crisis rocked the structure of global finance by threatening to bring down large commercial banks, which had considerable debt exposure. More than 80 percent of total third world debt was owed to about 200 western banks, but about half the debt was owed to only 20 banks, seven from the United States, four from United Kingdom, three from Germany, three from France, two from Japan, and one from Canada. The vulnerability of the major western financial institutions and the attendant potential for serious economic disruption was the key to western strategies designed to prevent debt default.

The debt, referred to as "sovereign debt" because it was incurred by sovereign countries, had been contracted with private bank which were simply recycling surplus dollars accumulated by the Organization of Petroleum Exporting Countries (OPEC) and deposited in Western banks. OPEC's surplus liquidity, known as petrodollars, had been boosted by a quadrupling of oil prices following the Arab–Israeli war of 1973. The rapid expansion of commercial lending benefited from deregulation of international financial activities, and from extended reach of financial intermediaries resulting from improved communications technology.

The crisis was testimony to the expanded role of commercial banks in the global financial regime. Their role and importance had grown markedly after the oil crisis of 1973 and the collapse of the Bretton-Woods system, which initiated a period of floating exchange rates. The immediate outcome of the oil crisis was to distort the spread of international liquidity and the commercial banks, which received the oil wealth as deposits, became the major instrument for a necessary redistribution and circulation of liquidity.

Prior to the easy availability of petrodollars from commercial banks, assistance to developing countries was given either directly by Western governments or by the two Bretton-Woods institutions. The IMF provided funds, known as program aid, to countries experiencing balance of payments difficulties while the World Bank provided funding for large projects, such as infrastructural developments in the developing countries. IMF loans were conditional loans and borrowing countries were required to implement economic policies that would ensure their ability to meet debt service obligations. Typically, this meant restructuring the economy toward export markets rather than domestic consumption. IMF programs were designed to restore a country's macroeconomic stability through spending cutbacks and budgetary restrictions. The onerous nature of IMF loans usually produced higher unemployment and inflation, leading to a social crisis involving labor unrest and militancy. In the Philippines, such a crisis led to the collapse of democracy and imposition of martial law by President Marcos in September 1972. Not surprisingly, the IMF loans were not looked upon with much favor by developing countries.

Escape from the IMF conditionality came in the 1970s when private sector capital flows to developing countries dwarfed the IMF and other official aid programs. Commercial banks became agents for recycling "petrodollars," and they targeted developing countries partly because growth in developed countries had slowed and there was insufficient demand to absorb the available liquidity. On the other hand, growth prospects in the middle-income developing countries looked promising. Banks did not regard such loans as risky because of the perceived negligible risk of loan default. For instance, Walter B. Wriston, Chairman of Citicorp, was fond of repeating that "sovereign nations don't go broke."[2]

Commercial banks were reassured also by the knowledge that international loan losses were only a small proportion of their total non-performing loans. For the ten largest American banks, international net loan losses were only 0.1 percent of average international loans in 1980 and constituted only 15 percent of total losses incurred by these banks. Consequently, as mentioned above, foreign lending was not considered very risky. Moreover, as Wiarda suggests, if American bankers did, in fact, recognize the riskiness of the loans, they were also convinced that the US government would be obliged to bail them out and not risk a collapse of the banking sector. Still, they were selective in their lending programs. Banks lent mainly to the rich Latin American and Asian countries rather than to the poorer African and South Asian countries, which were presumably a higher risk proposition. The primary risk, nonetheless, was defined in political terms as unwillingness to repay, rather than inability to repay. The debt crisis, however, demonstrated that countries, like firms and individuals, could also become insolvent.

With relatively easy lending available to them, developing countries accumulated debt at a rapid rate through the 1970s. They were encouraged to borrow by a regime of high inflation and low interest rates, which meant that the real cost of borrowing and interest payment was small and negligible. For some countries, the real cost of borrowing was negative. For the period 1977–1982, the real interest rate in Bolivia was −10.1 percent and that for Ghana was −32.8 percent which meant that borrowing, instead of incurring real costs, was actually profitable.[3] Low interest payment on sovereign loans probably encouraged the developing countries to borrow more than they would have if the cost of borrowing had been higher. Total LDC debt increased from US$167 billion in 1977 to US$248 billion in 1979 and to about US$400 billion in the critical year of 1982. Some of the largest debtor countries in 1982 were Brazil (US$93 billion), Mexico (US$86 billion), Argentina (US$44 billion), Venezuela (US$32 billion) and the Philippines (US$25 billion). Total accumulated debt would not have become a problem if borrowing had been directed to project development and other productive purposes. But borrowing, instead, sustained a conspicuous consumption and import pattern. In Mexico, for example, the import bill increased from US$6 billion in 1977 to US$23 billion in 1981. Moreover, the lending institutions had little information of how the loans were being employed and were unaware, even, of the total debt burden of each debtor country. East Asian countries, like South Korea, also increased their debt liabilities through the 1970s but avoided the Latin American contagion by investing in productive activities to generate export revenue. This enabled them to keep debt servicing to manageable proportions.

Debt servicing involves payment of interest on loans, in foreign currency, and requires a debtor country to generate sufficient export revenue to finance both its import requirements and interest payment on loans. It is commonly assumed that a safe level of external debt means a debt servicing ratio of no more than 25 percent of export revenue. Table 6.1 shows the magnitude of the debt problem for the 15 heavily indebted countries.

The Causes of the Latin American Debt Crisis

The causes of the debt crisis might be separately classified as those originating within the developing countries and those beyond their control, such as the rapid increase in real interest rates, which exacerbated their debt servicing burdens. As far as conditions within the developing

Table 6.1. Debt indicators of 15 heavily indebted countries.

	1970–1979	1980	1981	1982	1983
Total debt (US$b)	97.5	271.1	332.4	380.1	395.9
Debt service (% of exports)	26.0	29.4	38.9	49.8	39.9

Source: *World Economic Outlook*, International Monetary Fund, Washington, DC, October 1988, p. 40.

countries were concerned, a key factor was misuse of funds, and government policies, which encouraged a pattern of conspicuous domestic consumption rather than productive investment. The crisis also reinforced perceptions that developing countries were steeped in structural impediments to growth and development and that restoration of financial solvency and economic growth required structural reform and adjustment.

Externally, in the late 1970s, several factors combined to end the relatively comfortable position of the indebted developing countries. These included the oil crisis of 1979 and the fall of the Shah of Iran, and the renewed attempts to control the inflationary spiral in the West.

1. The fall of the Shah and the second oil crisis were reminders that market stability was fragile and the uncertainties made lenders more cautious. Although loans were still available, the terms were shortened and consequently for the LDCs, loan repayments became bunched together and this affected their ability to meet payment obligations.

2. The low cost of capital that the borrowing countries had exploited was only possible as long as inflation remained high. In 1979, however, President Carter, initiated a policy that was very un-Democratic and instead of fighting unemployment, chose to concentrate on inflation. To reduce inflation, the Federal Reserve Bank under Paul Volcker initiated a tight monetary policy. This was successful but in the process, it increased the cost of borrowing for other countries. A similar restrictive monetary policy in England and widening US federal budget deficits reinforced the upward trend in interest rates. The problems for many developing countries were compounded by the fact that loans had been contracted at floating interest rates. For

example, more than 75 percent of Brazil, Argentina, and Mexico's total debt had been contracted at a floating interest rate. This meant interest rates at market prices and as the US tightened monetary policies, market interest rates went up. The upward drift in American prime lending rate or the London Interbank Offer Rate (LIBOR)[4] directly affected the cost of debt servicing. Some countries, however, ignored the risks of high interest rates. Mexico, for example, confident that its oil wealth would enable it to make timely repayments continued to borrow into the early 1980s. In 1981 alone, it added US$21 billion to its total debt. Moreover, the high interest rate policy in the US and elsewhere, encouraged business to run down inventory levels because it is more costly to hold inventories when interest rates are high. The reduction of inventory levels initiated a collapse of commodity pries and by reducing export revenue, worsened the capacity of debtor countries to service their debts.

3. Progressively through the 1970s, the ability of developing countries to service their debt was undermined by the rise of protectionism in the developed countries. This affected export revenue and made it harder to service debt.

4. The debt crisis began in Latin America and can be partially attributed to the Falklands War, which began when Argentina invaded the Falklands in April 1982 to wrest control of the island from Britain. Other Latin American countries like Venezuela, in a show of support for Argentina, switched deposits out of London banks. This prompted the British government to urge banks to reassess risks across the continent which, given that most Latin American countries already had a poor liquidity position and high accumulated debt levels, resulted in a general downgrading of their credit ratings.[5] As credit rating declined, interest rates shot up. This affected Mexico the hardest because, in the interest of securing lower interest rates, it had opted for short maturity periods. This meant that Mexico was dependent on its ability to roll over existing loans but once its credit ratings were downgraded, it became harder to refinance existing loans. In August 1982, Mexico was forced to seek debt relief. The international debt phenomenon had come a full cycle. The 1973

Arab–Israeli War and the oil crisis had ushered in a period of easy credit whereas the Falklands War, in so far as it was one of the many factors, brought it to an end less than ten years later.

Debt Management Strategies

Most analysts agree that the debt crisis had the potential to seriously undermine international financial stability if it led to large-scale collapse of major western banks. This reflected the growing importance of commercial banks within the monetary regime and their role in international liquidity recycling. From the viewpoint of commercial banks, it was necessary to ensure that developing countries continue to service the debt, and not repudiate or renege on their debts. Debt write-off was unacceptable because of the precedent it would establish and also because banks did not have sufficient loan loss provisions to undertake debt forgiveness. By contrast, the only real solution for debtor countries was debt relief and debt forgiveness but this did not happen until much later.

In order to protect the lending institutions and safeguard global financial stability, the response of the IMF and western governments was primarily to restore debtor countries to acceptable levels of solvency. The fact that this was also a crisis of development for the developing countries was a secondary concern. It mattered even less that the involvement of the IMF and western governments highlighted a policy contradiction. They had intervened in capital markets in violation of market principles to save banking institutions that "deserved" to go bankrupt. At the same time, they insisted that debtor countries adopt a more *laissez faire* approach themselves and allow the market to reassert itself, in the expectation that this would revive growth and ease their debt servicing problems.

The three debt management strategies adopted by Western countries were the Mexican model; the Baker plan; and the Brady plan. Apart from management strategies at the official level, commercial banks also, at a later stage, introduced various measures, like debt swaps and debt discounting, to deal with the crisis and these will be considered further below. The distinction between official and private sector responses is somewhat arbitrary since many of the official initiatives also included specific steps to be taken by commercial banks.

Before discussing the three debt management strategies, it is useful to briefly describe the institutional fora for debtor countries to renegotiate and reschedule their debt. The institutional umbrella for debt management were the Paris and the London Clubs. The Paris Club had been formed in the 1950s as a forum for debtor and creditor governments to negotiate public sector debt rescheduling. The London Club was a later addition, modelled on the Paris Club, to deal with private sector debt rescheduling. The Paris and the London Clubs are similar in that both are *ad hoc* creditor groups without any formal mandate or rules of procedure. The main difference is that while the Paris Club deals with public sector lending to private or public sector borrowers in the debtor countries, the London Club deals only with private sector credits. The London Club also has a broader scope and is able to negotiate new credits whereas the Paris Club only renegotiates the terms of existing credits. The Mexican model and the Baker plan were based on guidelines already existing within the Paris Club, and both clubs were important as "implementors" of debt management strategies in the 1980s.

The Mexican Model: The Mexican model was a case-by-case approach to debt management, beginning with Mexico and later applied to other debtor countries. Within two days of the Mexican notification that it was unable to keep up interest payment, the United States had arranged an emergency assistance package of US$4 billion, with US$3 billion coming from the US. Of this US$3 billion, US$2 billion was advance payment for purchase of oil from Mexico and the balance was comprised of bridging loans from a group of central bankers. This was a short-term package to ensure that Mexico kept up interest payment but the United States also forced Mexico to negotiate with the IMF for long-term credit arrangement. On 10 November that year, an agreement was reached between the Mexican government and the IMF for a credit line of US$3.84 billion for the period 1983–1985, in return for strict austerity measures. The IMF conditions were

1. reduction of public expenditure from the 1982 figure of 16.5 percent of GDP to 8.5 percent of GDP in 1983 to 5.9 percent in 1984 and down to 3.5 percent in 1985;
2. liberalization of the economy. Mexico had maintained a protectionist import substitution industrialization strategy which undermined its export potential by keeping import prices, and prices of intermediate imported inputs high. Liberalization, it was believed, would enhance export competitiveness and increase export revenue, much as had happened in the East Asian economies;
3. elimination of new state investment plans;
4. increase the prices of goods and services in the public sector; and
5. negotiate with commercial banks for debt rescheduling, i.e. arrangements to stretch out interest repayment and extend maturity of loans to lessen the repayment burden.

The bailout package negotiated for Mexico established the precedent for a central role for the IMF in future debt management. Although the debt was owed to commercial banks, these banks refused to reschedule debts without prior agreement between the debtor countries and the IMF on domestic economic restructuring which would eventually enhance their capacity to repay. The role of the IMF was central because commercial banks, themselves, could not presume to impose conditions on sovereign countries. In 1982–1983, 39 countries negotiated similar arrangements with the IMF. This number, however, declined to 23 by mid-1986. The table below gives the number of such agreements concluded on a yearly basis between 1983–1989.

The decline was not necessarily an indication of a general improvement in the debt position of developing countries but rather a reflection of difficulties debtor countries faced in complying with IMF conditions. Even Mexico was unable to meet its obligations and withdrew in 1985. The austerity conditions demanded by the IMF seriously strained domestic political legitimacy of governments that had bought popular support through profligate spending. Usually, they found ways around the austerity conditions. For example, in 1985, under the watchful eyes of visiting IMF delegates, the Mexican government retrenched 50 000 public sector employees, "... but then rehired 35 000 of them in the next few

Table 6.2.   Debt rescheduling agreements.

Year	Number of countries
1983	20
1984	17
1985	16
1986	12
1987	17
1988	10
1989	9

Source: *International Capital Markets: Development and Prospects,* International Monetary Fund, Washington, DC, April 1990, p. 31.

weeks when it thought no one was looking, and by the end of the year had found ways to put the rest — and more patronage persons besides — back on the public payroll.[6] Miles Kahler correctly summed it up by stating that "Latin American elites were restorationists, not reformers."[7]

It was ironic that strict fiscal austerity induced economic deflation and low growth at a time when the debtor countries required high growth rates to be able to pay off their debt. Structural adjustment, however, was considered essential to restore viable long-term growth even at the risk of short-term difficulties. Fiscal austerity also resulted in higher unemployment and lower wage levels. For example, between 1982 and 1987, real wages in Mexico declined by 51 percent. The weakness of IMF conditionality was that it left the overall debt burden of debtor countries unchanged and, moreover, threatened to unleash domestic political instability.

There was no provision for debt reduction or forgiveness, nor was there any, even temporary, debt relief. Western governments and lending institutions enforced loan conditions to avert a crisis of confidence in the international financial structure. For them, the debt crisis would *become* a crisis only if the developing countries either repudiated or were granted a reprieve from their contractual obligations. In contrast, the developing countries remonstrated for debt relief. The Cartegna Declaration, issued by 11 Latin American countries following a meeting in Cartegna, Colombia in June 1984, pleaded for a fair resolution of the crisis, including deferral of interest payment without penalty to the debtor countries. Rather than ask for a debt write-off, they sought deferral that could be paid out from a certain portion of future export receipts until the full amount had been repaid. Debt relief, however, did not become part of the debt management strategy until the late 1980s.

The Baker Plan: The Baker plan was announced by US Treasury Secretary James Baker at a joint IMF–World Bank meeting in Seoul in October 1985. The plan was not markedly different from the Mexican model. It was still based on a case-by-case approach but did give the World Bank a greater role in helping the poorest debtor countries of Africa. It also acknowledged US governmental responsibility in managing the debt crisis and while the plan did not include significant financial outlays, was an important transitional stage to a more comprehensive approach, the Brady plan. The Baker plan, at least acknowledged that austerity and slowdown of economic growth were not the answer to the difficulties in debt servicing and, consequently, emphasis shifted to measures promoting growth. The three main principles of the Baker plan required

1. debtor countries to implement macroeconomic and structural policies to promote growth, reduce inflation, and become more export competitive;
2. the IMF to remain the central player but financial aid to be provided by other development banks as well; and
3. increased lending by commercial banks.

As before, the Baker plan rejected debt reduction because it would undermine the return to credit worthiness of the debtor countries by witholding new loans from financial institutions, and because stretching out repayment was believed sufficient to restore prosperity. Debt forgiveness also was not considered seriously because it would make private lending institutions wary of new loans to sovereign countries, at a time when there was high demand for such funds in Eastern Europe and Russia, and which the Western governments wanted to encourage. The Baker plan ran for three years and called for additional new bank loans of US$20 billion, which was more or less followed up and provided. A total of 15 debtor countries participated in the Baker plan and had to introduce drastic domestic structural adjustment.

The Brady Plan: The Brady plan was announced by the new US Secretary of the Treasury, Nicholas Brady, in March 1989. The main architect of the plan was David Mulford, Under Secretary of the Treasury, who, earlier, as Assistant Secretary of the Treasury, had also helped draft the Baker plan. In the Brady plan, Mulford embraced the idea of debt relief, although he had previously dismissed it as "bonehead."[8]

The plan reflected a belated acceptance by the United States that the debt problem could not be approached simply at the technical level of ensuring short-term debt servicing by the developing countries and required hard political decisions to reduce overall debt levels and create conditions for economic growth. It had become obvious that existing arrangements were not producing the desired result. The plan also mirrored concern for the future of fledgling democracies in Latin America. The year 1989 not only began a new administration in the United States but also witnessed the installation of new governments in Mexico and Venezuela, and democratic elections in Argentina, Brazil, Chile and Uruguay. Debt reduction, in this context, was one way of strengthening the incipient democracies in Latin America. These countries, in turn, used their democratic transition as a bargaining chip to obtain more advantageous debt management strategies. As emerging democracies, they felt that insistence on strict austerity and repayment of debt in full would alienate a newly empowered electorate and jeopardise the survival of democratic regimes. President Garcia of Peru had, in September 1985, stated very bluntly that, "We are faced with a dramatic choice: it is either debt or democracy."[9]

Until 1988, the commercial loans contracted by the developing countries were being fully serviced but financed by the IMF and other multilateral development banks. This at a time when the banks themselves had shown, by their actions, a readiness to accept losses on their loans by increasing loan loss reserves. On 19 May 1987, Citicorp led other commercial banks in announcing an addition of US$3 billion to its loan-loss reserve fund to cover possible losses on its sovereign debt of US$14 billion. This signalled the banking community's willingness to write down assets (loans) and it, also, enhanced their capacity to resist arm-twisting by the Treasury or the Federal Reserve to provide new loans.

Rather than simply continue to provide new loans, the banks, enabled by their own loan-loss provisions, added debt discounting to their debt-conversion strategies. Prior to this, the more common practice was to exchange debt in the form of a straight asset swap, with no discount on the face value. The two are no longer mutually exclusive and combined debt-conversion and debt-reduction strategies have included debt-for-equity swaps, debt-for-nature swaps, and debt-for-development swaps. By engaging in debt discounting, the banks demonstrated a readiness to accept losses by selling their loans to other institutions at discounts of, as much as, twenty cents to the dollar. The benefit of this type of debt discounting, however, did not always flow back to the developing countries, because they could still be required to service their debts as before.

The Brady plan, instead, emphasized debt reduction and relief for the developing countries. The objective was to reduce both the outstanding debt and the interest payable by the debtor countries. More specifically, it was expected that commercial banks would cut about US$70 billion of the US$340 billion owed to them by 39 developing countries and that the banks would also reduce by US$20 billion the total interest that they would be owed over the next three years. It was anticipated that only those countries that had initiated structural adjustment to improve economic efficiency would qualify for consideration under the Brady plan.

With regard to the objective of providing debt relief, the Brady plan encouraged commercial banks to choose from the following three general options:

1. To reduce the principal, commercial banks could exchange, or buy back, existing debt for long-term bonds with discounted face values. Debtor countries could avail of this facility with funds provided by the IMF and the World Bank, and commercial banks could, in turn, dispose

the bonds the bond market and exit the business of sovereign lending. Under the Plan, IMF/IBRD extended credit to Mexico, Costa Rica and other countries, with Japan providing another US$10 billion in supplementary lending. An example of debt buyback was Chile which, in 1988, bought back US$439 million of its debt with US$248 million of its own resources. The buyback formula in this case was as follows:

US$299 million in November 1988 at 56 cents per dollar
US$140 million in November 1989 at 58 cents per dollar.

2. To reduce the debt service burden, commercial banks could exchange existing debt for bonds at lower interest rates.

3. To reverse the flow of capital, commercial banks were encouraged to provide new loans to debtor countries.

Depending on which options that the banks chose to accept, actual debt reduction ranged from 23 percent of present value to about 35 percent. For Peter Kenen, however, even the higher estimate was insufficient debt relief and he advocated approximately 50 percent as the desirable rate for debt reduction.[10] Robert Wesson went a step further and argued for totally abolishing all debt. He wrote that "If as acknowledged by the Brady Plan, it would be a good idea to cut it [debt] by 20%, it is a better idea to cut it more. *Any* capital transfer from the Third World is undesirable. That is, the debt should be abolished."[11]

By 1992, debt reduction packages had been completed for six countries — Mexico, Costa Rica, Nigeria, the Philippines, Uruguay and Venezuela and their debt was reduced by about two-fifths of the total, or US$38 billion in present value terms.[12] Overall, the plan brought only modest improvement to the debt-financing difficulties of the debtor countries. The following table gives a complete breakdown of debt reduction in the period 1987–June 1992.

As mentioned, the Brady Plan was indicative of a new approach and deviated from earlier strategies by giving commercial banks a restricted menu of options from which to chose the appropriate strategy. This was only begrudgingly accepted by the banks and even this did not obviate the need for lengthy negotiations on each individual case. In the meantime,

Table 6.3.   Debt reduction 1987–June 1992 (US$ billion).

	Debt reduction	Debt-service	Pre-payments	Total reduction
Bolivia	0.5	–	–	0.5
Chile	0.4	–	–	0.4
Costa Rica	1.0	0.2	–	1.2
Mexico	7.9	7.0	7.7	22.6
Mozambique	0.2	–	–	0.2
Niger	0.1	–	–	0.1
Nigeria	3.4	0.6	0.4	4.3
Philippines	2.6	0.7	0.5	3.9
Uruguay	0.6	0.2	0.1	0.9
Venezuela	1.9	2.7	1.7	6.3
Total	18.6	11.3	10.3	40.2
Of which: since March 1989	16.7	11.3	9.8	37.8

Source: Clark, J. and Elliot Kalter, "Recent Innovations in Debt Restructuring," Finance and Development, September 1992, p. 7.

however, while refusing to be regulated by national decision makers, credit institutions evolved a complex set of reform measures to deal with the debt problem through market mechanisms. One interesting innovation was the debt-for-development swap which involved discounted sale or donation of debt to charitable institutions which, in turn, could swap it with the debtor country for payment in local currency. Such swaps were established in 1987 and examples include the Bank of America (BOA) announcement that it would donate up to US$6 million, over a three-year period, to Conservation International and the World Wildlife Fund, the advisors, to fund debt-for-development swaps in Latin America. The BOA gift was specifically earmarked for rain forest conservation and required the environmental organizations to swap debt with governments at 100 percent of the face value, but in local currency.[13] The funds thus raised were to be used for conservation purposes.

Critics of the Brady Plan inveighed against the fact that it contained no enforcement mechanism. Indeed, commercial banks were not compelled to participate. The creditor institutions could simply endorse it without taking concrete actions and as already mentioned, banks were not favorably disposed large-scale debt reduction. More seriously, it left open the possibility of some banks "free riding" on the efforts of other financial institutions. The free rider problem presented itself because debt reduction was voluntary and banks that held out could improve their net position after others banks had entered into debt buyback schemes. The objective of the Brady Plan was to reduce total debt so as to ensure that the remaining debt was at least repayable. To the extent that the remaining debt was repayable, debtor countries also improved their credit rating and credit worthiness. Credit worthiness can be conceptualized as a public good that would benefit all credit agencies regardless of whether or not the costs had been socialized. As such, if, some creditor institutions chose to hold out and not participate in buyback schemes, they could be in a better position than before, even though they had not borne any of the costs of the buyback mechanism. Apart from the free rider problem, another flaw of the debt buyback scheme was that it was not universally advantageous to the debtor country, especially if debt buyback was only partial and did not include total outstanding debt. This and the free rider problem can be illustrated through the Bolivian debt buyback scheme.

Total Bolivian debt in early 1988 were US$670 million and in March that year, the Bolivian government used US$34 million of its own resources plus donated resources from Spain, the Netherlands, and Brazil, to buy back US$308 million of total debt at a discount of eleven cents to the dollar. Total remaining debt was reduced to US$362 million but as Rogoff explains, the entire scheme was of dubious merit, as far as Bolivia was concerned.

The net result of the buyback deal was that Bolivia had used US$34 million dollars to secure debt relief of only US$4 hundred thousand dollars. Bolivia, Rogoff argued, would have been unambiguously better off if it could have bought back all of its US$670 million debt for US$40.2 million (US$670 million × 0.06 cents = US$40.2 million). The partial debt buyback offered no significant real debt relief to Bolivia. The above example also illustrates the free rider problem in that where

Table 6.4.   The 1988 Bolivian debt buyback.

	Before buyback	After buyback
Secondary market price times	0.06 cents	0.11 cents
Debt outstanding equals	$670 million	$362 million
Total market value	$40.2 million	$39.8 million
Total benefit to Bolivia	= $40.2 − $39.8	= $0.4 million

Source: Rogoff, K., "Dealing with Developing Country Debt in the 1990s," *The World Economy*, Vol. 15, No. 4, July 1992, p. 480.

creditors, before the buyback, could only expect to receive six cents to the dollar, after the buyback, they could expect to receive 11 cents because Bolivia was now assumed to have improved its credit worthiness, regardless of whether or not they participated in the buyback scheme.

Apart from the practical inefficiencies of the system, debt reduction and bailout were criticized also for benefiting mainly the Highly Indebted Countries which, in 1987, had an average per capital annual income of US$1430 and, therefore, undeserving of the limited pool of international capital for development purposes. Critics argued that it was morally indefensible to bankroll the relatively rich at the expense of the deserving needy, and to allow aid decisions to be straight jacketed by decisions of commercial banks in 1970s. Under the Brady Plan, about US$30–40 billion dollars were pledged by the West and multilateral institutions for debt buyback purposes when the poorer countries of Asia and Africa were in much greater need of these funds.

The 1994 Mexican Crisis

In late 1994, Mexico reignited the fuse of another debt crisis when a sharp collapse of the Mexican currency spread fears that Mexico might default on debt repayment. Several factors contributed to the crisis, including the rapid appreciation of the Peso. Between 1990 and 1994, the real value of the Peso had appreciated approximately 20 percent and this eroded the country's international export position. The crisis was also a result of political instability. In January 1994, the Zapatista rebels launched an uprising in the state of Chiapas and in March the presidential candidate of the ruling party was assassinated at a political rally. These were indicators of social problems and inequalities, and contributed to a climate of uncertainty for international investors.

In the period before the crisis, foreign capital had continued to flood the Mexican economy, fooled by deceptive information and data released by the Mexican government, which painted a rosier picture of the economy than was warranted.[14] Mexico was touted as Latin America's miracle economy but, according to Sebastian Edwards, this was an "invented" miracle.[15] Capital inflows reached 10 percent of the GDP in 1993 and fuelled expansionary credit, excessive consumption and increasing current account deficits. On 20 December, the Mexican government announced plans for a controlled devaluation of the peso by 13 percent. Markets, however, were not convinced that such a devalua- tion, after years of determined resistance to currency realignment, could be executed.

The problem was that by the time of the announcement, the Mexican government had already depleted its foreign reserves and had little fighting fund to manage a controlled devaluation. An overvalued peso together with political uncertainties within Mexico had encouraged domestic capital flight and, consequently, an erosion of the international reserve base of the Mexican central bank. Instead of a controlled devalua- tion, the peso collapsed from 3.45 peso to the dollar to 5.57 in early January 1995, a devaluation of more than 60 percent. The root of the problem was growing current account deficits fuelled by an overvalued currency. The devaluation was a positive development for exporters in Mexico but added to the debt servicing difficulties. This was compounded by the fact that approximately US$17 billion of the debt was to mature within the next six months.[16]

As in the earlier crisis, the US government quickly announced plans to extend large-scale loan guarantees to the Mexican government. However, with uncertainty over whether the US Congress would approve the plan to provide US$40 billion in loan guarantees, President Clinton by-passed the Congress and promised US$20 billion from US currency stabilization fund and also committed the Bank of International Settlement and the International Monetary Fund for additional loan guarantees of nearly US$30 billion. The European leaders were displeased at the lack of adequate prior consultation but, nonetheless, agreed that decisive measures were needed to avert a repeat of the debt crisis. Mexico's quick recovery was assisted also by easy access to the US market as a result of the North American Free Trade Agreement (NAFTA) which came into effect in 1994 and liberalized trade between US, Canada and Mexico. According to Nora Lustig, one indicator of NAFTA's role Mexican recovery was that "The average rate of growth of Mexican exports to the United States was more than ten percentage points higher after 1994 than in the period 1991–1993."[17]

The East Asian Currency Crisis of 1997

At the time of the Latin American debt crisis, the contrast with East Asia was striking. Many of these countries, too, had high debt levels but still managed to keep debt service ratios to within manageable limits by pursuing export-oriented growth strategies to generate adequate foreign exchange revenues. Very simply, the debt crisis of 1982 was seen as a vindication of export-oriented industrialization (the East Asian model) and a castigation of import substitution industrialization (the Latin American model). Bolstered by economic success through the 1980s, these countries continued to benefit from readily available investment capital from overseas to sustain and boost economic growth. This private sector capital inflow continued unabated through the mid-1990s. Foreign capital supplemented domestic savings which was high by international standards but insufficient to meet domestic investment needs. A significant portion of this capital inflow was short term which, in Thailand, accounted for as much as 5 percent of GDP during 1994–1996.[18] The attraction of short-term lending for creditors was that it entailed fewer risks and for borrowers that it came with a reduced interest rate because of the shorter maturity. The danger, of course, was that any loss of investor confidence would reverse capital inflow and make it difficult to either rollover existing debt or to meet debt service obligations.

In the lead-up to the debt crisis, most accounts presented a glowing picture of development and industrialization in East Asia. A World Bank report, prepared a few years earlier, referred to these as "miracle economies" because of their sustained and equitable economic growth. The World Bank attributed this miracle to good macroeconomic policies and selective state intervention in the economy to channel investment to growth industries or to compensate for periodic market failures. That state intervention had been beneficial was an important and controversial acknowledgment, especially in the context of dominant economic theories and principles that underpinned World Bank and IMF structural adjustment programs. However, the World Bank did add a note of caution that state intervention in Southeast Asia was often less constructive than in Northeast Asia.[19]

A somewhat less glorious explanation was provided by Paul Krugman, who argued that there had been no miracle because the East Asian growth cycle was premised simply on factor input growth rather than productivity growth. Denying that the East Asian had achieved a miracle, he argued that once "One accounts for the role of rapidly growing inputs in these countries' growth, one finds little left to explain."[20] The conclusions reached by Krugman generated considerable controversy but it needs to be reiterated that the East Asian miracle was not simply the achievement of high growth but rather growth with equity. Despite the controversy sparked by Krugman, the mood of optimism about East Asian growth remained strong.

Few detected any signs of serious troubles on the horizon. In a report released in 1997, but before the Asian currency crisis could be factored in, the World Bank sounded a positive note on the East Asian lending situation. It pointed out that, unlike Mexico, countries like Indonesia, the Philippines, and Thailand had been able to avert a banking crisis because of their sound macroeconomic fundamentals.[21] Somewhat more cautious was a report published by the Institute of Developing Economies, Tokyo, in July 1997, just as the crisis was beginning to unfold. It raised concerns about the economic outlook for East Asian countries.

The most telling sign was the decline of export growth which pointed to future difficulties in servicing existing foreign debt. Once the currency

Table 6.5.   Economic indicators for nine East Asian economies.

	Actual economic growth (%)			Rate of export growth (%)		Trade balance (US$ million)	
	Average of 1986–1995	1995	1996	1995	1996	1995	1996
Korea	8.9	9	7.1	30.3	3.8	−4 328	−15 278
Taiwan	7.8	6	5.7	20.1	3.9	8 109	14 704
Hong Kong	6.8	4.7	4.7	14.9	4	−19 001	−17 800
Singapore	8.3	8.8	7	22.5	5.8	−6 208	−6 320
Malaysia	7.9	9.5	8.2	25.8	5.9	−3 778	−196
Thailand	9.4	8.6	6.7	24.7	−1.3	−14 335	−17 245
Indonesia	7.2	8	7.6	13.4	9.7	4 760	6 991
Philippines	3.5	4.8	5.5	29.3	18.3	−9 168	−11 786
China	9.6	10.5	9.7	20.3	1.6	16 692	12 270

Source: Kitamura, K. and Tanaka, T. (eds.), *Examining Asia's Tigers: Nine Economies Challenging Common Structural Problems*, Institute of Developing Economies, Tokyo, 1997, See Executive Summary.

turmoil set in, focus quickly shifted to the macroeconomic weaknesses. The rapidity with which the economic miracle was reduced to a meltdown also raised questions about the role of governments in achieving economic growth. The crisis, blamed on political mismanagement, undermined the credibility of arguments supportive of state intervention in the market. But rather than dismiss government intervention as detrimental, it might be sufficient to caution about the possibility of periodic government failure. Market failure is a recognized occurrence and government failure may belong in the same category. The lesson of the Asian financial crisis is that in a global economy with rapid capital mobility, prudential economic management is particularly important to avoid panic in the market.

The East Asian crisis was triggered by a dramatic loss of investor confidence in these economies. This reversed capital flows and resulted in sharp currency devaluation. The countries most severely affected were Malaysia, Thailand, Indonesia and South Korea. The last was particularly spectacular because it, together with Taiwan, Hong Kong and Singapore, was one of the original newly industrializing countries and widely recognized as an East Asian success story. Interestingly, while South Korea was gripped in currency turmoil, Taiwan remained relatively unaffected by the conflagration raging around it. In 1997, the decline in the value of the Taiwan currency was modest and its stock exchange was the only major Asian market to post a gain for the year.[22] Consistent with what we would expect from a capital surplus countries, the private sector in Taiwan had low exposure to foreign debt and this fact, by itself, ensured that Taiwan would escape the worst of the debt crisis. An advantage for Taiwan was that its industrial structure was dominated by small firms which had less access to foreign capital than the large conglomerates, Chaebols, of South Korea. With limited access to "easy" foreign capital, investment decisions tended to be more prudent and this may have enabled the private sector to avert the trap of fanciful investments indulged in by some of the other East Asian countries. Taiwan also had an efficient capital market to channel savings to potential investors and, most importantly, large foreign exchange reserves to resist speculative pressures on the local currency.

The crisis had been gathering momentum, almost imperceptibly, for several years previously. However, a climate of economic optimism had inured East Asian governments and foreign investors to the dangers of profligate and uneconomic investment decisions. They had become so accustomed to high economic growth that they could not contemplate the possibility of a drastic slowdown. Investor confidence, too, was strong and even the Mexican crisis failed to significantly affect capital flows to these countries. One factor that contributed to the crisis was that foreign debt was being used increasingly not for productive purposes but for speculative investment in real estate, show-piece development, and for luxury and conspicuous consumption in a highly status-driven societal structure. Instead of market discipline, countries like Indonesia descended into crony capitalism, where political cronies and family members of President Suharto were permitted lucrative monopolies. This did not bode well for future debt servicing requirements. Currency devaluation in China in 1994 also had an adverse impact on regional exports. The massive devaluation of the yuan boosted China's export competitiveness relative to other East Asian countries. It led to an export boom and substantial increases in Chinese trade surpluses. By contrast, there was a rapid deterioration in the trade position of other East Asian economies. This deterioration was a result of factors mentioned above as well as the policy of maintaining exchange rate fixed to an appreciating US dollar. In 1993, for example, South Korea had a modest current account surplus of US$385 million but the surplus turned into a deficit of US$453 million in 1994 and a deficit of US$23 716 million in 1996. At the same time, its external debt increased from US$78.4 billion in 1995 to US$104.7 billion in 1996.[23] In 1996, Thailand's current account deficit was 8 percent of GDP, that of Malaysia was 5.5 percent and Indonesia had a deficit of more than 4 percent.

Large debt, speculative and wasteful investment in, for instance, a national aircraft industry in Indonesia, wastage through cronyism and corruption, and worsening trade situation spooked foreign investors who pulled the plug on foreign investment in East Asia. The dependence on borrowed international capital to sustain domestic growth had also increased the vulnerability of these countries to international speculative pressures. This could only be prevented with prudent macroeconomic management and exchange rate flexibility but easy credit appeared to obviate the need for macroeconomic discipline and prudence, and the East Asian government also had a policy of inflexible exchange rates. As their currencies were pegged to the US dollar, it was inevitable that as the dollar appreciated in value, these countries would lose their trade competitiveness. But rather than devalue, they persisted with a strong currency policy on an assumption that a strong currency reflected a strong economy. Later, because of total foreign debt, they became locked into defending their currencies because the loans would be unserviceable at a lower exchange rate. Nonetheless, while external factors, such as appreciation of the US dollar, devaluation of the Chinese yuan, and increase in global interest rates, contributed to the crisis, the role of domestic political corruption and cronyism, and economic mismanagement should not be underestimated.

In Malaysia however, Prime Minister Mahathir Mohamad insisted initially that the crisis was caused by panic resulting from currency speculation and capital flight. Capital flight from the five worst-affected Asian economies (South Korea, Indonesia, Thailand, Malaysia and the Philippines) amounted to US$12 billion in 1997 compared to an inflow of US$97 billion in 1996.[24] This capital shift of US$105 billion represented 11 percent of their collective GDP and was a strong vote of no-confidence in the affected regional economies.

Mahathir singled out George Soros as the most nefarious of all currency speculator, who had taken it upon himself to punish non-democratic regimes by undermining their economic growth and stability.[25] The allegations of a foreign conspiracy was reminiscent of earlier assertions that American objections to an exclusively East Asian regionalism were similarly inspired by a desire to contain East Asian growth and prevent the emergence of East Asian as a strong force in international political economy. Having externalized the source of the problem, Prime Minister Mahathir resisted the need to implement the necessary correctives and rebuild confidence about Malaysia in international markets. The Malaysian government refused to accept IMF loans or submit to IMF conditionality.

The first country to experience speculative pressures on its currency was Thailand. The Thai baht came under pressure in early May 1997, followed by similar pressures on other regional countries. The speculative attacks elicited a response of coordinated exchange rate intervention in defence of the pegged exchange rate. Governments in Thailand, Malaysia, and other Southeast Asian economies had pegged their currencies on an assumption that a strong currency was a sign of strong economy. As currencies tumbled, the East Asian governments intervened extensively in capital market and brought in new capital controls but failed to stem the tide. The Central Bank of Thailand lost US$30 billion in foreign reserves in its failed attempt to shore up the value of the baht. Eventually, governments succumbed to market pressures and in early July 1997, for example, the Thai government abandoned its defence of the pegged exchange rate.

Unlike the Latin American sovereign debt, East Asian debt was owed mainly by the private sector. Because of the large number of private borrowers, it was impossible to obtain an accurate assessment of the total debt burden but it was obvious, as soon as currencies depreciated, that these borrowers would be unable to roll over their debt or to service existing debt. As an example of the magnitude of the currency devaluation, the Indonesian rupiah declined from a pre-crisis rate of around 2 500 to 17 000 against the US dollar in January 1998. This had a severe impact on the capacity of borrowers to service their debt. The international implication of the crisis was that any large-scale failure of corporations and banking institutions would have important flow-on effects on their trade partners, lending institutions, and the rest of the world. To prevent this eventuality and forestall bankruptcies, the Indonesian government, in late January, provided a reprieve by announcing a short pause in debt repayments by Indonesian companies.

The East Asian currency meltdown again resulted in an extensive bailout operation led by the IMF. The IMF had assisted Mexico in its 1994 crisis, in what is widely acclaimed as a success since Mexico was able to repay its debt to the IMF ahead of schedule. In East Asia, IMF stepped into the breach with extensive aid packages for South Korea, Thailand, Indonesia, totalling US$109 billion. In return, each of these countries accepted strict austerity measures, cut subsidies on key commodities, and introduced measures to further deregulate their economies. IMF conditions came under some criticism on grounds that the directives went beyond what was required to manage a currency crisis. It was certainly understandable that the IMF should require greater openness and transparency in financial regulations and strengthening of the banking sector but it was not plainly obvious how, for instance, the demand for tariff reduction in the auto industry or the abolition of the Clove Marketing Board in Indonesia might help stablilze the Indonesian currency. As far as critics were concerned, the IMF was simply exploiting the opportunity to bring about massive changes in the economic structure. In defence of the IMF conditionality, it might be said that if liberalization did bring about more national investment policy decisions, abandonment of meaningless investment in a national car industry, which had more to do with prestige than economic rationality, then it was a step in the right direction toward sustained economic growth. Indeed, the the IMF was prepared to admit that its reform conditions in this debt crisis were markedly different from the IMF conditions in the 1980s, which had relied extensively on austerity measures. In East Asia, the objectives of reforms were to change domestic business practices, corporate culture and government behavior. The IMF justified its reform agenda as necessarily harsher and more far-reaching in order to restore market confidence and return these economies to viability.[26]

The Korean government also renegotiated extensions on US$24 billion of short-term loans with 13 creditor banks in order to ease its debt service burden. More importantly, the new loan conditions were not harsh. Initially, the creditor institutions insisted on an interest rate of at least 12 percent per annum for new loans while the Korean government argued that the interest rates should be less than 8.6 percent. In the end, the two sides agreed on new loans at around 8.4 percent. The low interest rate meant considerable savings for Korea since a difference of just 1 percent on debt of around US$25 billion results in savings of around US$250 million annually.[27]

The IMF reform and austerity conditions imposed considerable hardship on the people because the affect of reforms was to significantly lower the levels of economic activity. For example, before the crisis, in May 1997, the IMF had predicted a 1997 GDP growth rate of 7.4 percent and 7.0 percent for Indonesia and Thailand respectively but soon afterwards growth forecasts for 1997 were lowered to 2.0 percent and zero for these two countries. The IMF however, forecast a higher growth rate of 6.0 percent for South Korea, up from 5.6 percent, despite the financial crisis. This was perhaps because the South Korean crisis was managed very quickly and effectively by restructuring the country's debt.

The crisis will have major long-term consequences for the affected countries, perhaps not as severe as that confronted by the Latin American countries in the 1980s but serious nonetheless. The ambitious developmental objectives are the first obvious victims of the crisis and it is unlikely that Malaysia will now be able to achieve the status of a developed economy by the year 2020, as envisioned in the so-called "Vision 2020." The impact of the crisis will be most acutely felt by the common people who will be forced to endure a drastic reduction in their living standards.

Social unrest and rioting, however, was limited to Indonesia where economic difficulties aggravated popular discontent with the long established dictatorial regime of President Suharto. Here, economic crisis became a political crisis and the opposition forces rallied the people to demand change and an end to the system of political patronage and corruption that had allowed family members and close associates to obtain lucrative economic deals from the state. IMF conditionality placed the Suharto administration under pressure from two separate sources. Firstly, there was pressure from family members and political cronies, who had amassed enormous fortunes through their political connection, to maintain the level of public support for their various businesses. Secondly, there was pressure from the IMF, which demanded economic reforms, transparency of regulations, and policies to end anticompetitive practices within the Indonesian economy. The dilemma for the Suharto administration was that it was impossible to reconcile family interests with the national interest. The Indonesian government resisted scaling back several of the mega-projects in order to protect financial interests of the ruling and business elite. The government insisted on pushing ahead with its ambitious infrastructure projects even though it was now obvious that these projects were not viable.

The delays in implementing IMF directives further undermined international market confidence and renewed speculative pressures on the Indonesian currency. The rupiah depreciated and this only added to domestic inflationary pressures and economic hardship, as well as exacerbating debt servicing difficulties. The government toyed with the idea of re-pegging the currency at a much more favorable exchange rate and announced, in mid February 1998, a plan to establish a Currency Stabilization Board. The intention was to provide relief to local debtors and to political cronies but was immediately criticized by IMF and the international community, which maintained that any attempt to re-peg exchange rates would invite the same currency speculation that had triggered the crisis in the first place, especially if the peg was at inappropriate levels.

When Indonesia defaulted on promised reforms, the IMF withdrew its monetary support, adding to the economic uncertainty and chaos.

Confronted by a possibility of large-scale social dislocations, some western governments advocated a more measured pace of IMF reform. The reasoning was that political instability would impede a resolution of the economic crisis and that social and political instability in a large and populous country like Indonesia could also undermine overall regional stability. The Australian government was particularly concerned that social collapse would re-create a refugee problem in the region.

Finally, in April 1998, the Indonesian government relented and agreed to a new package of reform conditions, which Indonesia promised to implement faithfully and expeditiously. The new package permitted Indonesia to continue subsidies on some basic commodities in order to contain the possibility of a popular backlash against the government, but price rises in oil and some other commodities still unleashed a massive wave of social unrest and violence. A few months earlier, President Suharto had arrogantly brushed aside growing societal demand for political change and secured a fifth term as President. The price rises that followed inflamed popular resentment and led to rioting in Jakarta and elsewhere. The target of the protest movement was the Suharto administration but the immediate victims were members of the Chinese community, who seemingly had benefited from policies of the Suharto government to amass large fortunes. The Chinese became the scapegoats in the power-play but ultimately the protesters secured their objective and Suharto was forced to resign in May 1998. This ended more than 30 years of the "New Order" government.

The violence and political fallout of the crisis in Indonesia were dramatic but whether these can be read as precursors to liberal democracy is uncertain. Suharto's departure does not guarantee that liberal democracy will fill the vacated political space. Much will depend on the role of the military. Since its formation in the mid-1960s, the New Order regime had benefited from its close relationship with the military and the military, in turn, had obtained a political role for itself. For democracy to succeed in Indonesia, the military will have to give up its political role and become a professional institution but there is little to suggest that the military is contemplating such a transformation.

As the crisis stricken Asian economies struggle to recover, the Japanese role will be especially important. Through much of the post-war period, the Japanese government chose not to assume an assertive role in regional affairs because of lingering regional hostility for its wartime atrocities. The economic crisis, however, was an opportunity for Japan to play a constructive role if it mobilized its capital reserves to assist the regional economies or if it stimulated its own economy to provide a large market for regional exporters to regain previous production levels. Addressing the World Economic Forum, Thai Prime Minister Chuan Leekpai said that the Japanese economy had to be stimulated to act as "An engine for recovery in the region ... ."[28] If there was an opportunity for Japan to demonstrate leadership, the government, yet again, failed to seize it. Jeffrey Sachs had earlier criticized Japan for not playing a constructive role in the Russian economic transition and, in reference to the Asian financial crisis, the US Trade Representative described Japan's response as "woefully inadequate" while Deputy Prime Minister Anwar Ibrahim of Malaysia criticized Japan for being slow to respond to the crisis.[29]

The crisis also was an opportunity for China to repair its relationship with regional countries after the damage it had done to itself in the missile crisis of 1996. To demonstrate its goodwill, the Chinese government promised to refrain from any further currency devaluation that might exacerbate the situation in Southeast Asia. Whether the Chinese government will be able to keep its promise, and for how long, is uncertain, especially if the currency devaluation in Southeast Asia undermines Chinese export potential and its revenue base. If that were to happen, the temptation to devalue the yuan might become hard to resist, especially as China needs to generate sufficient revenue in order to undertake the pending reform of its state-owned enterprises and the banking sector.

Structural Adjustment and Change in Developing Countries

The structural adjustment programs introduced by the IMF following the onset of the Latin American debt crisis became a medium for rapid change in the developing countries. In the decade of the 1980s, apart from the former communist countries in Russia and Eastern Europe, a similar transformation toward greater openness and liberalization swept through the developing world.

The debt crisis provided a rationale for drastic economic restructuring in the developing countries, from import substitution industrialization (ISI) to export-oriented industrialization (EOI), and from economic regulation to market orientation. The primary focus of structural adjustment and reform was to enhance economic performance and export competitiveness in the developing countries. It was assumed that such reforms would boost economic growth and enhance their export earnings, which would lead to improvements in balance of payments position and enable them to finance their foreign debt. Structural adjustment programs promised a virtuous cycle of higher growth and higher exports. In the process, structural adjustment would also assist in the realization of wider adherence to liberal economic principles, as envisaged by the founders of, for example, the GATT. By the early 1990s, about 70 countries had embarked upon structural adjustment programs.[30]

The thrust of structural adjustment was to force developing countries to adopt export oriented and open economic structures in place of earlier policies that promoted import substitution behind protectionist trade barriers. It was, as mentioned above, a key component of the Baker and the Brady plan and was successfully implemented in many Latin American countries as part of IMF conditionality. The importance of openness has been strongly asserted by one recent study by Jeffrey Sachs and Andrew Warner in which the authors conclude that openness, along with private property, is a sufficient condition for growth in developing countries.[31]

Structural adjustment was not confined to the Highly Indebted Countries of Latin America but was imposed, with equal vigor, in the poorer countries of Africa and Asia. The former group of relatively rich developing countries turned to the multilateral agencies only after the debt crisis had blocked their capacity to borrow from commercial banks. The latter group of countries were considered a bigger risk and did not venture extensively into the commercial sector. Their borrowing was limited, to a large extent, to the multilateral agencies. For example, whereas more than 70 percent of the debt owed by poorer countries of Asia and Africa was either multilateral or bilateral debt, 70 percent of the Latin American debt was owed to private lending institutions.[32] For the poorer countries, structural adjustment was, from the beginning, a condition of multilateral financing.

The IMF and the World Bank were at the forefront of structural adjustment programs, providing not only financial assistance but also policy advice. The ideas informing structural adjustment had been articulated in various World Bank reports, including a 1981 report on economic stagnation in Sub-Saharan Africa. It observed that "Three major policy actions are central to any growth-oriented program: (1) more suitable trade and exchange-rate policies; (2) increased efficiency of resource use in the public sector; and (3) improvement in agricultural policies."

Structural adjustment programs were intricately linked with policies of trade liberalization and export promotion,[33] which created a bias in favor of export sales over domestic sales. Behind the push for economic rationality and export promotion, was the view that countries that permitted a greater play to market forces and encouraged exports (Taiwan, South Korea, Hong Kong and Singapore) achieved superior economic results than countries that regulated their economies and pursued import substitution industrialization. The incorporation of export-oriented policies into structural adjustment programs reflected the belief that the East Asian model was not historically unique and could be replicated in other developing countries.

Economic liberalization was necessary to enhance export competitiveness through lower prices for imported inputs and, together with export promotion, was essential to correct domestic price distortions. Given the practical difficulty of determining real market prices for any given economy, the IMF and the World Bank used world market prices as indicators. It was consequently necessary to liberalize their trade regimes to ensure that domestic prices reflected world prices. In general, the reform program can be discussed under the three headings of monetary measures; fiscal measures; and trade measures.

The monetary measures targeted high levels of inflation caused by profligate government spending. High inflation was considered a serious and threatening condition which eroded business confidence and signaled that the market was not performing to its full potential. Consequently, anti-inflationary policies formed the bedrock of the reform agenda, without which the reform measures were unlikely to succeed. Anne Krueger explained, "When public sector deficits are large, and/or inflation is proceeding at annual rates in excess of, say, 100 percent, major reduction in the size of the public sector deficit is a virtual necessary condition for the success of the reform effort."[34] IMF conditionality required a drastic reduction in government spending and increase in domestic interest rates to control and bring down inflation levels. Higher domestic interest rates had the additional advantage of encouraging private savings, reducing consumption, and discouraging capital flight.[35]

The fiscal measures concentrated around reducing the size of the public sector within the economy. This was the most painful aspect of structural adjustment because of withdrawal of various governmental services and subsidies. On the positive side, this curtailed investment in 'white elephant' projects and retrenched state involvement in inefficient public enterprises through forced privatization. Apart from reductions in government expenditure, structural adjustment also entailed reforms in the tax structure. Instead of relying on export and import taxes for revenue, the IMF reforms required states to raise revenue by taxing domestic sales and excise taxes, or income tax. This was not very successful given the inadequacies of the adminstrative bureaucracy to monitor and collect taxes from a broad domestic base.

The trade measures were largely designed to encourage exports and reduce barriers to imports. This involved liberalization of tariff schedules, tariffication of trade restrictions, and exchange rate adjustments. Many developing countries had introduced exchange restrictions and also maintained an overvalued exchange rate on the dual assumption that export demand for their products was unlikely to expand significantly and that import demand was constant and the essential imports could not be reduced. Under these assumptions, countries tried to minimize their total import bill by maintaining overvalued currency rates. Unfortunately, an overvalued currency also made imports cheaper and it created a dependency on imports. Between 1977 and 1981, for example, Mexican imports grew at 35 percent each year. Nigel Harris wrote that, "For an import substituting economy, this was poor performance. Some saw it as intrinsic to the imperfect structure of the economy, its "dependency," but a simpler explanation related it to the value of the peso; dollar denominated imports were generally cheaper than domestic produced goods. Thus, the advantage of protection was nullified by the exchange rate."[36]

At the same time, cheaper imports, of at least capital and intermediate producer goods, were considered desirable for the domestic industrialization program. To prevent luxury imports from benefiting from overvalued exchange rates, many countries introduced dual or multiple exchange rate system such that a lower rate applied for non-essential luxury imports.[37] Overvalued exchange rates were a tax on exports and while multiple exchange rates solved the problem of luxury imports flooding the domestic market, such a system also produced negative externalities.

Under structural adjustment programs, countries were forced to adopt a unitary exchange rate and one that did not penalize exports but rather encouraged it. They were also forced to remove quantitative import restrictions. A measure of the importance of exchange rate changes in IMF lending practices can be seen in the fact that while exchange rate actions were required in only 31 percent of the Fund programs during 1963–1972, such actions were part of 64 percent of the programs during 1981–1983.[38] For a group of 15 developing countries undergoing reform, the exchange rate by 1987 had depreciated by around 40 percent compared to the 1965–1981 levels.[39]

On specific trade restrictions, Krueger argued that non-prohibitive import restrictions and rent seeking activities eroded peoples confidence in the market mechanism because of the perception that the rich benefit or were successful as rent seekers "Whereas the poor are those precluded from or unsuccessful in rent seeking ... ."[40] This set off a political vicious circle where the government was 'forced' to intervene to correct market distortions which only further distorted the economic payoff structure. A logical corollary of this, not pointed out by Krueger, was that such a system should lead to political instability whereas a transition to liberal trade and freeing up of the market mechanism should restore faith in the market and enhance political legitimacy.[41]

Structural adjustment programs were for fixed periods and both the IMF and the World Bank provided special structural adjustment loans to make the transition easier for developing countries. The World Bank classified its financial assistance programs as Structural Adjustment Loans (SALs) and Sectoral Adjustment Loans (SECALs). The latter was narrowly focused but both had the same objective of improving market efficiency and resource allocation. Between 1980 and 1987, the World Bank provided a total of US$15 billion to 51 countries under the two loan programs.[42]

Social Impact of Structural Adjustment Policies

The developing countries shouldered a disproportionate share of the cost of stabilizing the international financial system. Rather than receive foreign aid and capital, debt servicing, in the 1980s, meant a perverse flow of capital from the developing to the rich countries. In 1981, the developing countries' net receipt (new debt less total debt repayment) was US$36.5 billion but by 1986, this had turned into a deficit of US$19.7 billion and to a deficit of US$42.9 billion in 1989.[43] Within the developing countries, the worst affected was the poorer segment of the population because governments pared welfare spending to meet interest payments.

Structural adjustment policies imposed a regime of openness on developing countries and thrust them into the global economy. The result was to enhance the degree of integration of the developing economies into the global economy. Most developing countries except in Latin America and the Caribbean substantially increased the ratio of their trade to GDP between 1985 and 1995 and also benefited from vastly expanded inflow of foreign direct investment. In 1990, FDI brought US$24.2 billion of investment to developing countries but by 1995 this had increased to US$91.8 billion.[44]

Confirming expectations that liberalization would enhance growth prospects in developing countries, the World Bank issued its finding that reforms had been generally successful in promoting growth. According to the Bank, between 1985 and 1987, economic growth in countries with a strong reform program averaged 3.8 percent a year whereas economic growth in countries with weak or no reform was only 1.5 percent a year.[45] Another World Bank study of 29 Sub-Saharan African countries reached similar conclusions, that countries that persevered did better than countries which vacillated on the implementation of reforms. The study acknowledged that growth had failed to meet expectations but according to Christine Jones and Miguel Kiguel, the inability to generate growth was because reforms had not been sustained, and not due to a failure of the reforms themselves.[46]

Other studies reached similar conclusions. Even though structural adjustment policies led to immediate negative impact, the longer-run results have been seen as generally beneficial to the developing countries. Not only that, according to Lawrence Summers and Lant Pritchett, those countries that underwent 'intensive structural adjustment,' that is those countries which had at least two structural adjustment loans between 1986 and 1990, "... enjoyed faster growth, higher export and savings shares, and lower fiscal deficits in the second half of the 1980s, both compared with other countries and compared with their own earlier performance."[47]

Critics of greater integration into a global economy, however, argued that it would lead to large western transnational corporations dominating the economies of the third world. According to Martin Khor, the developing countries, by hitching into a system over which they had little control, risked losing their "Indigenous skills, their capacity for self-reliance, their confidence, and, in many cases, the very resource base on which their survival depends."[48]

Apart from the introduction of inappropriate technologies, critics argued that developing countries could also become dumping grounds for pollutants generated elsewhere. These are essentially problems that result from institutional weaknesses and structural inadequacies, such as in legal systems, to deal with the forces of globalization. If true, then the developing countries may be underprepared to partake of the benefits of economic globalization. For developing countries, the putative advantage of participating the globalized economy was a prospect of eventual convergence of incomes and standards of living. By late 1990s, however, no convergence had taken place, even if some developing countries had narrowed differentials against developed countries. In its world economic and financial surveys in 1997, the International Monetary Fund acknowledged that "... on average, there has been no convergence of per capita income levels between the two groups of countries [developed and developing]; in fact, in absolute terms there has been a widening."[49] This is a serious indictment of the failings of the openness programs as they were implemented.

Whether this was a conceptual failure or one of implementation, structural adjustment programs, following the 1980s debt crisis and the Indonesian debt crisis of 1997, were criticized for their neglect of political and social considerations. The burden of structural adjustment was placed squarely on the developing countries, much as the Bretton-Woods agreement placed the onus for adjusting to payments difficulties squarely upon the deficit countries. Structural adjustment also imposed tremendous hardships on the poorer segment of the population because cutbacks in government services meant the withdrawal of a social safety net.

When structural adjustment programs began in the early 1980s, it was assumed that the adjustment would take no more than a few years and that the hardship too, would be a short-term phenomenon before the benefits started flowing in. However, the process of adjustment continued longer than expected, with little relief for the worst-affected. It resulted in significant declines in the standard of living in many countries. In Peru, for example, from 1985 to 1990, average consumption declined by over 50 percent but the poorest decile (10 percent) was the worst affected. Its monthly per capita consumption declined by 62 percent.[50] Indeed, the 1980s was a decade that was lost to development in that, according to Hans Wolfgang Singer and Sumit Roy, "Attention shifted to debt settlement, stabilization, adjustment, structural change, liberalization, and so on — often at the expense of everything that had previously been understood as development, whether growth, employment, redistribution, basic needs or reduction of poverty."[51]

With the emphasis on fiscal discipline and cutbacks on welfare programs, the poor were left to fend for themselves. Likewise, the emphasis on producing cash crops for exports rather than food crops for domestic consumption added to the people's misery and, when global agricultural prices declined, contributed to the crisis of hunger and famine in Africa. For these people, the possibility that structural adjustment would lead to long-term economic prosperity was cold comfort, considering their immediate hunger and impoverishment. The failure of structural adjustment to quickly reverse declining economic fortunes of the developing countries led to new criticisms from dependency theorists that structural adjustment programs merely reproduced dependent development by emphasizing international economic linkages and that such programs were unlikely to alleviate poverty or produce autonomous development. In Nigeria, according to Julius Ohinvbere:

> At the end of 1989, students, workers, peasants, market women, bankers and indigenous entrepreneurs have pronounced the adjustment package a total disaster. Only transnational corporations, speculators, drug pushers, currency traffickers, consultants and middlemen, as well as top army officers and bureaucrats, are full of praise for the SAP [structural adjustment program].[52]

In 1988, after the collapse of the Egyptian structural adjustment program because of domestic political repercussions, President Mubarak likened the IMF to an unqualified doctor who prescribed life-threatening dosages of medicines.[53] Because structural adjustment programs affected the poorest segment of the population, it became necessary to search for ways to alleviate their immediate hardships. In Ghana, the government in 1987, was forced to adopt a Program of Action to Mitigate the Social Costs of Adjustment (PAMSCAD), and alleviate the suffering caused by rising unemployment. The government allocated US$90 million to the PAMSCAD in an effort create employment, improve health care, nutrition and other basic needs. Commenting on the economic crisis in Ghana, John Loxley stated that, "It is a sad reflection on [the] Fund/Bank thinking that such considerations were not, and generally, still are not, built directly into adjustment programmes. PAMSCAD was tacked onto the end of the body of the reform package as a reluctant afterthought, under pressure from UNICEF and concerned bilateral donors. The IMF did not even see fit to send a representative to the meetings in which PAMSCAD was developed."[54]

Because of the socio-political costs, many developing countries were forced to amend and temper the pace of reform. Countries like Egypt, for example, found it extremely difficult to persist with structural adjustment even if the Egyptian government recognized the importance of economic reform. As a result of structural reform, the Egyptian government was able to reduce its budget deficit from 20 percent of GDP in 1991 to around 4–5 percent of GDP in 1993, and similarly reduce inflation from 22 percent in 1990 to around 11 percent in 1993. Despite these successes, the period 1991–93 witnessed declining real GDP growth and unemployment at around 20 per cent. Such conditions, Bromley and Bush point out, are incubators of social unrest and political instability.[55] The Egyptian government was conscious also of the fact that IMF reform programs and forced austerity had results in food riots in 1977.

Conclusion

The Latin American debt crisis was the single most important source of potential instability in international monetary relations in the 1980s. It was, like the two other debt crises, also a crisis of development and the decade of the 1980s is often regarded as a decade lost to development. The western crisis management strategy largely focused on maintaining the viability of the international financial system although, arguably, the structural adjustment programs were designed to relaunch the developing countries onto a more sustainable developmental trajectory.

By the early 1990s, it appeared that while the Latin American debt problem had not disappeared, it was no longer a compelling issue. The developing countries still remained burdened by high levels of debt and their debt service burden, at the end of the 1980s, had declined only marginally to 33 percent, but the danger that debt repudiation might severely stress the pillars of international financial stability had faded.

The commercial banks, in the meantime, increased their loan-loss provisions and were in a better position, than before, to absorb loan default. Moreover, since the early 1980s, the commercial banks also increased their equity capital dramatically and reduced their LDC loan assets as a percentage of total bank assets. For the banks, the storm appeared to have passed. With its passing, they returned, once more, as lenders to developing countries. Since the onset of the debt crisis and until 1991, international aid agencies, including the World Bank, were the main donors to developing countries but in 1992, private lenders overtook international agencies. In 1994, private institutions lent well over US$150 billion to developing countries compared to slightly over US$50 billion for the World Bank and other international agencies.

In managing the Latin American crisis, western governments and the IMF were concerned mainly with ensuring the survival of lending institutions and the stability of the international financial system. As a measure of the success of this approach, it might be noted that not a single major financial institution declared bankruptcy as a result of bad loans. Debt, however, continued to be a serious problem for several countries, especially in Latin America and sub-Saharan Africa, even if the debt-service ratios were more manageable. The table below provides a summary of the debt situation in the early 1990s.

The Mexican debt crisis of 1994–1995 and the East Asian debt crisis of 1997–1998, unlike the Latin American crisis, were also crises resulting

Table 6.6.   Developing countries' debt indicators (US$ billion; %): total debt stock debt service ratio.

	1991	1992	1991	1992
All developing countries	1 605.9	1 662.7	18.6	18.7
East Asia	293.8	320.1	13.4	12.9
Africa and middle east	386.9	383.1	17.8	25.7
Latin America and Caribbean	488.4	496.3	25.9	29.8

Source: Compiled from World Debt Tables, 1993–1994, Vol. 1, The World Bank, Washington, Summary Tables, pp. 170ff.

from the globalization of international capital. These two crises were the result of speculative capital flows and capital flight from the affected countries. They highlighted the vulnerability for countries participating in a globalized system with weak and small domestic financial structures. Certainly there are advantages arising out of participating in the global economy but there are also pitfalls if domestic financial structures are poorly prepared to cope with the demands of a global economy. The IMF strategies in dealing with these crises have included measures that might enhance the resilience of the financial sector in the affected economies. The unfolding of the Indonesian drama, however, reveals that a transition to a more effective economy might require some prior political liberalization.

Of the four main affected countries in the East Asian crisis, Indonesia's performance in implementing the IMF reforms was particularly poor. This was, at least partly, a result of the government's determination to protect economic interests of Suharto and the political cronies who had benefited from the corrupt practices of the regime. The prescribed reform measures were designed to prepare Indonesia to cope with the demands of participation in a global economy but the outcomes were compromised by the irresponsible attempts to preserve entrenched family interests. The Indonesian example suggests that economic reform may also have political conditions and that successful economic reforms might require a measure of political liberalization. In the absence of democratic accountability, the Suharto regime was more intent on protecting family interests than national interests. This prompted Michel Camdessus, Managing Director of the IMF, to remark that democracy and effective economics were sisters. As to whether this was unnecessary intrusion into domestic politics, he added that, "... it would be pointless, indeed reckless, and contrary to the IMF's charter, for the IMF to use its members' resources to support these programs unless there were strong reasons to believe that they would be successful in restoring market confidence and economic growth."[56] The concern was that unless Indonesia faithfully implemented the reform measures, it would leave itself vulnerable to future crises of a similar nature.

The Asian currency crisis highlighted the importance of good governance in the age of economic globalization. An important lesson of the crisis was that, in the age of globalization, market signals are quickly relayed across the globe and that political failure is punished quickly and ruthlessly. While the Latin American debt crisis had been an indictment of import substitution policies, the East Asian crisis was not a result of flawed developmental strategy but, in part, of policies hijacked and derailed by corrupt practices and political cronyism. As a result of increasing corruption, Indonesia pursued many ambitious national projects, such as national car production, but instead of contributing to growth, such investment was detrimental to growth because it channelled capital into sectors with low productivity.[57]

The events surrounding the Mexican and the East Asian crises also revealed flaws in the existing system of international monetary surveillance. The IMF had played a leading part in managing the debt crisis in the 1980s but still had woefully inadequate surveillance powers to ensure sound international financial management. At a minimum, the events of 1995 underscored the importance of establishing a code of conduct to ensure that member governments adhered to standards of transparency. Few countries, however, publish their economic statistics, provide details of foreign exchange operations, or collect important economic information. The East Asian economic crisis highlighted, for example, the basic gaps in understanding the nature of the crisis because there were no aggregate statistics on firms' foreign indebtedness.[58] If the Mexican and East Asian governments had been obliged to publish details of reserve movements and short-term liabilities, financial markets and commercial banks would have been better informed about their overall exposure.

A problem for the IMF, however, is that, apart from conditionality, it has no mandate to dictate policies to its members, except when they borrow on their credit tranche. Instead, the members control the IMF and even when the danger signals are present, the IMF cannot force them to alter policies. Prior to the East Asian crisis, the Thai government had ignored policy advice by the IMF when it became concerned with the direction of the Thai economy.[59] But when conditions did deteriorate, the Thai government did not shy away from seeking IMF assistance.

Inevitably, the IMF's bail-out operations leave the impression that the IMF will always step in to fill the breach. Thus, the bail-out of Mexico in 1995 may have added to the poor investment decisions that created the crisis of 1997. Rescue packages carry the attendant risk of diminishing even more the need for prudential and disciplined investment decision when the lesson of a crisis must be to introduce greater discipline. Bail-outs thus create the problem of "moral hazard" by eliminating the risk factor that must be the base of all market-based economic activity. The succession of debt and currency crises reveal that there is a fine line between the problem of moral hazard and the need to ensure continued system stability.

The Indonesian crisis highlighted also the importance of political consideration for the success or failure of reform packages. It is obvious, for example, that the first two IMF rescue packages for Indonesia had to be abandoned because they were political infeasible. That, however, raises the vexed question of whether reform policies should be dictated by what is political feasible or whether they should be based solely on economic merit, regardless of political and social consequences. With respect to Indonesia, the Australian government actively lobbied the IMF to reconsider its reform package on political grounds. It maintained that political instability in Indonesia would have adverse regional consequences and that it was imperative, therefore, not to destabilize the Suharto regime. These are vexed issues that will eventually have to be resolved but there are no easy solutions.

Notes

1. Cline, William R., *International Debt and the Stability of the World Economy*, Institute for International Economics, Washington DC, September 1983, p. 11.
2. Neikirk, William B., "Mexico Dropped Like a Bombshell," *Asian Finance*, 15 October 1987, p. 57.
3. Krueger, A. O., *Economic Policy Reform in Developing Countries: The Kuznets Memorial Lectures at the Economic Growth Center, Yale University*, Blackwell Publishers, Mass. 1992, pp. 48–49. The

average real interest rate on sovereign loans during the period 1974–1978 was only half a percent per year and this increased to more than 7 percent in 1981 and 1982. Real interest rate is defined as the London Interbank Offer Rate (LIBOR) on three-month US dollar deposits less the rate of change of the GNP deflator in the US. See *World Economic Outlook*, International Monetary Fund, Washington DC, April 1984, p. 65.

4. LIBOR is the rate used between the banks when they provide loans in Eurocurrencies to each other. Lending to developing countries is usually at rates that are 2–3 percentage points higher than the LIBOR rates. It has been estimated that, given total accumulated debt, a 1 percent increase in LIBOR directly translated to an additional US$850 million in interest payment for Brazil and US$790 million for Mexico.

5. Credit rating is important in securing new loans or to roll over existing loans.

6. Wiarda, Howard J., "The Politics of Third World Debt," *PS: Political Science and Politics*, Vol. 23, No. 3, September 1990, p. 414.

7. Kahler, M., "Conclusion: Politics and Proposals for Reform," in Kahler, H. (ed.), *The Politics of International Debt*, Cornell University Press, Ithaca, New York, 1986, p. 259.

8. Ipsen, E., "The Brady Plan's Enforcer," *Institutional Investor*, Vol. 23, No. 8, July 1989, p. 179.

9. Kahler, M., Op. Cit, 1986, p. 267.

10. Andrews, S., "Slouching Toward Forgiveness," *Institutional Investor*, Vol. 23, No. 6, May 1989, p. 88.

11. Wesson, R., "Wrapping Up the Debt Problem," *PS: Political Science and Politics*, Vol. 23, No. 3, September 1990, p. 423. Italics in original.

12. Clark, J. and Eliot Kaltor, "Recent Innovations in Debt Restructuring," *Finance & Development*, September 1982, p. 6.

13. Sung, W. and Rosaria Troia, *Developments in Debt Conversion Programs and Conversion Activities*, World Bank Technical Paper No. 170, The World Bank, Washington, DC, 1992, pp. 28–29.

14. See, Blaine, Michael, J., "Déjà Vu All Over Again: Explaining Mexico's 1994 Financial Crisis," *The World Economy*, Vol. 21, No. 1, January 1998, p. 34.

15. Edwards, S., "The Mexican Peso Crisis: How Much Did We Know? When Did We Know It?" *The World Economy*, Vol. 21, No. 1, January 1998.

16. See *The Economist*, 7 January 1995, p. 36.

17. Lustig, N. C., "NAFTA: Setting the Record Straight," *The World Economy*, Vol. 20, No. 5, August 1997, p. 607.

18. "Economic Crisis in Asia," Address by Shigemitsu Sugisaki, Deputy Managing Director of the International Monetary Fund at the 1998 Harvard Asia Business Conference, Harvard Business School, 30 January 1998 (http://www.imf.org/external/np/speeches/1998/013098.HTM).

19. *The East Asian Miracle: Economic Growth and Public Policy*, Published for the World Bank by Oxford University Press, New York, 1993, p. 7.

20. Krugman, P., "The Myth of Asia's Miracle," *Foreign Affairs*, Vol. 73, No. 6, November/December 1994, p. 70.

21. *Private Capital Flows to the Developing Countries: The Road to Financial Integration*, A World Bank Policy Research Report, Oxford University Press, New York, 1997, p. 257.

22. Tanzer, A., "Tight Little Market," *Forbes*, 12 January 1998, p. 52.

23. *IMF Survey*, Vol. 26, No. 23, 15 December 1997, p. 389.

24. "The Perils of Global Capital," *The Economist*, 11 April 1998, p. 62.

25. Mahathir may have reached this conclusion based on the activities of the Open Society Fund which George Soros had established in 1979 to, by his own account, subvert and undermine non-democratic systems. The OSF's first major undertaking was in South Africa but its first success was in Hungary in the 1980s. See Soros, G., "The Capitalist Threat," *The Atlantic Monthly*, Vol. 279, No. 2, February 1997. Soros, however, vigorously denied the allegations that he was responsible for the crisis in Asia and in the end, Mahathir was forced to retract the allegations against Soros.

26. See *IMF Survey*, Vol. 27, No. 4, 23 February 1998, p. 49.

27. "Debt on Korea's Terms," *Asiaweek*, 13 February 1998, p. 46.
28. *The Australian*, 31 January–1 February 1998, p. 11.
29. See *The Australian*, 28 January 1998, p. 7 and 31 January–1 February 1998, p. 11.
30. Chowdury, A., "Soviet Implosion Paves Way for Market Economy," *Asian Finance*, Vol. 17, No. 9, September 1991, p. 44.
31. See Sachs, J. D. and Andrew Warner, "Economic Convergence and Economic Policies," NBER Working Paper No. 5039, National Bureau of Economic Research, Massachusetts, 1995.
32. Bradshaw, Victoria W. and Ana–Maria Wahl, "Foreign Debt Expansion, the International Monetary Fund, and Regional Variation in Third World Poverty," *International Studies Quarterly*, Vol. 35, 1991, p. 252.
33. In general, developing countries have the option of choosing export-oriented or import substitution policies to promote development and industrialization. Although the two sets of policies are not mutually exclusive, developing countries have emphasized one or the other as the most suitable to their particular condition. In the post-war period, the Latin American countries pursued import substitution policies whereas the East Asian countries opted for export-oriented policies. However, the adoption of export-oriented industrialization strategies by the East Asian economies in the 1960s did not immediately lead to general renunciation of import substitution or to a general withdrawal of protection given to domestic industries.
34. Krueger, Anne O., *Economic Policy Reform in Developing Countries: The Kuznets Memorial Lectures at the Economic Growth Center, Yale University*, Blackwell Publishers, Cambridge, Mass. and Oxford, 1992, p. 94.
35. Capital flight is determined by a number of factors including low interest rates. Other factors include expected currency depreciation, political instability and macroeconomic mismanagement. Capital flight has been a serious problem in many of the developing countries. For the period 1980–1984, capital flight has been estimated at US$16–17 billion for Argentina, $40 billion for Mexico and $27 billion for Venezuela. See *World Development Report, 1991*, The World

Bank, Washington, DC, Oxford University Press, New York, 1991, p. 124.

36. Harris, N., *The End of the Third World: Newly Industrializing Countries and the Decline of an Ideology*, Penguin Books, London, 1986, p. 81.

37. See Todaro, Michael P., *Economic Development in the Third World*, 4th ed., Longman, New York and London, 1989, p. 447. Multiple exchange rates were specifically forbidden under IMF conditions of membership but many developing countries continued to openly flout their commitment to abide by their terms of membership and IMF, too, chose to overlook this breach of commitment.

38. Sachs, Jeffrey D., "Trade and Exchange Rate Policies in Growth-Oriented Adjustment Programs," in Corbo. V., Morris Goldstein and Mohsin Khan (eds.), *Growth-Oriented Adjustment Programs*, International Monetary Fund and The World Bank, Washington, DC, 1987, p. 292.

39. Thomas, V. and Ajay Chhibber, "Experience with Policy Reforms Under Adjustment: How Well Have Adjustment Programs Been Working?" *Finance & Development*, March 1989, p. 29.

40. Krueger, Anne O., "The Political Economy of the Rent-Seeking Society," *American Economic Review*, Vol. 64, No. 3, June 1974, p. 302.

41. In reality, however, structural adjustment led to, in many places, domestic political instability and eroded the legitimacy of the government. This in some cases led to reversal of reforms, although not on a large scale.

42. McCleary, William A., "Policy Implementation Under Adjustment Lending," *Finance & Development*, March 1989, p. 32.

43. See "Globalization — To What End?" Part II, *Monthly Review*, Vol. 43, No. 10, March 1992, p. 16.

44. See "Economic Trends in the Developing World," in *Finance & Development*, Vol. 34, No. 1, March 1997, p. 47.

45. Cited in Carol Lancaster, "Economic Reform in Africa: Is it Working?" in Obasanjo, O. and Hans d'Orville (eds.), *The Leadership Challenge of Economic Reforms in Africa*, Crane Russak, New York, 1991, p. 95.

46. Jones, C. and Miguel A. Kiguel, "Africa's Quest for Prosperity: Has Adjustment Helped?" *Finance & Development*, Vol. 31, No. 2, June 1994, p. 2.

47. Summers, L. H. and Lant H. Pritchett, "The Structural-Adjustment Debate," *American Economic Review*, Vol. 83, No. 2, May 1993, p. 384.

48. Khor, M., "Global Economy and the Third World," in Mander, J. and Edward Goldsmith (eds.), *The Case Against the Global Economy: And for a Turn Toward the Local*, Sierra Club Books, San Francisco, 1996, p. 48.

49. *World Economic Outlook, May 1997*, International Monetary Fund, Washington, DC, 1997, p. 72.

50. See *World Bank Policy Research Bulletin*, Vol. 3, No. 5, November–December 1992.

51. Singer, H. W. and Sumit Roy, *Economic Progress and Prospects in the Third World: Lessons of Development Experience Since 1945*, Edward Elgar, Hants, 1993, p. 40.

52. Ihonvbere, Julius O., "Structural Adjustment in Nigeria," in Turok, B. (ed.), Alternative Strategies for Africa: Debt and Democracy, Vol. 3, Institute for African Alternatives, London, 1991, p. 82.

53. See Seddon, D. "The Politics of Adjustment: Egypt and the IMF, 1977–1990," *Review of African Political Economy*, Vol. 47, Spring 1990, p. 96. Egypt has been very sensitive to domestic public reaction to reforms ever since the bread riots in 1977.

54. Loxley, J., "Structural Adjustment in Africa: Reflections on Ghana and Zambia," *A Review of African Political Economy*, Vol. 47, Spring 1990, p. 21.

55. Bromley, S. and Ray Bush, "Adjustment in Egypt?: The Political Economy of Reform," *Review of African Political Economy*, Vol. 21, No. 60, June 1994.
Qureshi, Moeen A., "The Banking System and the Indebted Developing Countries: Retrospective and Prospects," in Mikdashi, Z. (ed.), *Bankers' and Public Authorities' Management of Risk*, The Macmillan Press Ltd., London, 1990, p. 19.
Newsweek, 29 May 1995, p. 20.

56. See *The Australian*, 6 May 1998, p. 6.
57. For an analysis of corruption and its impact on growth, see Tanzi, V. and Hamid Davoodi, "Roads to Nowhere: How Corruption in Public Investment Hurts Growth," *Economic Issues*, No. 12, International Monetary Fund, Washington DC, 1998.
58. "The Perils of Global Capital," *The Economist*, 11 April 1998, p. 63.
59. "What Are the Lessons of the Southeast Asian Crisis?" *IMF Survey*, Vol. 26, No. 22, 1 December 1997.

Chapter Seven

POLITICAL ECONOMY OF FOREIGN INVESTMENT

International capital flows can be classified as either speculative or productive. Speculative capital flows are short-term transfers and determined mainly by interest rate differentials between countries and by exchange rate movements. In the contemporary period, such flows of capital have increased markedly and vastly exceed productive capital transfers or foreign direct investment. Short-term capital flows can undermine national monetary and economic objectives and, at worst, can lead to economic destabilization by undermining confidence in the local currency. To dampen speculative flows and sterilize national economies from the adverse consequences of speculative capital, various proposals have been put forward, such as the imposition of a tax on all such transactions. There is no agreement among governments, however, as to whether such initiatives will be effective or on the desirability of intervening in normal market activities. In this chapter, I will focus on foreign direct investments (FDI) and the efforts to create an international regulatory regime governing FDI.

Productive capital flows or foreign direct investment is generally a long-term commitment in the host economy. Foreign demand for a company's products can be serviced through either exports or local production but it is only after market presence has been clearly established that a company will consider local production. The advantages

Table 7.1.   The advantages of FDI.

Most Tangible	Reduce direct and indirect costs
	Reduce capital costs
	Reduce taxes
	Reduce logistics costs
	Overcome tariff barriers
	Provide better customer service
	Spread foreign exchange risks
	Build alternative supply sources
	Preempt potential competitors
	Learn from local suppliers
	Learn from foreign customers
	Learn from competitors
	Learn from foreign research centers
Most Intangible	Attract talent globally

Source: Ferdows, K., "Making the Most of Foreign Factories," *Harvard Business Review*, March–April 1997, p. 82.

of foreign investment in local production range include cost reduction and better customer service. According to Ferdows, the various advantages can be ranged from those that are the most tangible to the least tangible.

Most governments welcome foreign investment even if they insist on some performance criteria to ensure domestic benefits. Foreign direct investment has increased dramatically in recent years and in 1994, total global FDI was US$220 billion of which 80 percent came from Japan, the European Union and the US. More recently, South Korea and Taiwan have also emerged as important sources of foreign investment, particularly in Southeast Asia. Foreign direct investment also concentrates primarily in developed economies.

Even if FDI is largely a developed country phenomenon, developing countries with specific resource endowments, for example, were success-ful in attracting considerable foreign investment. In the early twentieth century, a significant share of FDI went into resource extraction and the major oil companies invested extensively in oil rich countries of the Middle East. Something similar — but on a smaller scale — happened in countries that produced bananas, sugar and rubber.[1] The benefit to these resource-based export economies remained small. The oil exporting countries of the Middle East benefited little from MNC investments because oil prices, controlled by the oil majors, were kept very low. This changed with the oil crisis of 1973, which shifted the balance of power between the oil majors and the oil-producing countries and brought wealth and prosperity to the Middle East. The benefit of foreign investment to resource rich developing was small also because MNCs, typically, engaged in little value-adding activities in these economies and tended, instead, to export commodities in crude form. Thus, foreign investment failed to stimulate industrial deepening and development.

However, in the 1980s, the East Asian economies demonstrated that it was possible to exploit foreign investment to promote industrialization. They successfully implemented an exported-oriented industrialization strategy, which relied extensively on foreign capital. It helped also that international developments, such as the appreciation of the Japanese yen after 1985, forced many Japanese firms to relocate production to cheaper cost countries in Asia in order to remain internationally competitive and service demand in third countries. In general, FDI flows to developing countries is increasing more rapidly than in developed countries. In the early 1980s, for example, developing countries received an annual average of US$12.6 billion, or only 20 percent of global FDI, but in 1994, FDI in developing countries had increased to US$70 billion, or 32 percent of total.[2] By 1996, net foreign investment in developing countries had increased slightly to over US$100 billion, nearly 60 percent of which went to Asian countries.

The increasing share of LDCs in investment inflows reflected passage of the Latin American debt crisis. In the aftermath of that debt crisis, private capital flows to developing countries had declined considerably, forcing them to rely mainly on international agencies like the World Bank and the International Monetary Fund. The return of private sector lenders was an indication that the worst of the debt crisis had been successfully negotiated. However, given the prominence of Asian countries as hosts of FDI, it is inevitable that the debt and currency crisis of 1997–1998 will be reflected in lower levels of FDI in developing countries over the coming few years.

One important development in the foreign investment flows has been the emergence of Japan as a major creditor country.[3] For much of the post-war period, for instance, Japanese companies relied on exports to meet overseas demand. In the US, in the late 1970s and after, there was a concerted push to force Japan to invest in local production rather than rely on exports. The reasoning was that local production by Japanese firms would create jobs, add to the industrial base and benefit the American economy, whereas exports appeared to undermine the target economy by eliminating local competitors. One of the motivations behind the American demand for voluntary export restraints on Japanese cars in the early 1980s was to force Japanese car manufacturers to invest in production in the United States. Not surprisingly, the boom in Japanese investment in the US began in the early 1980s and was led by investment in auto plants in the US. Along with export restrictions, which played a part in encouraging Japanese FDI in the US, the outflow of FDI from Japan received a fresh boost, in the mid 1980s, when exchange rate adjustments made Japanese exports less competitive.

The growth of Japanese FDI began in the mid 1980s and was briefly interrupted when the asset price bubble burst in early 1990s, plunging the economy into a recession. It, however, recovered a few years later.[4] In overall terms, the bulk of Japanese investment has been in the developed economies of North America and Europe. In 1994, FDI outflows to the US accounted for 43.7 percent of the total, the European countries received 19.4 percent and the Asian countries 16 percent.[5] Even though most Japanese FDI is in US, Japan is a major investor in the East Asian countries. The stock of Japanese FDI in Asia exceeds that of the United States and Japanese corporations loom large in the small economies of East Asia.

While Japan has emerged as a major source of FDI, inflows of FDI into Japan have remained relatively small. In 1993, the stock of FDI in Japan was US$29.9 billion while the stock of Japanese FDI abroad stood at US$422.5 billion. In 1996, total Japanese FDI overseas was US$49 billion (yen 5.5 trillion) whereas overseas FDI in Japan was only US$7 billion (yen 770 billion). By contrast, the comparative figures for the US were US$85.6 billion and US$78.1 billion in 1996. The imbalance in Japanese FDI flows is large but it should be noted that FDI flows into and from the United States were also highly unbalanced in the early post-war period and into the 1970s. In 1970, the US was the source of nearly 63 percent of FDI outflows and absorbed only about 16 percent.[6]

As mentioned above, a number of factors stimulated the growth of Japanese foreign investment, including protectionism in the United States, and currency realignment following the Plaza Accord of 1985, which made Japanese exports less competitive. As the yen appreciated and pushed up production costs in Japan, Japanese manufacturers began to relocate production to less costly countries. Japanese investments in East and Southeast Asia, according to Hatch and Yamamura, have also been motivated by a strategic vision, formulated by the Japanese Ministry of International Trade and Industry, to create a regional division of labor and integrate the entire region into a production network in order to pursue a global corporate strategy.[7] It is true that manufacturers in Japan have used East Asia as a production platform not only to satisfy demand in host countries but also in Japan and elsewhere. In 1992, the ratio of exports to total sales of Japanese affiliates in the manufacturing sector in Asia was 45 percent.[8]

The high proportion of exports to local sales for Japanese subsidiaries in East Asia is, however, part of a broader pattern of MNC activity. Studies have shown that foreign firms export a greater proportion of their production than do locally-owned firms. This can perhaps be explained by the fact that MNCs are the dominant source of FDI and they trade extensively among their own affiliates. There is evidence that intra-firm trade among MNCs accounts for a third of total world trade.[9] Moreover, to attribute Japanese FDI in East Asia to a grand MITI plan may be an exaggeration. MITI has much diminished powers to implement an industrial policy even within Japan.

The rapid expansion of Japanese foreign investment in East Asia produced worrying concerns within Japan that it will lead to a "hollowing out" of Japanese industry and ultimately to the erosion of Japanese industrial base. Such concerns are not without precedence. In the US, in the 1960s and 1970s, the outflow of American FDI had produced similar reactions. A spokesperson for the AFL-CIO stated that the transfer of production overseas was making the US "a nation of hamburger stands ... a country stripped of industrial capacity and meaningful work ... a service economy ... a nation of citizens busily buying and selling cheeseburgers and root beer floats."[10]

From the perspective of host countries, especially developing countries, concerns about FDI include its economic consequences. A common criticism, articulated by Sanjaya Lall and Paul Streeten is that "host economies do not gain much financial benefit from foreign direct investment, and would be seen to gain even less if hidden remittances in the form of transfer pricing were fully known."[11] Transfer pricing is a corporate tax minimization strategy, which MNCs may engage in by artifically fixing prices for intra-firm trade across borders to shift excess profits out of national jurisdictions with high taxation rates. Multinationals are ideally positioned to take advantage of these strategies because they operate in a number of national jurisdictions and source supplies from subsidiaries in other countries. Transfer pricing might have benefits for the MNC but a host government could potentially lose out in potential taxation revenue. The revenue losses for governments may be significant, especially for developing countries.

Other reasons why MNCs were presumed not to benefit developing countries was the imbalance of power between a large MNC and a poor developing country such that MNCs were able to extract a favorable deal, including tax holidays, that lowered benefits to the host economy. Another criticism was that MNCs tended to introduce capital intensive and sophisticated technology that was inappropriate to developing countries, which had a comparative advantage in labor intensive manufacturing. MNC reputation was tarnished also by a fear that these companies were agents of the home government and intervened in host country politics to advantage the home country. One of the best examples of this was the way the International Telephone and Telegraph Company (ITT), an American multinational, orchestrated a campaign against the democratically elected, but socialist, government of Salvador Allende in Chile in the early 1970s. ITT machinations induced massive capital flight and paralyzed the Chilean economy. The result was a bloody *coup d'etat* that toppled the government of Allende.

Finally, dependency theory also recommended a policy of self-reliance for developing country. Dependency theorists, like Raul Prebisch, and Andre Gunder Frank, argued that underdevelopment was a result of continued exploitation by western economies and that the developing countries should pursue inward-looking and autarchic policies and avoid or minimize economic exchange with western countries in order to promote development at home. They maintained that, historically, developing countries, with a reliance on primary exports, suffered deteriorating terms of trade which impeded their development and that there were structural restraints to successful industrialization, which was essential for development. Drawing on the experiences of Latin America, they maintained that it was no coincidence that Latin American industrialization had to wait the onset of the First World War when economic linkages with the western developed countries were markedly diminished. Since MNCs, essentially western-based, were a source of integration and linkages with developed countries, it was obvious that MNCs had to be controlled and limited in their ability to operate in developing countries. The evidence that MNC activity contributed little to developing countries might be that despite a long history of FDI in developing countries, there had been no appreciable improvement of economic conditions in a majority of the host countries.[12]

There were, of course, others who portrayed a more positive picture of MNC investment on grounds that this supplemented the small domestic capital base, brought in necessary technical and managerial skills, and built up an industrial base. Moreover, they argued that free movement of capital was more efficient than governmental regulation designed to influence free market forces. The debate may have excited passions but there was really no firm basis for reaching a conclusion that foreign investment was either hugely detrimental or beneficial to host developing economies.

In the 1980s, the debate over the role of multinationals and of foreign investment was considerably less strident. This was, perhaps, because levels of FDI in developing countries had declined substantially following the debt crisis. In the late 1980s and 1990s, FDI to developing countries increased dramatically and the share of FDI flows going to developing countries increased from 15 percent of total in 1990 to nearly 40 percent in 1996.[13] But concerns about the negative impact of FDI on development remained relatively dormant.[14] Indeed, the prevailing view is that, at its worst, FDI is a neutral phenomenon and usually a stimulant for growth and development. The growth in foreign investment can be attributed to liberalization and the abandonment of import substitution industrialization for export-oriented industrialization in developing countries. Not surprisingly, the World Bank and the IMF take some of the credit for the improved investment climate in developing countries following the structural adjustment programs of the early 1980s.[15]

Despite the increase in capital flows, there has been no major reopening of the debates of the 1970s. Pockets of unease about foreign investment may continue to linger but governments in developing countries have generally been more welcoming of foreign investment. It is felt that multinational corporations could play a useful role in expanding the export presence of developing countries. Nonetheless, many countries maintain a foreign investment review mechanism to scrutiny foreign investment proposals and ensure that the benefits of foreign investment outweigh costs. Countries may also designate certain industries as strategic and essential for national control and therefore off limits to foreign investors.

While competition to attract foreign investments might appear to weaken the bargaining power of host economies, especially the poorer ones, vis-a-vis the multinational corporations, they were, at the same time, also very successful in imposing conditions and performance criteria on foreign corporations.

Another argument that gained considerable importance was that in a global economy, capital and multinational corporations had become "nationalityless" commercial entities. American Secretary of Labor, Robert Reich, argued that US MNCs had become global citizens instead of serving American interests.[16] Moreover, it was clear that East Asian growth was underpinned by large capital inflows and under these circumstances, there was no support for the view that FDI could have a negative impact. Indeed as countries increasingly moves away from import substitution industrialization in 1980s to export-oriented industrialization, they emphasized the importance of foreign direct investment.

As foreign direct investment increased, the absence of uniform regulatory standards began to loom large as a hindrance to international capital flows. To simplify the regulatory environment, the Uruguay Round included foreign investment in its negotiations.

Uruguay Round and Trade Related Investment Measures

Trade related investment measures (TRIMs), such as local content or export requirements, were included in the Uruguay Round negotiating agenda in order to produce a more liberal investment climate. TRIMS can be classified either as input (local content requirement, local equity requirement, R&D requirement) or output (export performance requirement, export controls) measures. Some such as trade balancing requirements operate both as input and export measure because they require foreign investors to counterbalance imports of parts and raw materials with exports of finished commodities. TRIMs are widely used, and according to David Greenaway, have the three following objectives:

1. influence the location and pattern of economic activity;
2. ensure benefits to the host country; and
3. redistribute part of surplus generated by FDI away from MNCs and towards host countries.[17]

There was initial disagreement between the developed and developing countries as to whether TRIMs should be included as part of an agreement on international trade. Developing countries argued that TRIMs were an investment, and not trade policy measures, and, therefore, beyond the jurisdiction of the GATT. The gulf, however, was not, according to David Greenaway, "unbridgeable" and could be overcome with preferential treatment for the developing countries through an extended transitional period. At the same time, it was obvious that there could be no clear demarcation between developing countries as hosts of FDI and the developed countries as the home countries. In recent years, developing countries, too, have started investing overseas and this has blurred the divide between developed and developing countries. In 1989–90, for example, Taiwan's FDI was US$12 billion and South Korea's US$1.3 billion.[18] Even smaller countries like Thailand, Malaysia and the Philippines, have been investing in other countries.

Global business corporations were especially keen to see the establishment of standardized rules and regulations that did not arbitrarily restrict their global strategies. TRIMs, like local content requirements, are policy measures used by government to force foreign investors to achieve certain performance criteria. But local content regulations can restrict trade by forcing a company to procure locally what might otherwise be cheaply sourced from abroad. Similarly, minimum export requirements also distort and divert trade by substituting home country exports to third countries, with host country exports to such markets. The GATT's involvement with TRIMs was natural given its emphasis on trade creation, as opposed to trade restriction or trade diversion and its significance was not lost on global businesses.

Developing countries, however, resisted the pressure to force them to give up local content requirements, which they regarded as essential to their developmental objectives. By contrast, the OECD countries insisted that such measures distorted trade and should be part of the trade negotiating agenda. The Uruguay Round Agreement recognised the significance of TRIMS and applied the principle of national treatment (Article 3) to prevent discriminatory national policies. It, however, permitted developing countries an extended grace period to eliminate nonconforming TRIMs. The accepted schedule specified that developed countries had to remove all non-conforming TRIMs within two years, the developing countries within five years, and the least developed countries within seven years.[19] The agreement determined that local content requirements violated the GATT principles but, interestingly, did not address the question of export performance requirements. It was agreed also that the TRIMs agreement would be reviewed within five years of the establishment of the WTO to assess the need for more general disciplines on investment and the possibility of expanding the list of prohibited TRIMs.[20]

The Uruguay Round took the first step toward achieving a uniform and nondiscriminatory regulatory environment in international investments. The inclusion of Trade Related Investment Measures (TRIMs) in the negotiating agenda was of particular interest to global corporations, which hoped, thereby, to lower transactions costs and minimize the trade distortionary consequences of host country investment regulations.

Multilateral Agreement on Investment

In the absence of uniform standards, bilateral investment treaties proliferated and, according to UNCTAD, there were, at the end of June 1996, nearly 1 160 bilateral investment treaties, of which about two-thirds had been concluded during the 1990s.[21] This meant that foreign investors confronted a very complex and complicated legal environment and which also provided no certainty about the long-term investment climate.

To simplify and harmonize investment standards, the European Commission initially proposed that the WTO facilitate the development of a global investment treaty. The US argued instead that the venue for an investments treaty be the Organization for Economic Cooperation and Development (OECD), which comprised the leading industrial countries. The US had determined that a group of similar countries would be more conducive to the formulation of a treaty of very "high standards." It was also felt that negotiations on a uniform code for foreign direct investment under the auspices of the WTO would be complicated by the divergent interests of developed and developing countries.

To avert a possible deadlock in negotiations along the north–south axis, the OECD countries, in 1995, began the process of negotiating a multilateral agreement on investments (MAI). By negotiating initially within the OECD, it was expected that members would be able to agree on high standards that did not have to be watered down as a result of objections from smaller developing countries. OECD member countries are major players in FDI, accounting for 85 percent of FDI outflows and 60 percent of FDI inflows, or US$243 billion and US$191 billion respectively, in 1995.[22] As major players they expected to be key beneficiaries of a liberal code on investments. A Canadian study, for example, found that an increase of US$1 billion in incoming FDI produced, over a five-year period, an additional 45, 000 jobs and added US$4.5 billion to gross domestic product. It is understandable therefore, why the OECD countries were interested in a liberal and transparent code that was comprehensive and uniform.

The drawback of negotiations confined to the OECD countries was that it excluded the interests of developing countries. Foreign investment is a significant proportion of total domestic investment in many developing countries but these countries found themselves locked out of the negotiation process. Critics charged that the negotiations were motivated primarily by an interest to promote multinational corporations (MNCs), the majority of which were headquartered in the developed OECD countries.

If negotiations within the OECD were supposed to produce a relatively early agreement on the final terms of the treaty, such hopes proved unfounded. When the draft text of the treaty became public, consumer and citizens' groups within the OECD countries emerged as leading critics of the MAI, fearful that the outcome would diminish state sovereignty in favor of multinational corporations. OECD negotiations on the MAI began in 1995, with the expectation that an agreement would be achieved by May 1997. When that became unlikely, the deadline was extended to May 1998. The second deadline also passed without agreement but discussions were expected to resume later in the year. The delays point to the difficulties confronting negotiators amid the many criticisms that such an agreement would infringe national sovereignty and act to the detriment of the national interests of participating countries. The hurdles in the path of an agreement include the issues of labor and environmental standards and cultural protectionism. In April 1998, the OECD released a draft of the negotiating text of the MAI treaty listing all the major points of disagreement among the negotiating countries. These ranged from trivial disagreement on specific words and terminology to disagreement on more substantive issues, such as whether agreed upon rights and privileges should extend not only to citizens of contracting countries but also to permanent residents.

The main principles of the MAI were national treatment and Most Favored Nation treatment to foreign investors, and transparency of regulatory frameworks. The objective of the MAI was to create a liberal investment climate, which facilitated the expansion of global FDI. The MAI proposed to eliminate all discriminatory performance requirements, whether on the input or the output side of productive activities. It was to establish clear parameters, discipline state behavior and force compliance with established rules. To that extent, it would moderate state policies but according to the OECD, the advantage for states, and for investors, was that it would lead to a more open and transparent investment climate. However, governments were to permitted to declare a list of exemptions, identifying industries that would not be subject to the provisions of the MAI treaty. Most negotiating countries announced that they planned to prepare a list of exemptions, including for example, culture industries.

If successful, the proposed MAI would be a freestanding treaty among the 29 OECD member countries but accession would be available to non-OECD countries that were able to meet its obligations. Non-OECD countries that wished to accede to the MAI could also negotiate their entry conditions rather than confront a "take it or leave it" situation. However, the core obligations were declared non-negotiable.[23] The ultimate stated objective was that the MAI would, at some stage, be adopted also by the WTO. Indeed, the WTO secretariat, along with several other non-OECD members, participated in the MAI negotiations as an observer.[24]

Despite the advanced state of negotiations on the MAI, there emerged considerable pockets of resistance even within developed countries to the proposed standards. Critics charged that negotiations had been carried out in secrecy to benefit MNCs and without adequate safeguard of national interest. The assertion that the treaty privileged MNCs at the expense of states was premised on a widely held belief that, under the terms of the agreement, MNCs would be able to sue states for damages, a right that they did not currently possess and a right that was also not granted to local companies. The negotiating text of the treaty dealt extensively with dispute resolution mechanism and provided for a tribunal to be established to resolve disputes between an investor and a contracting party, if a contracting party failed to honor its commitments to the investor at the time of initial investment. Whether this eroded national sovereignty was extremely dubious and there were, in any case, safeguards provided to states in times of war and other international emergencies. As noted in earlier chapters, similar objections were raised when the International Trade Organization was proposed and, again, when the World Trade Organization was established. The objections really were an attempt to hold back the tide of globalization in the guise of protecting national sovereignty. In reality, governments would be free to regulate activities in most areas provided regulation was not discriminatory and treated foreign investors equitably.

Critics, however, charged that the MAI went beyond establishing a principle of nondiscrimination to positive discrimination in favor of MNCs. For instance, it was suggested that states would not be permitted to apply discriminatory performance standards (export quota; local content etc) on foreign investment, such that even "if a national government imposes these performance requirements on domestic companies, it cannot apply them to foreign-based corporations."[25] This was a misrepresentation of the principle of national treatment, which essentially obligated governments not to selectively discriminate against foreign investors.

If the MAI was deficient, it was in the fact that contracting parties were not very active in promoting the treaty to their domestic con-stituencies. This created a situation where critics of the MAI began to prevail in the propaganda war. Another long-term weakness was the exclusion of developing countries. This made sense in terms of the stated objective of achieving a treaty of high standards but it also made it less likely to attract support of a group of country that had no input in the formulation of this important treaty. Admittedly, the developing countries do not have to accept the MAI but if it is indeed intended to become a global treaty, a more inclusive approach might have yielded a more complete outcome.

In the end, critics of the MAI in the developed countries were responsible for its failure. The OECD countries were forced to let the negotiations lapse and resume it later as part of the next round of proposed WTO trade negotiations. Presumably, at that stage developing countries will also be involved in drafting the codes and regulations.

Conclusion

The overwhelmingly negative popular perception of multinational corporations is gradually being replaced by more realistic assessments that MNCs and foreign investment can be harnessed for national economic development. The negative perceptions in developing countries were based on experiences with tax evasion, transfer pricing, exploitation of labor, introduction of inappropriate technologies, and their negative impact on domestic competition and indigenous entrepreneurs, and poor safety standards relative to home countries. This last aspect of MNC investment in developing countries was most vividly highlighted by the large number of deaths in India resulting from a poison gas leak in the local Union Carbide factory. More recently, however, spurred by East Asian experiences, developing countries are eagerly trying to attract foreign investment. Another positive development is the gradual removal of the North-South divide in foreign investment, where the former group of countries provided foreign investment and the latter were mainly the host countries. Developing countries have also become foreign investors.

The increased global significance of foreign investment spurred international efforts to create a uniform regulatory code. This effort was led by developed countries with the objective of creating standards that conform to the highest common denominator. Having determined that standards must be high to be meaningful, it was clear that developing countries would not, in the immediate future, agree to be bound by such standards. Globalization of standards will necessarily be a gradual and slow process. Completion of the Multilateral Agreement on Investment was held up and stalled by disagreement within the small OECD grouping. This is testimony to the complexity of the problems but also did not speak well of the political management of the process. Critics of the MAI claimed that the negotiations were conducted in secret but this was not a valid criticism. If there was a failure, it was in preparing the groundwork within the national jurisdictions of each member country. Information on the MAI was widely available but governments were not very active or persuasive in explaining its importance and significance to their domestic constituency. The failure of the MAI negotiations was largely because of political naivete of the respective governments, not because of insurmountable technical difficulties.

References

1. Jones, G., *The Evolution of International Business: An Introduction*, Routledge, London and New York, 1996, p. 245.
2. *See Bergsman, et al., in Finance & Development*, December 1995, p. 6.
3. Inflow of foreign investment into Japan, however, remains small. In 1994, inflow of foreign investment into Japan was US$888 million and in 1995 it was only US$37 million. By comparison, inflow of foreign investment into the US in 1994 was US$49.5 billion and in 1995 it was US$74.7 billion. See Witherell, Willam H., "An Agreement on Investment," *The OECD Observer*, No. 202, October/November 1996, p. 9.
4. Bayoumi, T. and Gabrielle Lipworth, "Japanese Foreign Direct Investment and Regional Trade," *Finance & Development*, Vol. 34, No. 3, September 1997, p. 12.
5. Hatch, W. and Kozo Yamamura, *Asia in Japan's Embrace: Building a Regional Production Alliance*, Cambridge University Press, Cambridge, UK, 1996, p. 6.
6. Shepherd, William F., *International Financial Integration: History, Theory and Applications in OECD Countries*, Avebury, Aldershot, 1994, p. 32.
7. Hatch, W. and Kozo Yamamura, *Asia in Japan's Embrace: Building a Regional Production Alliance*, Cambridge University Press, Cambridge, UK, 1996, pp. 22ff.

8. World Trade Organization, *Annual Report*, Vol. 1, Geneva, 1996, p. 51.
9. World Trade Organization, *Annual Report*, Vol. 1, Geneva, 1996, p. 44.
10. See Barnet, Richard J. and Ronald E. Muller, *Global Reach: The Power of the Multinational Corporations*, Jonathan Cape, London, 1975, pp. 305–306.
11. Lall, S. and Paul Streeten, *Foreign Investment, Transnationals and Developing Countries*, Macmillan Press Ltd., London, 1977, p. 54.
12. According to Geoffrey Jones, the bulk of investment in the nineteenth century and into the inter-war years of the twentieth century was located in the developing countries of Asia and Latin America. See Jones, G., *The Evolution of International Business: An Introduction*, Routledge, London and New York, 1996, p. 225.
13. Private Capital Flows to Developing Countries: The Road to Financial Integration, *A World Bank Policy Research Report*, Oxford University Press, New York, 1997, p. 9.
14. Most FDI to developing countries have gone to a few select countries, dominated by China and other East Asian economies.
15. See, Private Capital Flows to Developing Countries: The Road to Financial Integration, *A World Bank Policy Research Report*, Oxford University Press, New York, 1997, p. 86.
16. Reich, R., "Who is Us?" *Harvard Business Review*.
17. Greenaway, D., "Trade Related Investment Measures: Political Economy Aspects and Issues for GATT," *The World Economy*, Vol. 13, No. 3, September 1990, p. 373.
18. Chan, S., "Introduction: Foreign Direct Investment in a Changing World," in Steve Chan (ed.), *Foreign Direct Investment in a Changing Global Political Economy*, Macmillan Press Ltd., Houndmills and London, 1995, p. 2.
19. The GATT Secretariat, "The Final Act of the Uruguay Round: A Summary," *International Trade Forum*, No. 1, 1994, p. 10.
20. Hoekman, B. and Michel Kostecki, *The Political Economy of the World Trading System: From GATT to WTO*, Oxford University Press, Oxford, 1995, p. 122.
21. World Trade Organization, *Annual Report*, Vol. 1, Geneva, 1996, p. 62.

22. *The Multilateral Agreement on Investments, OECD Policy Brief*, No. 2, 1997, p. 3. (http://www.oecd.org/publications/Pol_brief/9702_Pol.htm)
23. Witherell, William H., "An Agreement on Investment," *The OECD Observer*, No. 202, October–November 1996, p. 7.
24. Other observers to the MAI negotiations are Hong Kong, Argentina, Brazil, Chile and Slovakia.
25. Clarke, T., "MAI-Day! The Corporate Rule Treaty," http://www.nassist.com/mai/mai(2)x.html.

Chapter Eight

THE POLITICAL ECONOMY OF ENVIRONMENTAL MANAGEMENT

Environmental degradation is a direct result of human activity. In the process of transforming resources to satisfy our material needs, we release large quantities of toxic effluent and emissions into the environment. It is estimated that our daily impact on the environment includes a release of 17.3 million tonnes of carbon dioxide into the atmosphere; a loss of 64.8 million tonnes of topsoil; destruction 47 000 hectares of forest; desertification of 346 000 hectares of land; and the extinction of perhaps 100–300 species.[1] The doomsayers among us lament that this is unsustainable and that either we protect our ecology or accept our own extinction. Even if we forestall our extinction, there are predictions that, as a result of pollution and despite medical advances and better nutrition, human longevity could decline by 50 percent in the next century.[2] The doomsayers will no doubt disagree that we have changed our habits sufficiently but may be encouraged by the growing environmental movement and increased awareness of the adverse consequences of continued environmental degradation. We are more aware of our role in protecting the natural environment and the delicate ecological balance. The greening of our collective consciousness has encouraged individuals to modify consumption patterns and forced businesses to be environmentally responsible.[3]

The environmental movement is most active in western countries but, following the collapse of communism, has spread also to eastern Europe. Previously, central planners had dedicated themselves to increasing material output, regardless of environmental impact. The distorted domestic price mechanism and subsidies on energy resources also contributed to wasteful usage and higher levels of pollution. Pollution indicators improved significantly following the collapse of socialism, initially as a result of declines in industrial output and higher energy prices and later, as a result of industrial restructuring and modernization.[4]

The emphasis on environmental protection after 1989 can be attributed to several factors, including popular pressure to undo some of the damage caused by decades of environmental neglect, and the perceived need to harmonize policies with the West European countries so as to facilitate admission into the EU.[5] These countries required access to the larger European market for their domestic economic revitalization and East European governments recognized that regulatory harmonization, including environmental regulation, was a precondition to EU membership. For the West European countries, this was a welcome dividend of the collapse of communism. In the past, they had suffered from air pollution drifting in from unregulated industries in the East, but had been frustrated in attempts to resolve the trans-border pollution issue.

The European experience was not unique. Although atmospheric and water-borne pollution cannot be contained within national boundaries, it has been difficult to deal with them because of divergent state interests, lack of scientific evidence, or because of domestic political constraints. The record of global or regional environmental management is less than exemplary. In this chapter, I will look at the various obstacles to multilateral environmental management and recent efforts to link trade privileges to environmentally responsible production of goods and services.

The Basic Dilemma

Human activity, throughout history, has been propelled by a desire to assert dominance over nature. Whereas most living things adapt to their environment or face extinction, humans have survived by asserting mastery over the environment. This peculiarity of human interaction with nature continues to alter the "state of nature." In particular, since the industrial revolution, human activity has unleashed massive systemic changes in the environment. Increasingly however, it appears that our future will depend not on mastering the environment but rather on protecting it from stress induced by human activity. This is important especially because of uncertainty about the tolerance level of the global ecology, and the imperative, therefore, of not exceeding threshold levels.

Uncertainty, however, is a double-edged sword. It has lent an urgency to the task of environmental management and, at the same time, enabled others to dismiss environmentalists as befuddled prophets of doom obstructing the path of economic progress and development. If there is a tension, it is between environmental logic that puts a high value on the future and economic analysis that tends to discount future value. The absence of incontrovertible scientific evidence has allowed protagonists to vie for political influence in the struggle between environmental protection and development. The conflict between environmental and developmental concerns results from a persisting belief that pollution is the price of progress. However, as we shall see below, the contradiction between environment and development may be more imagined than real.

Environmental degradation is a direct result of human activity and predates the modern industrial period. The industrial revolution, however, added to the pressures on the environment by accelerating the pace and intensity of economic activity. The emphasis on productive activity sacrificed environmental and health safeguards, resulting in such tragic crises as the "black death," which affected coal miners in Britain. National response and responsibility for such localized suffering, however, were only grudgingly acknowledged. In a similar manner, today, even though environmental pollution has assumed global dimensions, international cooperation to establish global regulatory regimes have proved to be very difficult. Cooperative efforts have faltered over disagreement on how to allocate the cost of pollution abatement and on the unwillingness of states to sacrifice other desirable objectives.

The developing countries, for example, agree on the importance of protecting the environment but in the perceived trade-off between environment and development, remain committed to developmental objectives. This is especially true for countries where regime legitimacy is premised on economic performance criteria rather than on the democratic mandate. Democratic governments, which have to respond to public opinion, may be expected to be more environmentally responsible but with limited capital and technological resources, it is inevitable that investment in pollution abatement technologies in developing countries has lagged behind the drive to accelerate economic growth. Export-oriented industrialization strategies, which were an integral component of structural adjustment policies of the IMF, designed to accelerate economic activity and growth in developing countries, have further added to the pollution problem in these countries. According to Loxley, for example, export promotion policies resulted in serious ecological damage in Ghana, mainly through excessive deforestation.[6] Deforestation is also a problem in many Asian countries. In Malaysia, 1.2 percent of its forest resources are harvested each year and in Indonesia, plantation farmers have continued to burn large tracts of forests to bring more land under cultivation. Governments, however, have ignored these problems, likening them to the inevitable price of progress.

Environmental degradation in developing countries has also been attributed to a lack of resources. A World Bank report observed that "Poor families often lack the resources to avoid degrading their environment."[7] The report also acknowledged that while the Third World countries were guilty of environmental damage, they were not necessarily the main agents of environmental destruction. It admitted that "those who cause[d] environmental damage ... [were] likely to be the rich and influential, while those who suffer[ed] most [we]re often the poor and powerless."[8]

In developed countries, the problem is largely profligate and conspicuous consumption. Environmental damage is a function of production and consumption patterns, and the developed countries are a greater cause for concern. The developed countries are a primary source of pollution, including greenhouse gases like carbon dioxide. These gases tend to retain heat within the atmosphere, rather than allow dissipation into space, and have been associated with global warming. The developed country category, however, conceals considerable divergence. The average American, for example, consumes twice as much energy (and is responsible for more environmental damage) as the average Japanese.[9] This is a result of wasteful and inefficient consumption patterns and of a pricing structure that does not adequately reflect the environmental and social costs or the scarcity value of non-renewable energy resources. Energy efficiency was a major governmental objective in Japan after the oil crisis of 1973 and while the gains were significant, it is possible to achieve further improvements. The European countries, initially, lagged behind Japan but are now as energy efficient as Japan and more ambitious than Japan in future energy efficiency.

Although both developed and developing countries are responsible for environmental degradation, the environment is a also source of contention between them. In recent years, developed countries have emphasized the importance of protecting rain forests in developing countries, like Brazil and Malaysia, to avert future global warming. There exists well-documented evidence of the capacity of rain forests to act as a sink for greenhouse gases and the Brazilian rain forests have been likened to human lungs providing clean air to the world. The problem is that the forest cover is being rapidly diminished through developmental pressures, which will inevitably lower the quality of human life everywhere, including in Brazil and Malaysia. Unfortunately, these countries have been unprepared to sacrifice development for environmental protection, insisting upon their sovereign right to exploit domestic forestry resources for national economic development.

The position of the developing countries is not without precedent. Historically, development has been achieved through environmental compromises. Still, notwithstanding historical reality, an important question is whether development must necessarily be detrimental to the environment. The answer, of course, depends on how development is defined. To break with the tyranny of history, it is necessary not to equate development simply with rapid GNP growth. In practice, as gleaned from development policies of the Third World, development *is* narrowly defined as growth in income and industrialization. However, development can also be defined to include improvements in the quality of life and welfare. Such a redefinition would elevate environmental protection to a worthy developmental objective alongside material improvements, especially as environmental degradation can be correlated with diseases and a general deterioration in the quality of life indicators. These entail costs for the community, such as in terms of health care and lower productivity. In Bangkok, for examples, studies show that the average child "... lost four or more IQ points by the age of seven because of elevated exposure to lead, with enduring implications for adult productivity."[10] This is clear evidence that present production and income growth is being purchased at the expense of future productivity losses. Similarly, while deforestation in Latin America, Asia, and elsewhere may produce immediate and short-term economic gains, in the long-term, the loss of forestry cover could be detrimental to economic growth, through such aftereffects as soil erosion, loss of biological diversity, and desertification.

In recent years, the term "sustainable development" has gained greater acceptance as a way of underscoring the complementarity between income growth and environmental protection. The World Bank report, mentioned above, emphasized "sustainable development," as a challenge for the future. The first usage of the term is credited to the World Commission on Environment and Development. The WCED, in its 1987 report titled *Our Common Future* (also known as the Brundtland Report, after the Chairperson of the WCED, Norwegian Prime Minister Gro Harlem Brundtland), defined sustainable development as development "that meets the needs of the present without compromising the ability of future generation to meet their own needs."[11] There are many interpretations of what it actually means. Some use it to mean that there are "limits to growth" or that only "steady state economics" is consistent with sustainable development, whereas others have used it to mean a stretching of environmental limits to accommodate growth.[12]

As a concept, sustainable development attempts to reconcile differences between environmental and economic logic by emphasizing that environmentally unsustainable development might only exacerbate the quality of life rather than improve it. It seeks to balance the desirability of development with the environmental trade-offs. The necessary balancing act is not easy, nor carefully defined, but it has at least provided a basis for fuller assessment of the environmental impact of large projects. In a sense, sustainable development underscores the importance of appropriate technologies to achieve a particular objective, or to forego a project, for instance, which can not adequately safeguard the environment given existing technology. It, therefore, hinges around "technological appropriateness" and in this context has increased the importance of technology transfer from the developed to the developing countries.

Sustainable development applies to both developed and developing countries and, according to Stephan Schmidheiny, "... sustainable development will require the greatest changes in the wealthiest nations, which consume the most resources, release the most pollution, and have the greatest capacity to make the necessary changes."[13] The World Bank report emphasized the complementarity of development and growth on the one hand, and environmental protection on the other. Given that environmental damage is the result of economic activity, the report stressed the importance of not ignoring the environmental impact of economic decisions. It did not however, conclude that we must produce less, rather that we must produce differently and in a more environmentally conscious way, or produce more with less. To highlight the complementarity, the report pointed out that "... policies that conserve the quality of agricultural land and protect forests improve the long-term prospects for agricultural development. An increase in the efficiency of energy and material use serves ecological purposes but can also reduce costs."[14]

In its annual report for 1992, the World Bank urged a balanced approach to income growth and quality of life. It suggested that environment should not be sacrificed for income, but pointed also to the reverse danger. According to the World Bank, "... too much environmental quality is now being given up. There is, however, a danger that too much income growth may be given up in the future because of failure to clarify and minimize trade-offs and to take advantage of policies that are good for both economic development and the environment."[15] Evaluating the trade-off between costs and benefits of present and future generations is not easy but sustainable development suggests that environmental costs should be factored into all investment decisions. When such costs are factored in, certain investments may be unwise but, of course, the problem is in assigning values and determining appropriate discount rates. A study of Mexican livestock industry suggested that adjustments for the costs of soil erosion sharply reduced this industry's net value added. The World Bank was cautious in stating that such studies did not in themselves indicate to "... policymakers as to whether Mexico's use of natural capital has been in the country's best interest, but they can be useful in reminding policymakers of potential tradeoffs and can assist in setting sectoral priorities."[16]

The idea of sustainable development also logically leads to the notion of sustainable population. Given that human activity is the cause of pollution and environmental degradation, it is obvious that the attempts to clean up the environment must also include measures at population control. Focusing on one without the other will weaken whatever positive gains are made. Population puts immense pressure on the environment, especially in the conversion of natural habitat for agricultural production. With a total world population of 5.3 billion, even the most optimistic projections suggest that total population will double to 10.1 billion by the middle of the next century, with most of the growth in the developing countries.

For sustainable development to become a practical reality, there will have to be large transfer of resources and technology from the developed to the developing countries. However, as we shall see further below, developed countries have not been altogether generous in their largesse.

The Changing Nature of Environmental Concerns

The issues of environmental damage and protection have been with us since the industrial revolution, but became more prominent with rapid industrialization beginning in the nineteenth century. For example, rapid Japanese industrialization in the late nineteenth century and "economic miracle" after the Second World War produced some of the worst excesses of industrial pollution. During this time, pollution was largely seen as a local issue. In Japan, the initial push for environmental protection and compensation was spearheaded by local communities directly affected by industrial emissions. The clean-up, however, began only after pollution and its consequences; Minamata mercury poisoning, the Yokkaichi asthma, and the "itai itai" disease, had assumed crisis proportions and the national government was forced to act. The "Pollution Diet" of 1969 passed a series of laws to protect the environment and settled also the issue of compensation for victims of pollution.

An OECD report in 1991, documenting the significant gains over the last 20 years in protecting the environment, reducing particulate emissions and increasing forest cover in the OECD countries, singled out Japan as the exemplar among OECD countries with emissions of sulfur oxides, particulates, and nitrogen oxides as a share of GNP at one-quarter the OECD average. The environmental gains in OECD countries have come at a price. Annual expenditure, since the 1970s, on anti-pollution policies ranged between 0.8 and 1.5 percent of GNP.[17]

In the latest stage of environmental consciousness, activists have spearheaded a push to win recognition of the indivisibility of the global ecology. The environmental movement embraced the idea of a single ecosystem in which the effects of pollution could not be localized, in space or in time, or prevented from affecting the entire ecosystem. Pollutants in the air and water are transmitted across national boundaries by regional and global atmospheric and tidal patterns. The most dramatic evidence of this was the Chernobyl nuclear accident, which resulted in radioactive fallout across many European countries. It contaminated the food chain and will continue to affect the lives of present and future generations.

The global nature of the environmental problem highlights the shortcomings of a purely national approach to protecting the environment. Left to national strategies, public spending on environmental protection is likely to be sub-optimal because each country will obtain only marginal benefits from efforts to protect the ecosystem. Moreover, the public goods nature of the environment may also tempt free ride and avoidance of responsibility. The environmental challenge, today, is first, to devise and implement a coordinated response and second, to develop strategies that not only react to environmental disasters but also anticipate and prevent damage to the environment. The recurrence of environmental crises and the costliness of clean-up efforts suggest that it is more cost effective to avert potential damage than to reverse the aftereffects of a real disaster. It is necessary, therefore, to develop, according to Moomaw and Kildow, the environmental equivalent of military deterrence.[18] Moreover, environmentalists argue that the ecosystem might be approaching saturation point as a consequence of "planetary overload."[19] Under these circumstances, to allow a disaster to happen before attempting to deal with it might be too late to reverse the damage.

Managing the Global Environment

In international trade and financial relations, the US had exercised leadership in establishing rules to facilitate transactions, not necessarily through a brute application of power but through negotiated settlements. A hegemon can use superior bargaining advantages and other power resources to structure a regime and secure compliance. The US, however, has not displayed the same commitment and determination to produce a negotiated outcome in environmental protection. Although State Department Counsellor Tim Wirth proclaimed that, "We're moving to new missions and our new missions are democracy, sustainable development, population ... the environment ...,"[20] at the Rio summit (discussed below), the United States was the only developed country to refuse to sign the Biological Diversity Convention and it also opposed the Climate Change Convention. A Greenpeace spokesperson stated that "by opposing the Climate Change Convention with commitments to cut polluting emissions, the United States has forfeited its claim to global political or environmental leadership. Again, prior to the 1997 Kyoto summit on global warming, the US Senate passed a unanimous resolution demanding that the Clinton administration reject any treaty that was either not binding on developing countries or which could potentially harm the American economy."[21] National interest considerations have weakened American resolve to act decisively and to provide leadership.

Any effective environmental regime must, of necessity, be intrusive but the objections raised by states are not simply that a regime would transfer sovereignty to a potentially supranational institution but also that there remain uncertainties about the cost-benefit calculations. Despite high global environmental interdependence, the benefits of operating within a regime framework are not manifestly obvious. In the case of pollution control and environmental protection, the present costs of environmental cooperation are perceived to be high compared to uncertain and intangible future returns. Although some countries, like Japan and Singapore, have turned the cost-benefit matrix to their advantage by developing and exporting pollution abatement technology and devises, many other countries remain unconvinced that the huge investments required to improve environmental quality and introduce controls on pollutants are justified. This is not surprising given that scientific evidence is inconclusive and the scientific community itself is divided on what measures should be taken to protect the environment.

Thus, despite environmental interdependence, the cost of environmental pollution is not uniformly assessed as high by all countries to ensure demand-driven global regime creation. Some countries have introduced stringent environmental standards, but global consensus has eluded negotiators. Creating global environmental regimes is handicapped by several factors, including the "tragedy of the commons,"[22] and the public goods dilemma. The commons include resources that are non-excludable, such as air, water, biosphere, and territories beyond national jurisdiction, such as the high seas. The enjoyment of commons cannot be denied and rational self interest dictates maximum enjoyment without particular consideration to protecting it. The tragedy of the commons is that while everyone benefits, it is in no one's individual interest to protect it or to limit consumption to sustainable levels. The public goods dilemma of environmental protection, on the other hand, refers to consumption without cost sharing. Walter C. Swap explained that the difference between the two concepts is that the first involves a failure to restrain use of resources (tragedy of the commons) and the other a failure to contribute resources/costs (public goods dilemma).[23] If clean environment is a public good, then the problem of free ride complicates and bedevils the production of such goods. Another source of difficulty, as indicated above, is the lack of overwhelming scientific evidence.

Even if the above difficulties can be surmounted, there still remains the problem of securing agreement to a specific set of rules. Given the improbability of political sovereignties disappearing in the near future, we cannot rule out conflicts of interest. The US, for example, is the largest producer of greenhouse gases but rejects international controls on grounds that it is capable of solving the problem without international standards. Malaysia, similarly refuses to accept internationally mandated restrictions to its logging operations and China insists on proceeding with the Three Gorges Dam regardless of the environmental consequences. [24] The Indian Minister of Environment, Kamal Rath, also accused the United States of imposing tougher environmental standards on developing countries than were required of the US and other industrialized countries in their early stage of industrialization and development.[25]

The difficulties in reaching a common accord are not simply a manifestation of the North-South divide. There also exists considerable disagreement among developed countries on the recognition and solution of environmental problems. The US and Canada, for example, have a history of acrimonious debate on the issue of acid rain, with Canada demanding urgent reduction of sulfur emissions by the United States and the US consenting only to further investigation and study before taking concrete steps. A regime cannot exist without rules but the contentious issue that had still not been resolved is which rules to adopt.

Commercial considerations have also complicated the creation of environmental regimes because business groups have been reluctant to assume the costs of pollution abatement. In 1997, some American corporations lobbied extensively against any US action on climate change. Industries are the most prevalent source of pollution and, yet, have been free to pursue their private gains while the costs of pollution control have been socialized. Businesses have a well-deserved reputation for opposing stricter environmental regulations. The US producers of ozone-depleting chlorofluorocarbons (CFCs) and the electronics industry effectively prevented a global ozone protection policy for more than a decade after scientists had identified the harmful consequences of CFCs.[26]

One concern of business corporations is that stricter environmental regulation at a national level will benefit competitors operating in countries with weaker regulatory regimes and the concern for policymakers is that national legislation will only encourage a horizontal movement of industries to areas with less stringent environmental policies. It is suggested that Japanese direct investment in East Asian countries may, at least partially, have been the result of tougher environmental controls in Japan in the early 1970s.

Increasingly however, businesses have recognized that environmental consciousness can be an important marketing advantage. This has led to a "greening" of business. In the US, a group of business leaders called CEO Environmental Technologies Coalition envisions corporate sector as leading the efforts to reduce greenhouse gas emissions. The greening of business and the rising trend of globalization has increased the level of support from the business community for uniform regulations, at least regionally. Multinational and global corporations have indicated their preference for cross-national and uniform anti-pollution measures so as to harmonize business costs. According to Anthony McGrew, "With the increasing internationalization of business the logic of more harmonized regional and global environmental regulation has a certain appeal since ... it prevents the costs being borne solely by one competitor in the global market."[27] Even if the situation is changing, multinationals were guilty of double standards in the past. The Bhopal accident (December 1984) that resulted in the death of an estimated 2 000 people was partly the result of inadequate safety features in the Union Carbide plant in Bhopal, India. A similar plant in West Virginia had more sophisticated safety features and this belied initial assertions by Union Carbide officials that both plants complied with their own internal safety standards.[28]

It is heroic to assume that a global order can be created out of purely rational considerations and a spirit of cooperation and, indeed, business preference for uniform cross-national regulations may be an attempt to blunt the environmental movement. This was, allegedly, true of the chemical companies' support for international agreement on CFC emissions because they expected an international protocol "to be weaker than the most likely domestic US regulations."[29]

Before discussing strategies for environmental protection, it is useful to ask whether environmental management is best achieved through global, regional, or national agreements. According to David Robertson, international treaties are time-consuming and also ignore that "... many of the so-called global problems result from the spilling over of national and regional pollution, and that national measures can make important contributions to reducing global environmental problems." He claimed that international treaties are simply convenient tools used by governments "... to divert attention from their own failure to deal with domestic pollution ..." and blame other countries for lack of progress.[30] This argument needs to be taken seriously especially as many countries, such as developing countries and former centrally planned economies, have poor and inadequate national legislation to protect their environment. Yet, it must be acknowledged that global environmental interdependence has created also the need to step beyond national legislation.

Ozone depletion, in the southern hemisphere for example, is largely the result of CFC production in the northern hemisphere countries and requires global standards to reduce CFC production. Management of the commons and global issues, like climate change, are only be possible through broad-based accord. The indivisibility of the global eco-system means that no part of the world can be insulated from damage inflicted to the environment in another part. Yet, despite high interdependence, there has been little success in attempts to devise a multilateral and global environmental agreement with a uniform of standards applicable to all countries.

The regional approach to environmental management, on the other hand, may hold greater promise. The Promethean efforts that would be necessary for global regime creation might be better spent in searching for regional alternatives or for agreement among smaller groups of countries. Thus, in the case of forestry management, Stanley Johnson suggested that negotiations be limited to the 53 major forest nations. If a majority of these countries agreed to a common set of rules, then others could be expected to bow to international pressure.[31] This formula appears to have worked for the regime in CFC reduction. In 1989, when the Montreal Protocol entered into force, only 23 countries had ratified the Protocol. That number, by 1995, had increased to more than 100 countries.

It is also interesting to note that environmental treaties have progressively included fewer countries. For example, between 1920 and 1973, 65 multilateral environmental treaties were signed and of these 54 percent involved 16 or more parties. By contrast, between 1974 and 1990, 67 treaties were signed and only 37 percent of treaties involved such large numbers and nearly 50 percent involved fewer than nine countries.[32]

Regional approaches have been reasonably successful, with the Mediterranean Action Plan (Med Plan) serving as the exemplar. The Med plan was signed in 1976 and has expanded to include all 18 littoral states. Most remarkably, the Med Plan has managed to overcome the North-South divide. Initially, the developing countries around the Mediterranean, such as Algeria and Egypt, were strongly opposed to it and saw pollution abatement proposals as a threat to their development. The Algerian President Houari Boumediene, for example, in the early 1970s, declared that "If improving the environment means less bread for the Algerians, then I am against it."[33]

In the end, the developing countries moderated their hostility and acquiesced to the Plan after strong scientific data to recommend a regulatory regime, and under pressure from a united scientific community. The scientific community, according to Peter Haas, was able to usurp the policy making process and established a strong regional network that overcame the resistance of domestic oriented ministries in the various countries. Consensual knowledge, he argued, "served largely as a power resource for members of the epistemic community. With no basis for challenging their authority, they were able to use consensual knowledge to bolster their policymaking advice."[34]

The regional approach to environmental protection has also produced opportunities for middle powers to take the lead in environmental management. While there may be hegemonic advantages in the establishment of large overarching international regimes, in specific issue areas, smaller countries do have a capacity to play a leadership role. They may be able to do this by concentrating their energies, by clever diplomatic maneuverings, or by taking advantage of a fortuitous policy environment to influence international agenda.

Two middle powers, Australia and France, played a key role in establishing a regulatory regime, protecting the Antarctica from commercial mining. Even though Australia had played a leading role in negotiating the 1988 Convention for the Regulation of Antarctic Mineral Resource Activities (CRAMRA) that permitted mining, the following year it declared its opposition to the Convention. The decision to reject CRAMRA was conditioned on several factors, including the view that Antarctica had already become too crowded because all human activity had become concentrated in the 1 percent of the Antarctica that was ice-free and accessible.[35] Following on this, and the campaign of the environmentalist movement led by Jacques Cousteau, there was also the fear that any mining could seriously disturb the fragile ecosystem. Moreover, the CRAMRA was also deficient in establishing, with any clarity, the conditions under which mining would be permitted. For example, it prohibited resource activities that might have "significant" environmental consequences but failed to define what might constitute significant environmental impact.[36] Nonetheless, proponents of the treaty felt that reopening a completed agreement was foolhardy and for various reasons, suggested that a complete ban should be a two-stage strategy, the first step being the acceptance of CRAMRA.[37]

In May 1989, the Australian government proposed that Antarctica should be given the status of a wilderness reserve. The following month, France, under similar domestic pressures, expressed support for the Australian proposal. In 1975, New Zealand had floated a similar proposal for an Antarctic World Park but was unsuccessful and, instead, in 1982, initiated negotiations for regulated mineral exploitation.[38] When Australia revived the idea of a wilderness park in 1989, the New Zealand Foreign Minister Russell Marshall stated that the chances of securing a stronger convention were zero and that Australia was seriously mistaken.[39] However, as support for the wilderness park grew, the New Zealand government added its support as did such a diverse group like the former Soviet Union, Belgium and India.

The campaign by Australia and France led to the Protocol on Environmental Protection to the Antarctic Treaty which was accepted by Treaty countries in June 1991. The Protocol imposed a complete ban on mining activities and, in Article 2, designated Antarctica as "a natural reserve, devoted to peace." This was very similar to the Australian proposal. The Protocol also established an Advisory Committee for Environmental Protection but not, as proposed by Australia and France, the establishment of an environmental commission, a secretariat, and inspection and monitoring corps.

Australian success in persuading other countries, including the United States, to agree to a complete ban largely owed to the environment movement and heightened level of popular environmental consciousness and the view that no mining convention could be compatible with environmental protection. Without domestic publics that were sympathetic to the environmental cause, it would have been much more difficult to carry the proposal through to successful completion. Apart from popular support, various nongovernmental organizations (NGOs) also played an important role in negotiating the protocol. Organizations such as Greenpeace, the Wilderness Society, and Foundation Cousteau joined the negotiations either as members of national delegations or as lobbyists. The rejection of CRAMRA in favor of the protocol vindicated the position of the NGOs against CRAMRA and as Blay stated, "... on balance, the influence and positive role of the organizations were well established and their usefulness in the future consultations of the Treaty states accepted."[40]

Despite examples of success at the regional level, it is true that, as mentioned above, issues like climate change cannot be tackled through regional efforts.

The Role of Scientific Community

Scientific evidence and consensus have, in the past, been useful in establishing relevant international regulatory frameworks. For instance, international cooperation in disease prevention was in abeyance for nearly a century until scientific consensus provided an impetus to the formation of an international regime.[41] Similarly, we might expect science to provide compelling reasons for environmental management and, as mentioned above, scientific consensus and evidence was, indeed, an important factor in the success of the Med Plan. However, in many cases like global warming, there is, as yet, no conclusive scientific evidence on the nature and cause of environmental damage. With clear scientific evidence on damage to the environment, it might be possible for countries to approach the task of environmental protection as a technical-functional, rather than political, problem and to cooperate in the development of comprehensive guidelines.

Unfortunately however, there is, at present, no consensus on the significance of existing scientific data. Nor is there a full understanding of the various issues. For example, while it is certain that CFCs in the atmosphere deplete the ozone layer, it is not known how CFCs and other greenhouse gases interact to affect the ozone layer. Moreover, if greenhouse gases are a factor behind global warming, estimates of the magnitude of global warming vary sufficiently enough to prompt suggestions that the problem of global warming is misconceived.

Some scientists also question the validity of conclusions reached by projections into the future of present trends. Even if there is evidence to suggest an increase in carbon dioxide and other greenhouse gases in the atmosphere, according to Richard Lindzen, Professor of Meteorology at

Table 8.1.   Global warming forecasts.

Year of forecast	Rate of warming	Greenhouse effect by 2030	
		Temp. rise	Sea level rise
1988	0.8 C/decade	3.0 C	20–150 cm
1990	0.3 C/decade	1.2 C	15–40 cm
1995	0.2 C/decade	0.8 C	5–35 cm

Note: Forecast for 1988 is from the 1988 "World Conference on the Changing Atmosphere: Implications for Global Security," conference in Toronto, Canada. The 1990 and 1995 forecasts are by the UN's Intergovernmental Panel on Climate Change. Source: "Global Warming Earth Summit Fact Sheet: The Greenhouse Effect and Global Warming," Global Warming Information Center (http://www.nationalcenter.inter.net/KyotoFactSheet.html), April 23, 1998

the Masachussetts Institute of Technology, it is a "questionable contention
... that those increases will continue along the path they have followed for
the past century."[42] Predictions based on current trends may, indeed, be
erroneous because they do not account for future technological shifts and
other influences on the trend line. Many dire predictions of the past have,
consequently and fortunately, fallen well short of target. Some 200 years
earlier, Thomas Malthus had predicted famine and starvation in England
based on his understanding of population growth and its capacity to feed
itself but improved agriculture and lower population growth rates proved
him to be very wrong in his conclusions.

From an environmentalist's point of view, the danger is that inaction
until gaps in our knowledge have been overcome may be too late to repair
or reverse the impact of environmental damage. It is sobering also to
know that six of the seven warmest years on record occurred between
1980 and 1990.[43] The ideal solution would be to establish a structure of
preventative regulations rather than react to a situation that has deteriorated beyond repair. Precedents for this do exist, as in the case of
governments intervention and legislation to require warning labels on
cigarette packs in the absence of "firm" evidence linking tobacco with
cancer. The environment may be an issue area where we cannot wait till
we have hard data or complete consensus within the scientific community.

There are gaps and *lacunae* in our knowledge but the worst case
scenarios are too critical to be ignored. Data on global temperatures do
not go very far back in history but it is known that there has been
statistically significant global warming over the last 100 years. This is
consistent with the increased concentration of greenhouse gases in the
atmosphere but it is also true that there existed similar variations in
temperatures in earlier times without concommitant variation in levels of
carbon dioxide.[44] Thus, it is by no means certain that the increase in
global mean temperature, 0.3–0.6 degrees Centigrade over the past 80–
100 years, is due to carbon dioxide. However, the level of global warming
is consistent with existing models on the link between carbon dioxide and
climate change and, given the long-lived nature of greenhouse gases, it
may be foolish to ignore the potential danger. Admittedly, as the table
above showed, the potential danger has been revised downwards

significantly in only one short decade. It is clear also that the exact magnitude and nature of the "danger" is not very well understood.

Proponents of appropriate environmental regimes argue that evidential weakness actually strengthens the case for early action since incontrovertible scientific evidence might not be obtained in time to prevent planetary overload. Even if this logic is sufficient to cause demand for environmental regimes, the supply of regime is still hampered by considerations of national interests.

If environmental regimes are the ultimate objectives, several scholars have suggested that the vigor of global discourse on the environment together with an expansion of various environmental organizations have already constitutes a global environmental regime.[45] There is no doubt that the activities of various nongovernmental organizations have elevated global environmental consciousness and, with a time lag, facilitated the establishment of various multilateral and international agencies to manage specific environmental issues, but it is premature to suggest, as do Meyer *et al.*, that the global discourse on environment is embedded in universalistic and authoritative discussion and communication. As mentioned above, the scientific community is divided and the global environmental discourse weak because there is incomplete evidence about the magnitude of the environmental problem. This has, of course, not prevented the establishment of environmental associations and treaties, such as the United Nations Environment Program (UNEP), the Convention for the Protection of the Ozone Layer, the Montreal Agreement etc., but these are pockets of environmental action and concern. The associations and treaties are, in most cases, limited by membership and scope and the articulation of individual associations not clear.

The Role of the United Nations

The 1987 report of The World Commission on Environment and Development argued in support of creating a global institutional framework under the aegis of the United Nations. This was not surprising since the commission had been established by the UN Secretary General in 1983. Gro Brundtland and the commissioners, despite the declining fortunes and funds of the United Nations in the 1980s, optimistically argued that given its universal nature and with proper organizational reforms, "... the UN can and should be a source of significant leadership in the transition to sustainable development and in support of developing countries in effecting this transition."[46]

Following the submission of the report, the UN General Assembly, in December 1989, adopted resolution 44/228 to prepare for a global environmental conference in June 1992. Several prior meetings laid the groundwork for the United Nations Conference on Environment and Development, at Rio de Janeiro in June 1992 (commonly known either as the Rio summit or the Earth summit). The Rio Summit was a follow-up to a similar conference convened 20 years ago. The Stockholm Conference on the Human Environment (1972) was of little significance, however, because while it produced numerous agreements, none were actually implemented. With no support for the establishment of another layer of international bureaucracy, a limited and small UN Environment Program (UNEP), rather than an environment agency, was set up to collect and disseminate information, and to promote environmental cooperation among states.[47] UNEP's main instrument for monitoring the environment is GEMS, the Global Environmental Monitoring System. It tracks changes in the atmosphere, climate, ozone depletion, air pollution and various other indicators, through a network spanning more than 140 countries.

One of the priority areas of the UNEP was the protection of regional, enclosed and semi-enclosed seas which were identified as more at risk from pollution.[48] In response, the UNEP set up the regional seas program which led to eight regional agreements, the most successful of which was the Mediterranean Action Plan.

In 1988, the UNEP and the World Meteorological Organization (WMO) established the Intergovernmental Panel on Climate Change (IPCC) which submitted its Report in 1990. The report identified four greenhouse gases that had contributed to global warming: carbon dioxide produced by the burning of fossil fuels; halocarbons (CFC); methane (produced by rice paddies, cattle farms); and nitrous oxide. Of the four, methane is the least innocuous as it has a short lifetime of about ten years, meaning that quick results can be obtained by lowering methane emissions.[49] Of the other three, atmospheric carbon dioxide was identified as the main contributor and therefore of immediate concern. Given the long life of carbon dioxide (50–200 years) the report recommended immediate reduction of carbon dioxide emissions by 60–80 percent in order to stabilize atmospheric carbon dioxide to present day levels by the year 2050.[50] This can presumably be achieved by switching to more efficient fuel sources. It is estimated that a simple substitution of gas for coal would halve carbon emissions in powers stations.[51] For halocarbons and nitrous oxide, the IPCC report advised immediate emission reduction of at least 70 percent.

A January 1992 update of the 1990 findings reported that while some of the estimations used for arriving at the various recommendations had to be revised, given new information, there was no reason to alter the main conclusions regarding carbon dioxide emissions.[52] On the other hand, the prospects for halocarbon reductions improved significantly as a result of the London Amendment to the Montreal Protocol. The Montreal Protocol had been signed in 1987 and came into force on 1 January 1989, following ratification of the Protocol by 23 countries. The London Amendment was agreed to in 1990 and it set more ambitious targets for reduction of atmospheric halocarbons than had been contained in the Montreal Protocol. The revised targets were as below[53]:

- CFCs to be reduced by 20 percent in 1993, 50 percent in 1995, 85 percent in 1997 and phased out in 2000;
- halons to be reduced by 50 percent by 1995 and phased out by 2000;
- carbon tetrachloride to be reduced by 85 percent by 1995 and phased out by 2000;
- methyl chloroform to be reduced by 30 percent in 1995, 70 percent in 2000 and phased out by 2005; and
- other fully halogenated CFC to be reduced by 20 percent in 1993, 85 percent in 1997, and phased out in 2000.[54]

In 1994, the IPCC reported that atmospheric levels of carbon dioxide, the main greenhouse gas produced by burning fossil fuels, had increased by 0.4 percent a year, in the period 1980–1989 and that methane levels had increased by 0.8 percent a year, in the period 1980–1990. On a more optimistic note, the report observed that depletion of ozone was likely to peak around the year 2002 and that in the first half of the twenty-first century, ozone levels were likely to recover.[55]

The organizers of the Rio summit hoped to go beyond the limited achievements of the Stockholm summit. The summit itself was a grand occasion and attended by 175 countries, more than one hundred heads of government, about 1 500 officially accredited non-governmental organizations (such as the Greenpeace), and 7 000 journalists. The summit adopted an 800-page document (40 chapters) titled *Agenda 21*, on measures to clean up the environment. Agenda 21 was intended as a guideline for future national and international action in the field of environment and development.[56]

The document contained nothing that was mandatory and the conference produced little concrete understanding. As expected, the North-South divide proved difficult to bridge and the document was heavily laden with hortatory statements on the need for "capacity building" through technology sharing etc., to enable developing countries to realize sustainable development. The developed countries were keen on reaching agreement in the forest protection but the developing countries refused to accept the Western agenda and, "... the G77 led by Malaysia and India said 'no' from the start and went on saying 'no' to the bitter, very bitter, end."[57] The Malaysian government insisted on its sovereign right to exploit forestry resources to further developmental goals. The West might have secured support of the developing countries by sweetening the deal with financial assistance but that was not forthcoming. Organizers of the summit had hoped to secure Western commitments of at least US$10 billion but actual commitment fell short of the target.[58]

Besides Agenda 21, two conventions on Biological Diversity, and on Climate Change were signed by most countries present at the summit. The United States refused to sign the Convention on Biological Diversity, fearful that the stipulation on technology transfer would undermine the profits of firms engaged in biotechnology research and development.

The Convention on Climate Change did not include any targets for the reduction of carbon emissions despite pressure to do so in the interest of preventing global warming.

It had been expected that the Rio summit would lead to agreement on reduction of carbon emissions.[59] As mentioned above, carbon emissions can be reduced significantly simply by switching to more efficient energy sources, which could be encouraged either through carbon taxes or tradeable carbon emission permits. In either case the principle was that the polluter should be assessed a net cost for polluting the environment. Carbon taxes could be assessed depending on the carbon content of the actual energy source used by industries and such a tax would, arguably, be an incentive to use fuels with low carbon contents, such as natural gas or nuclear energy instead of coal or oil. The expectation that Rio would produce an agreement was understandable as the potential danger posed by carbon emissions was undeniable. The IPCC report, which highlighted the dangers of carbon emissions, was also generally acknowledged as thorough in incorporating latest scientific evidence. The United States, however, remained unmoved and rejected attempts to establish specific target levels to reduce carbon emissions. The oil-producing countries, too, did not want significant reductions in energy consumption because they were afraid of losing oil profits.[60]

Like the UNEP born out of the Stockholm summit, the Rio Summit agreed to establish a new international institution called the Commission for Sustainable Development (CSD) that would report to the Economic and Social Council (ECOSOC) of the UN. In his commentary on the Agenda 21, Stanley Johnson expressed concern that CSD would compete with UNEP and that "the net outcome of all the institutional debate at Rio might be, to put it in crude but simple terms, to undermine fatally the institutional achievements of Stockholm. At the very least, the scarce intellectual energies and scarcer financial resources which will now be devoted to 'getting CSD off the ground' will not be available to strengthen those other bodies in the UN system, particularly UNEP, whose 'strengthening and enhancement' is also called for in Chapter thirty eight [of Agenda 21]."[61]

The Rio summit was followed up by the Kyoto Earth Summit in December 1997. The agenda was climate change and global warming and the meeting was attended by 150 countries. Prior to the summit, the American Congress had passed a resolution opposing any targets on reducing greenhouse gas emissions unless developing countries reduced their own emissions. Nonetheless, the meeting produced an agreement requiring industrial countries to reduce emissions, by 2012, to levels below that in 1990. This committed the EU to an 8 percent reduction of greenhouse gases, 7 percent for the US, and 6 percent for Japan. The agreement, however, will only slow the process of global warming since there are no requirements on developing countries which continue to produce greenhouse gases and are likely even to increase their per capita production of such gases. According to Geoff Hogbin, halting global warming will require much larger cuts in greenhouse gas emissions and in the case of carbon dioxide (CO_2) require reductions of 60 to 80 percent below current levels for both developed and developing countries.[62] Compared to what is required, the Kyoto agreement was only a small step forward.

Nonetheless, the United Nations has had some limited success in securing agreements on environmental protection. It is impeded, however, by the unanimity rule and the difficulty of reconciling divergent national interests. It was impressive that 175 countries participated in the Rio summit but the large number of participants was also a drawback in securing agreement since it meant that many more interests had to be mediated before a decision could be reached.

Considering the difficulties in the path of UN leadership, Stanley Johnson argued that a successful treaty on forest management will require action outside the UN, among only the concerned countries, and by casting aside the tyranny of the consensus rule.[63] Even so, as Falk observed, the UN still performed a useful role as an important medium for transmitting the important message of environmental preservation and as a tool for international socialization. Eventually, he argued, despite the difficulties, "The UN is likely to play a very much more important role in world affairs once the evidence of the perils to the planet begins to be understood."[64]

The Role of Trade Related Measures

Trade can be an instrument for environmental protection but there is considerable disagreement whether the appropriate trade policy is free trade or trade sanctions against countries that damage the environment. On one hand, trade bans have been effective in protecting endangered species. In 1989, the Convention on International Trade in Endangered Species (CITES) introduced a ban on ivory trade which was instrumental in reducing the poaching of elephants. On the other hand, liberal trade theory maintains that free trade enhances productive efficiency and hence minimizes environmental damage. It is also assumed that trade, in itself, is not the source of environmental degradation, which is a result of market failures and inability of markets to include environmental costs in the final cost of products. From this perspective, rather than restrict trade to force compliance with good environmental practices, it might make more sense to use liberal trade to promote more efficient use of resources and lessen environmental damage.[65]

Some western countries have tried to use trade liberalization as a lever to force other countries to comply with their own standards on environmental protection. The US Marine Mammal Protection Act, for instance, prompted the American government to impose a tuna import ban because tuna fishing resulted in large numbers of dolphins being caught and destroyed. Such unilateral actions have been criticized by developing countries, which have limited institutional (well-functioning markets) and financial capacity to deal with their environmental problems. Unilateral trade measures have also raised concerns that the trade weapon could potentially be used simply as an instrument of protectionism in the guise of environmental protection. At a minimum, unilateral trade measures have highlighted the potential for conflict between provisions of national environmental legislation and GATT principles of Most Favored Nation and national treatment. In terms of specific instruments, the GATT also prohibits the use of trade bans to restrict trade, except in a limited number of cases, such as in products that contain prison labor. The GATT rules also do not permit trade restrictions related to how imported goods are produced.[66]

When the GATT was established, the environmental principle was, understandably, not high on the agenda but when the Uruguay Round Agreement was approved by members in Marrakesh in April 1994, trade ministers also agreed to establish a WTO Committee on Trade and Environment (CTE). The function of the CTE is to study the relationship between trade and environment and make recommendations to promote sustainable development. One of the main issues confronting the CTE is the ambiguity surrounding the use of trade sanctions by countries to achieve goals and objectives contained in multilateral environmental agreements. The Committee submitted its first report to the WTO Ministerial Conference in Singapore in 1996. The report emphasized the liberal principles of removing barriers to trade in order to benefit both trade and the environment but noted also that it may be necessary to include trade measures in multilateral environmental legislation, especially "... where trade is related directly to the source of an environmental problem."[67] The report also reflected the basic divide separating developed and developing countries. The latter group of countries remains concerned that environmental objectives might be abused to provide protection to domestic producers. Given the complexity of the task, CTE deliberations have not, as yet, produced a final resolution of the important linkages between trade and environment.

Conclusion

The importance of protecting our natural environment is now readily acknowledged but that does not render the task of environmental protection any easier. The gap between acknowledgment and action is still wide and this can be attributed to weak political will. The tragedy of environmental damage is that, globally, the funds and the technology do exist to prevent it. If in the past, economic decisions were based largely on a narrowly based cost-benefit analysis, the challenge now is to introduce an environmental calculus into economic policies. This needs to happen both at the micro level of individual investment decisions but also at the macro level of national accounts. Only by this can we heighten our environmental awareness. Measuring the environmental impact is not easy but models have been developed jointly by the World Bank and the UN Statistical Office to have the environmental impact reflected in figures for net domestic product (NDP). While not a perfect system, it nevertheless highlighted the significance of the environment. For example, according to its calculations, Mexico's environmentally adjusted net domestic product in 1985 was only 87 percent of NDP.[68] At present, such estimates are no more than conscious-raising exercises and not very useful as a guide to policy makers but their utility cannot be questioned. These may, in the end, prompt a sound environmental management program through a cooperative international regime.

References

1. United Nations Environmental Program (UNEP) press release, 1 March 1995.
2. See, Mungall, C. and Digby J. McLaren (eds.), *Planet Under Stress: The Challenge of Global Change*, Oxford University Press, Toronto, 1990, p. 23.
3. For example, several major US firms introduced better environmental systems to reduce wastage and pollution. These efforts had brought Northrop Corporation an estimated savings of US$20 million by January 1992, and Polaroid Corporation had reduced chemical usage by 20 percent in 1988–1990 as a result of a waste reduction program which was begun in 1988. See Pollack, S., "Cleaner Production Makes Money," *Our Planet*, Vol. 5, No. 3, 1993.
4. Schnoor, J. L., James N. Galloway, and Bedrich Molden, "East Central Europe: An Environment in Transition," *Environmental Science & Technology*, Vol. 31, No. 9, September 1997, p. 415A.
5. Levy, Marc A., "East-West Environmental Politics after 1989: The Case of Air Pollution," in Keohane, R. O., Joseph S. Nye and Stanley Hoffmann (eds.), *After the Cold War: International Institutions and State Strategies in Europe, 1989–1991*, Harvard University Press, Cambridge, 1993. In 1990, the government of Poland, for example, outlined a program to harmonize its environmental policies with those of western Europe over the next seven to ten years. See Zylicz, T.,

"Environmental Policy Reform in Poland," in Sterner, T. (ed.), *Economic Policies for Sustainable Development*, Kluwer Academic Publishers, Dordrecht, 1994, pp. 85–86.

6. Loxley, J., "Structural Adjustment in Africa: Reflections on Ghana and Zambia," *A Review of African Political Economy*, Vol. 47, Spring 1990, p. 18.

7. *World Development Report 1992*, The World Bank and Oxford University Press, New York, 1992, p. 30.

8. *World Development Report 1992*, The World Bank and Oxford University Press, New York, 1992, p. 43.

9. See Ehrlich, P., "Too Many Rich People," *Our Planet*, Vol. 6, No. 3, 1994, p. 13.

10. Schwarz, A., "Looking Back at Rio," *Far Eastern Economic Review*, 28 October 1993, p. 48.

11. *Our Common Future, The World Commission on Environment and Development*, Oxford University Press Australia, Melbourne, 1990, p. 87. The Brundtland Report also provided the initial stimulus for the Rio Earth Summit of 1992.

12. Dieren, Wouter van (ed.), *Taking Nature Into Account: A Report to the Club of Rome*, Springer-Verlag New York Inc., New York, 1995, p. 95.

13. Schmidheiny, S., *Changing Course: A Global Business Perspective on Development and the Environment*, The MIT Press, Cambridge, MA., 1992, p. 6.

14. *Our Common Future. The World Commission on Environment and Development*, Oxford University Press Australia, Melbourne, 1990, p. 106.

15. *World Development Report 1992*, The World Bank and Oxford University Press, New York, 1992, p. 35.

16. *World Development Report 1992*, The World Bank and Oxford University Press, New York, 1992, p. 36.

17. *See World Development Report 1992*, The World Bank and Oxford University Press, New York, 1992, p. 40.

18. Moomaw, William R, and Judith T Kildow, "International Environmental Decision Making: Challenges and Changes for the Old Order,"

in Chechile, Richard A. and Susan Carlisle (eds.), *Environmental Decision Making: A Multidisciplinary Approach*, Van Nostrand Reinhold, New York, 1991, p. 271.

19. McMichael, T., *Planetary Overload*, Cambridge University Press, Cambridge, 1993.

20. *The Straits Times*, 11 June 1993, p. 2.

21. *The United States and Japan in 1993: Impact of Domestic Change*, Paul H. Nitze, School of Advanced International Studies, Johns Hopkins University, Washington, DC, 1993, p. 89.

22. This borrows the title of Garrett Hardin's article titled, *The Tragedy of the Commons, Science*, No. 168, 1968.

23. Swap, Walter C., "Psychological Factors in Environmental Decision Making: Social Dilemmas," in Chechile, Richard A. and Susan Carlisle (eds.), *Environmental Decision Making: A Multidisciplinary Perspective*, Van Nostrand Reinhold, New York, 1991, p. 21.

24. Taylor, L., "Rio 1992: Earth Summit," *The Weekend Australian*, 16–17 May 1992, p. 22.

25. D'Monte, D., "A Dam Too Far," *Far Eastern Economic Review*, 28 October 1993, p. 62.

26. Porter, G. and Janet Welsh Brown, *Global Environmental Politics*, Westview Press, Boulder, 1991, pp. 65–66.

27. McGrew, A., "The Political Dynamics of the 'New' Environmentalism," in Smith, D. (ed.), *Business and the Environment: Implications of the New Environmentalism*, Paul Chapman Publishing Ltd., 1993, p. 24.

28. Gladwin, Thomas N., "A Case Study of the Bhopal Tragedy," in Pearson, Charles S. (ed.), *Multinational Corporations, Environment, and the Third World*, Duke University Press, Durham, 1987, p. 233.

29. Porter, G. and Janet Welsh Brown, *Global Environmental Politics*, Westview Press, Boulder, 1991, p. 66.

30. Robertson, D., "The Global Environment: Are International Treaties a Distraction?" *The World Economy*, Vol. 13, No. 1, March 1990, p. 111.

31. Johnson, S., "Rio's Forest Fiasco," *The Geographical Magazine*, September 1992, p. 28.

32. Haas, Peter M. with Jan Sundgren, "Evolving International Environmental Law: Changing Practices of National Sovereignty," in Choucri, N. (ed.), *Global Accord: Environmental Challenges and International Responses*, The MIT Press, Cambridge, MA., 1993, pp. 405–406.

33. Haas, Peter M., "Do Regimes Matter? Epistemic Communities and the Mediterranean Pollution Control," *International Organization*, Vol. 43, No. 3, Summer 1989, p. 379.

34. Haas, Peter M., "Do Regimes Matter? Epistemic Communities and the Mediterranean Pollution Control," *International Organization*, Vol. 43, No. 3, Summer 1989, p. 398.

35. Brown, A., "New Proposal: The National Park," in Verhoeven J., Philippe Sands and Maxwell Bruce (eds.), *The Antarctic Environment and International Law*, Graham & Trotman/Martinus Nijhoff, London, 1992, p. 98.

36. Blay, S. K. N., "New Trends in the Protection of the Antarctic Environment: The 1991 Madrid Protocol," *American Journal of International Law*, Vol. 86, April 1992, p. 382.

37. See, for example, Shapley, D., "Polar Thinking on the Antarctic," *New York Times*, 17 October 1989, p. 27(I).

38. James, C., "The Fragile Continent: Australia and France Push Antarctic Treaty Alternative," *Far Eastern Economic Review*, Vol. 144, No. 23, 8 June 1989, p. 40.

39. James, C., "The Fragile Continent: Australia and France Push Antarctic Treaty Alternative," *Far Eastern Economic Review*, Vol. 144, No. 23, 8 June 1989, p. 40.

40. Blay, S. K. N., "New Trends in the Protection of the Antarctic Environment: The 1991 Madrid Protocol," *American Journal of International Law*, Vol. 86, April 1992, pp. 298–399.

41. Richard Cooper cited in Horne, J. and Paul R. Masson, "Scope and Limits of International Economic Cooperation and Policy Coordination," *Staff Papers, International Monetary Fund*, Vol. 35, No. 2, June 1988, p. 281.

42. Lindzen, R. S., "Global Warming: The Origin and Nature of the Alleged Scientific Consensus," *Regulation: The Cato Review of*

Business and Government (http://www.cato.org/pubs/regulation/reg15n2g.html).

43. Postel, S., "Denial in the Decisive Decade," in *State of the World 1992*, W.W Norton & Co., New York, 1992, p. 3.

44. It is believed that western Europe, Iceland and Greenland were exceptionally warm between the late tenth and early thirteenth centuries. Following this the world experienced a 'Little Ice Age' from around the mid sixteenth to the mid nineteenth centuries. Thus, according to the IPCC report, 'some of the global warming since 1850 could be a recovery from the Little Ice Age rather than a direct result of human activity.' See *Climate Change: The IPCC Scientific Assessment* (eds. Houghton, J. T., G. J. Jenkins and J. J. Ephraums), Cambridge University Press, Cambridge, 1990, p. 203.

45. Meyer, John W., David John Frank, Ann Hironaka, Evan Schofer and Nancy Brandon Tuma, "The Structuring of a World Environmental Regime, 1870–1990," *International Organization*, Vol. 51, No. 4, Autumn 1997.

46. *Our Common Future, The World Commission on Environment and Development*, Oxford University Press Australia, Melbourne, 1990, p. 361.

47. The UNEP is headquartered in Nairobi, Kenya and, in 1992–1993, had a budget of US$150 million.

48. Tolba, Mostafa K., Osama A. El-Kholy *et al.* (eds.), *The World Environment, 1972–1992: Two Decades of Challenge*, Chapman & Hall, London, 1993, p. 766.

49. The other three gasses have atmospheric lifetime of between 50 to 200 years.

50. *Climate Change: The IPCC Scientific Assessment*, Report Prepared for the IPCC by Working Group 1, Cambridge University Press, Cambridge, 1990, p. 18.

51. The carbon content of coal is 25.1 grams carbon per 1, 000 British Thermal Units whereas that for gas is only 14.5 grams. See, Pearce, D., "The Role of Carbon Taxes in Adjusting to Global Warming," *The Economic Journal*, Vol. 101, July 1991, p. 939, fn. 4.

52. Leggett, J., W. J. Pepper and R. J. Swart, "Emissions Scenarios for the IPCC: An Update," *Climate Change 1992: The Supplementary Report to the IPCC Scientific Assessment*, Cambridge University Press, Cambridge, 1992, p. 93.

53. Tolba, M. K., Osama A. El-Kholy *et al.* (eds.), *The World Environment, 1972-1992: Two Decades of Challenge*, Chapman & Hall, London, 1993, p. 37.

54. This amendment to the Montreal Protocol became effective in May 1992 after it had been ratified by 20 countries. The Montreal Protocol itself had, by this time, been ratified by nearly 80 countries.

55. *The Sunday Mail*, 16 October 1994, p. 65.

56. Johnson, Stanley P., 1993, p. 5.

57. Johnson, Stanley P., *The Earth Summit: The United Nations Conference on Environment and Development (UNCED)*, Graham & Trotman/Martinus Nijhoff, London 1993, p. 5.

58. Johnson, Stanley P., *The Earth Summit: The United Nations Conference on Environment and Development (UNCED)*, Graham & Trotman/Martinus Nijhoff, London, 1993, pp. 6–7.

59. See, for example, Pearce, David, "The Role of Carbon Taxes in Adjusting to Global Warming," *The Economic Journal*, Vol. 101, July 1991, pp. 940–941.

60. Hemming, J., "Reactions to Tio," *The Geographical Magazine*, September 1992, p. 23.

61. Johnson, Stanley P., *The Earth Summit: The United Nations Conference on Environment and Development (UNCED)*, Graham & Trotman/Martinus Nijhoff, London, 1993, p. 489.

62. Hogbin, G., "Global Warming: The Mother of All Environmental Scares," *Policy*, Vol. 14, No. 1, Autumn 1998, p. 32.

63. Johnson, S., "Rio's Forest Fiasco," *The Geographical Magazine*, September 1992, p. 28.

64. Falk, Richard A., *This Endangered Planet: Prospects and Proposals for Human Survival, Vintage Books*, New York, 1972, p. 320.

65. van Bergeijk, Peter A. G., *Journal of World Trade*, December 1991, pp. 105ff. For a good discussion of trade and environmental issues, see Schmidheiny, S., *Changing Course: A Global Business Perspective on*

Development and the Environment, The MIT Press, Cambridge, MA., 1992, pp. 69–81.

66. Schlagenhof, M., "Trade Measures Based on Environmental Processes and Production Methods," *Journal of World Trade*, Vol. 29, No. 6, December 1995, p. 127.

67. Hunter, David B. and Michelle Billig, "International Economy and the Environment," *Yearbook of International Environmental Law*, Vol. 7, 1996, p. 253.

68. Steer, A. and Ernst Lutz, "Measuring Environmental Sustainable Development," *Finance & Development*, Vol. 30, No. 4, December 1993, p. 21.

Chapter Nine

THE POLITICAL ECONOMY OF INTERNATIONAL LABOR STANDARDS

One of the more contentious aspects of contemporary international political economy is that of defining and enforcing minimum universal labor standards to eliminate unfair competition based on exploitative labor conditions. A number of western governments have supported proposals for linking labor standards to trade privileges which, if accepted by all members of the World Trade Organization, might also include trade sanctions against countries that export goods produced using labor that is denied minimum labor conditions. Some aspects of the proposals on labor standards, for example, the prohibition of slave labor, are uncontroversial but not all countries agree that trade sanctions are a desirable method for ensuring compliance. Many of them also feel that social requirements are an unwarranted intrusion into the domestic affairs of sovereign countries. This latter group, primarily developing countries have, therefore, stubbornly resisted attempts to include a social clause in trade agreements.

In general, labor standards in developing countries are either non-existent or inadequately enforced. These countries also have abundant supplies of low-cost labor and an export competitive advantage in labor intensive industries, such as textiles and garments manufacturing. Consequently, they are concerned that implementation of labor standards could become a vehicle for the protection of labor intensive industries in developed countries from cheap developing countries' exports. This fear of labor standards as a western "Trojan horse" to undermine the export capacity of developing countries explains the hostility to universal labor standards. The concern is not without some justification since labor groups, such as textiles workers in the US, have, in the past, successfully obtained protection from cheap imports.

One source of the variance in labor standards is the restriction on labor mobility across borders. In a global era, where the flow of capital, merchandise and technology is relatively unrestricted, there remain extensive restrictions on international labor movements. Without such restrictions, labor standards would inevitably move towards some convergence, either up or down, as labor migrated from areas of poor conditions to where work conditions were superior. However, even in the absence of labor mobility, the labor market has been effectively globalized as a result of intensifying economic exchange. Bloom and Brender asked us to, "Consider, for example, a British entrepreneur who hires an Italian company to design a new line of clothing, then has those designs sent for production in southern China, and has a shipping company in Hong Kong send the finished product for sale in the United States. Without the entrepreneur or any worker having to cross a national border, this example involves the labour services of workers in five countries being exchanged."[1]

One concern is that despite restrictions on labor mobility, effective globalization of labor markets can, according to proponents of labor standards, lead to a decline in labor standards globally as capital migrates from high labor cost countries to low cost countries, where labor standards are either rudimentary or where the enforcement of it is lax. The greater the differential in labor standards and costs, the greater the temptation for firms to shift capital to exploit those conditions. This is not to suggest that investment decisions are based on labor cost considerations alone but they are one important factor in the decision matrix of foreign investors. Capital flight may put pressure on wages and labor conditions in the developed countries and produce a movement toward convergence but at the lower end of the spectrum. The "race to the bottom" might accelerate if governments in developed countries try to attract and retain capital investments by weakening labor standards. In the context of a heightened quest for trade competitiveness, there is concern that low standards in developing countries inevitably put pressure on wages, social benefits, and labor standards in developed countries. Ray Marshall, a former US Secretary of Labor, pointed to census data that suggested that, in the United States, the median hourly wage of men was 14 percent less in 1989 than it was in 1979. Income decline was not across the board but that only highlighted the growing wage inequality which, if left unchecked, could potentially provoke domestic social and political problems.[2]

One option for the West would be to ameliorate wage-based disadvantages by increasing labor productivity. Decline in wages and labor standards, and income inequality can be averted with increase in labor productivity but this is not easily achieved given adversarial labor-management relations. If a race to the bottom is a distinct possibility and increased productivity difficult to achieve, then the available options are to secure universal acceptance and compliance with a "minimum package of labor standards,"[3] and "upward harmonization"[4] of transnational labor standards.

A North-South Divide on Labor Standards

The debate on labor standards can not be neatly, or exclusively, segmented along the North-South axis but, in general, western governments have adopted a position of advocacy and the developing countries that of resistance. The advocates of labor standards, including the United States, maintain that the World Trade Organisation should be actively involved in the development of international labor standards and empowered to oversee its application under threats of sanctions. Admittedly, not all western countries accept and support the need for uniform standards. Proponents of linking labor standards to trade believe that this could help raise standards in developing countries. Labor unions in developed countries may regard such moves as a way of demonstrating their concern for working conditions in poorer countries and as a way of expressing solidarity with workers in those countries. There is, according to Torres, evidence to support this proposition based on past experience with the American Generalised System of Preferences (GSP). The GSP was introduced by developed countries to provide easy market access to exports from developing countries, at low or zero tariffs, to assist with their development objectives. The American scheme included a social provision which favored those developing countries which respected minimum labor standards. According to Torres, an analysis of the American "... GSP suggests that the system has played a part in improving core labour standards in some countries."[5] The GSP is not part of the GATT system and each country has its own GSP program but the demand now is to include respect for labor standards as part of the WTO system.

The United States placed the issue of labor standards on the agenda of world trade at the Marrakesh Ministerial Meeting which concluded the Uruguay Round negotiations. The US however is not a new convert to labor standards nor is the idea of linking labor standards to trade a recent phenomenon. The issue of labor standards has been debated since the nineteenth century and gained prominence especially in times of high levels of international trade, or interdependence. For example, the establishment of the International Labor Organization (ILO) in 1919 followed "... a hundred years of proposals and conferences,"[6] and came at the end of a period of "rapid growth of international trade and the associated demand for international labour standards."[7] The mandate of the ILO is to lead to improved labor standards among member countries. The American commitment to improved standards was reiterated by President Roosevelt in 1937 when he argued that "Goods produced under conditions which do not meet a rudimentary standard of decency should be regarded as contraband and ought not to be allowed to pollute the channels of interstate commerce."[8] In the GATT, however, only one specific labor standard was included: to forbid the export of goods produced with prison labor.

The American position on labor standards has been supported by some European countries but these countries have, thus far, failed to place the issue firmly on the WTO agenda by leading to the establishment of either a working party or a committee. The lack of progress can be

attributed to a lack of consensus on how to proceed with establishment of labor standards and whether this is at all desirable. As mentioned,
universal minimum labor standards have been rejected by developing
countries and also by many western multinational corporations,[9] which
suspect that their operations in developing countries could be adversely
affected by universal standards. However, it is the activities of some
prominent multinational corporations that have added urgency to the
entire debate on labor standards. MNCs have been criticised for exploiting
cheap labor in developing countries to produce goods for markets in
developed countries. Here, western motives may not simply be to improve
working conditions in developing countries but include also a degree of
self interest. Indeed, by most accounts, multinational corporations may be
using cheap labor but they also tend to pay their workers more than local
corporations in the host economies. US pressure for global labor standards
stems partly from a concern that multinational corporations, by relocating
their production to low wage countries, were displacing workers and
creating unemployment in developed countries.

The contemporary push for universal standards also stems from a
concern that in a global economy without universal standards, labor
conditions everywhere will be whittled away as multinational corporations
relocate productive activities to low cost areas. The resulting army of the
unemployed could then be expected to put pressure on existing labor
conditions in developed countries and initiate a race to the bottom. Labor
will be the ultimate loser if, in the process, hard won labor conditions are
placed in jeopardy. Understandably therefore, labor unions in the West
have been vocal in demanding the adoption of universal standards in order
to protect work conditions for workers. For example, the "International
Confederation of Free Trade Unions (ICFTU), and notably one of its
members, the International Metalworkers Federation (IMF), which
represents 165 engineering and metalworking trade unions in 70 countries
worldwide, have spearheaded a campaign to link trade preference
agreements to the maintenance of labour standards."[10] Organised labor
may be concerned about losing its gains but governments in many western
countries were, in the 1980s and 1990s, engaged precisely in a campaign
to curtail the rights and privileges of labor groups.

The western apprehension that rising unemployment and wage inequality are results of trade with developing countries is disputed, however, by Eddie Lee. He points out that the price in the United States of labor intensive manufactured goods has risen compared to skill-intensive ones and that this is contrary to what should obtain if trade with developing countries is the cause of inequality in the West. He wrote that, "It is thus unlikely that trade with low-wage countries has been a major cause of either the relative fall in the demand for unskilled labour or the rise in wage inequality."[11]

Supporters of international labor standards acknowledge the diverse motives of states, including expressions of solidarity with workers in developing countries, achieving minimum human rights, and protecting domestic working conditions. There may even be a more base protectionist motive underpinning the demand for labor standards, especially from those sectors of the economy that are unable to compete with developing countries' exports. However, regardless of the motives, Langille says that the message of improved labor standards ought to be universally welcomed, that we should not ignore the message because of the messenger. The demands, he argues, are for ethical standards that should apply everywhere. According to Langille, "... it is necessary to focus on the validity of the arguments, not the motivations of those advancing them."[12] The difficulty, however, is that the validity of the argument for international standards is not beyond question.

Developing countries argue that labor standards, like human rights, are the products of specific historical and cultural experiences and western demands are a veiled attempt to export their notions of appropriate labor standards to other countries. Westerns demands are based on a supposition that labor standards are universal values and should be upheld everywhere. In contrast to this universalist liberal approach, critics and communitarians maintain that value systems are a derivative of each community's social and cultural heritage and cannot be universalized. This disagreement is reminiscent of the contemporary debate between proponents of liberal democracy on the one hand, and advocates of "Asian democracy" on the other. Southeast Asian advocates of Asian democracy, where the individual is subordinate to the group and where individual rights take second place to societal rights and privileges, insist that it is inappropriate for western governments to push liberal democracy on these countries because liberalism is not a part of their cultural tradition. Westerners, however, reject these arguments as a self-serving defence of the privileges enjoyed by the ruling authoritarian regimes in several of these countries.

Even if there is no clear resolution of the communitarian and liberal approaches, developing countries are on firmer grounds when they reject uniform and minimum standards as a surreptitious attempt to protect western markets and to exclude cheap exports from developing countries.[13] They maintain that western demands amount to denying developing countries their legitimate international trade advantage in labor intensive manufacturing. Having obtained significant concessions from developed countries in the Uruguay Round of trade negotiations, developing countries fear that gains, in textiles for example, could be undermined through the imposition of labor standards and the threat of trade sanctions. The fears are not entirely unwarranted as it is entirely reasonable to assume that the withdrawal of MFA quotas on LDC export of textiles will impose severe pain on textile industries in the western countries.

Relatedly, the rejection of universal, and higher, labor standards is also premised on the assumption that high standards would jeopardise trade expansion and their developmental objectives by undermining their comparative advantage. Developing countries characterize the western push as a way of denying developing countries export opportunity to achieve economic development. They claim that the West is interested primarily in obstructing developing country exports. From their perspective, the western countries should provide better market access rather than threaten to restrict access on grounds of poor labor standards. And they might point to the experiences of the East Asian Newly Industrialising Countries that have achieved remarkable economic development, and in the process improved labor standards, through a policy of export-oriented industrialization. Developing countries are wary also of the perceived hypocrisy whereby having restructured their economy, under

IMF and World Bank guidance and encouragement, to become more internationally competitive and outward looking, they are now being threatened with potentially reduced market access.

That would be the case if higher standards became a negative influence on capital inflows and reduced the levels of investment in productive activities. Many developing countries have relatively low savings rate and foreign capital inflow is an important supplement to available domestic resources for investment purposes. If higher labor standards reduced that inflow of capital, it would have the inevitable effect of dampening their growth prospects. There have also been arguments that low standards attract foreign capital because it enhances managerial autonomy and guarantees labor peace and stability. These arguments are also often made by governments in developing countries as reasons why they cannot afford higher standards. However, Linda Lim found that, at least in the case of Singapore, growth and export competitiveness were not significantly explained by restrictions on labor and that controls on labor served a political rather than an economic function. Controls on labor were a part of an overall government policy to limit political freedoms and democratic participation. She argued that labor controls are not necessary either for industrial peace or for attracting foreign capital.[14]

In addition, developing countries have argued that labor standards should be a matter for the International Labor Organization (ILO) to deliberate rather than be brought under the purview of the World Trade Organi-zation, where it would be easy to link the social clause to trade benefits. Further, they argue that if the West wanted to use trade to promote social justice in developing countries, they should liberalize trade rather than threaten trade sanctions, because trade can be the engine of growth and improved welfare for all.

Apart from the appropriateness of labor standards, developing coun-tries also point to the difficulty of enforcing standards given the nature of standards and the institutional capacities of governments. Standards are often devised for factory type production organizations but actual pro-duction may take place in unorganized structures or on a self-employed basis.[15] Enforcement of standards in such diverse production processes can be difficult and developing countries also point out that institutional capacities of government are inadequate to police and enforce standards. Institutional weakness may be one reason why developing countries have been relatively disinterested in accepting the various ILO conventions on labor standards.

As a subtext to the above, it might be mentioned, as well, that the capacity of developing countries to conform with existing ILO conventions have been eroded by the structural adjustment requirements imposed by the IMF and the World Bank following the debt crises. Structural adjustment programs have typically included public sector cutbacks resulting in increased unemployment and a worsening of labor conditions, even in those instances where developing countries have ratified ILO conventions. Roger Plant argued that the early structural adjustment programs of the World Bank were also based on a fundamental theoretical hostility to labor standards as unnecessary interference with market principles. He wrote that, "The theoretical assault on labour standards as 'distortions' to the market can find expression in overall adjustment policies, and in some cases in specific structural adjustment programmes. Some criticisms are that excessive regulations ... can raise labour costs ... restrictions on hiring and firing can impede economic restructuring ... and minimum wage-fixing machinery can impede macro-economic stabilisation, facilitating an inflationary spiral."[16] If early structural adjustment programs were antithetical to high labor standards, the World Bank and the IMF, in the 1990s, appeared more prepared to accept the importance of state regulatory intervention in facilitating economic growth and it would be inappropriate to say that the hostility to labor standards had remained high. Nonetheless, it must be acknowledged that the capacity of developing countries to fulfil the intent of ILO Conventions was severely impaired during the 1980s.

However, if labor standards are eventually introduced the "institutional capacity" escape route may only be available to the least developed countries. The Marrakesh Agreement of 1994 which established the WTO stipulated that least developed countries, as recognized by the United Nations will "only be required to undertake commitments and concessions to the extent consistent with their individual development, financial and trade needs or their administrative and institutional capabilities" (Article 11, para 2).

Core Labor Standards

One of the main shortcomings of the debate on labor standards has been the difficulty in identifying which standards deserve inclusion. To be meaningful, the standards have to modify behaviour, otherwise it will be an exercise in futility. But because a basic agreement on the desirability of labor standards and linkage to trade is missing, there has been no collective effort to try and identify some of the possible standards.

To clarify the debate about labor standards and trade, the OECD has tried to identify core labor standards that presumably would be acceptable to all countries. These include

1. the elimination of exploitative child labor;
2. the abolition of forced labor;
3. nondiscrimination in employment; and
4. freedom of association and collective bargaining.[17]

These core rights are not inconsistent with Charter of the United Nations or the Universal Declaration of Human Rights but not all countries abide by all of the identified core rights. Children, for example, continue to work in hazardous factory jobs or in the mining industry or in industries such as carpet making. Most countries have no difficulty in supporting the principle of eliminating child labor but according to ILO estimates, there are 120 million children engaged in gainful commercial work.[18] Many developing and emerging economies have also not found it acceptable to them to grant workers the right to free association and collective bargaining. Most importantly, the core rights identified by the OECD are process rights rather than substantive outcome, on the presumption that if workers acquire, for example, the right to collective bargaining they will be able to achieve suitable outcomes in wages and other conditions of employment.[19] In the end, therefore, even if the core demands are process conditions, the expectation must be that through, for example, the right to collective bargaining, labor cost in developing countries will rise and that, consequently, wage differentials will be reduced to deny developing countries a comparative advantage in labor intensive production. This may not necessarily be the case if employers succeed in trading-off higher labor standards for lower wages. But where labor costs are already low, there is a limit to further reductions. Without a rise in wages in developing countries, standards will offer no relief to developed countries and this must be the expected outcome of universal standards.

The question remains whether trade policy should be used to enhance social justice in an intrusive manner. From an economic point of view, sub-standard labor conditions in developing countries are not a product of deliberate policy choice but a result of the overall context of poverty and backwardness. Developing countries do not have inferior standards in order to gain an unfair trade advantage and to single out labor standards as requiring elevation might be inappropriate. It could be argued that if the West was concerned, it should be concerned with poverty alleviation in general. Andre Sapir argued that if social clauses were introduced in trade agreements and used to deny trade opportunities, it would exacerbate poverty rather than benefit the poor.[20] Similarly, Chris Milner emphatically asserts that a social clause in trade agreements is undesirable because it would only discipline conditions in traded goods sectors and because it would be much better to try and improve labor standards through improved (rather than restricted) trade access and foreign aid.[21]

An Evaluation

As noted above, the issue of formulating international labor standards has created a sharp divide between the developed and developing countries.

There are no easy solutions to the problems and recognising the intractable nature of the dispute, the Director General of the ILO proposed that instead of taking the route of codifying universal labor standards in legalistic terms, a better way might be to institute a system of dispute resolution using agencies like the ILO. The ILO has in fact been involved in dispute resolution between countries, as between France and Panama, and according to Servais, such an approach "would allow for flexibility and pragmatism in seeking solutions to these thorny problems."[22] However, while ILO involvement might be useful in disputes involving small countries or middle ranking countries, disputes involving large countries, like the US and another ILO member country, would be extremely difficult to resolve. The same, of course, holds true for the WTO dispute resolution mechanism and, indeed, during the 1995 US–Japan auto dispute the Director General of the WTO, Renato Ruggiero, urged the two countries to resolve their difficulties bilaterally rather than through the WTO. Another problem with entrusting ILO with dispute resolution is that it is a very weak international institution. Its conventions, which might become guidelines for dispute resolution have a poor record of ratification by member countries. Since its establishment, for example, the ILO has passed more than 170 conventions but many countries have only adopted a limited few. The US, as of 1994, had accepted less than two dozen ILO conventions.[23]

Developing countries insist that their labor standards are appropriate to existing social conditions and that any attempt to impose higher standards would only create domestic social dislocations. It cannot be denied that labor conditions were tightly regulated by governments in the Asian newly industrializing countries, such as South Korea, Taiwan and Singapore, and that their economic miracle provided for a relatively equitable economic growth. In these societies, an organised and independent labor movement did not develop until much later but labor conditions did improve progressively. Countries at a lower level of development argue that they, too must be permitted to regulate labor conditions in order to generate growth.

Nonetheless, a social clause need not be seen only as a brake on development. Higher labor standards can also be a source of opportunity and dynamism. Even if neoclassical economic theory is less convinced of the merits of regulation, according to neo-institutional economics labor standards could become a catalyst for progress and development. In this alternative perspective, "... insufficient labor standards regulation in the international economy will lock some firms and countries into low-productivity production methods that not only deprive workers of basic rights but also produce poor economic outcomes."[24]

Here the example of the East Asian economy is worth keeping in mind. The East Asian economies progressively moved up the technology spectrum as they became proficient in low level manufacturing and as their low-cost labor intensive product exports increasingly came up against protectionist restrictions in developed countries. While such protectionism was undesirable, it at least provided opportunities to progressively do more value adding to cross the bar. It is also unlikely that labor regulations will erode the trade competitiveness of any single developing country, provided that the standards are universally applicable. External pressure impeding the retention of existing competitive advantage can become a catalyst for further economic development. When Singapore, for example, was no longer able to compete internationally with low cost labor intensive manufacturing, "the government made extensive investment to upgrade Singapore's technology and services to attract higher, value-added activities."[25]

If developing countries do exploit labor standards to move up the technology ladder, it can be expected to create some domestic dislocation. Given their comparative advantage in labor intensive manufacturing, given a large pool of cheap and abundant labor force, they can expect an immediate worsening of unemployment unless there is compensating growth in the other trade sectors of the economy. For off-setting increase in the growth sectors they will require open trade opportunities rather than sanctions of the threats of sanctions. Without that assistance to restructuring, developing countries will find it hard to vacate labor intensive manufacturing. At the same time, this will also require restructuring in developed countries. Therefore, restructuring is imperative in both developed and developing countries if there is to be much headway in the universal acceptance of international labor standards.

What the developing countries should focus on, instead, is to ensure that a social clause does not become a pretext for protectionism. It might be worthwhile, therefore, to introduce standards that do not attract trade sanctions for noncompliance. That linkage, if necessary, could be left for a later stage. If a two-stage process is what may work, we have to question whether efforts are at all meaningful since many of the standards that might constitute a set of minimum universal standards are already included in the ILO conventions and recommendations. The problem is not that standards do not exist but that many of these have not been ratified by the member countries. Of the 174 ILO conventions, only 11 have been ratified by more than half of ILO members. The US, despite championing labor rights has only ratified 11 conventions.[26] This does not mean that the US is guilty of breach, but simply that it needs to lead by example and demonstration.

The developing countries, too, have been delinquent in ratifying ILO conventions. This may be because they were not actively involved in the formulation of these conventions and if that has indeed held back the ratification process, then, one option would be to reopen up the convention to input from developing countries in order to give them a stake in the system. Alternatively, it may be better to restart the process in a different forum, such as the WTO, to rejuvenate the issue of standards.

Essentially, it is unreasonable to try and impose a one-dimensional resolution to the complex problem of labor standards. As mentioned at the outset, there are several options available to developed countries in deal with the trade competitiveness of LDC, such as withdrawal from affected industries, structural adjustment and a race to the bottom. Labor standards are an alternative to those possible policy responses but a meaningful solution would incorporate elements of each of these, in particular the importance of industrial restructuring in both developed and developing countries.

References

1. Cited in Lee, E., "Globalization and Employment: Is Anxiety Justified?" *International Labour Review*, 1996, p. 491.
2. Marshall, R., "The Importance of International Labour Standards in a More Competitive Global Economy," in Sengenberger, W. and Duncan Campbell (eds.), *International Labour Standards and Economic Interdependence*, International Institute for Labour Studies, Geneva, 1994, p. 67.
3. Emmerij, L., "Contemporary Challenges for Labour Standards Resulting from Globalization," in Sengenberger, W. and Duncan Campbell (eds.), *International Labour Standards and Economic Interdependence*, International Institute for Labour Studies, Geneva, 1994, p. 322.

4. Barenberg, M., "Law and Labor in the New Global Economy: Through the Lens of United States Federalism," *Columbia Journal of Transnational Law*, Vol. 33, No. 3, 1995, p. 449.
5. Torres, R., "Labour Standards and Trade," *The OECD Observer*, No. 202, October–November 1996, p. 12.
6. Hansson, G., *Social Clauses and International Trade: An Economic Analysis of Labour Standards in Trade Policy*, Croom Helm, London and Canberra, 1983, p. 182.
7. Milner, C., " 'New Standards Issue' and the WTO," *Australian Economic Review*, Vol. 30, No. 1, March 1997, p. 91.
8. Collingsworth, T., J. William Goold and Pharis J. Harvey, "Time for a Global New Deal," *Foreign Affairs*, Vol. 73, No. 1, January/February 1994, p. 10.
9. Collingsworth, T., J. William Goold and Pharis J. Harvey, "Time for a Global New Deal, *"Foreign Affairs*, Vol. 73, No. 1, January/February 1994, p. 9.
10. Sengenberger, W., "Restructuring at the Global Level: The Role of International Labour Standards," in Sengenberger, W. and Duncan Campbell (eds.), *Creating Economic Opportunities: The Role of Labour Standards in Industrial Restructuring*, International Institute for Labour Studies, Geneva, 1994, p. 410.
11. Lee, E., "Globalization and Employment: Is Anxiety Justified?" *International Labour Review*, 1996, p. 487.
12. Langille, Brian A., "Eight Ways to Think about International Labour Standards," *Journal of World Trade*, Vol. 31, No. 4, August 1997, p. 35.
13. See Langille, Brian A., "Eight Ways to Think about International Labour Standards," *Journal of World Trade*, Vol. 31, No. 4, August 1997, p. 31. However, according to Louis Emmerij, optimists might argue that inclusion of labor standards might actually halt the growth in protectionism by removing the perception of unfair trade practices. See, Emmerij, L., "Contemporary Challenges for Labour Standards Resulting from Globalization," in Sengenberger, W. and Duncan Campbell (eds.), *International Labour Standards and Economic Interdependence*, International Institute for Labour Studies, Geneva, 1994, p. 323.

14. Lim, Linda Y. C., "Singapore," in Herzenberg, S. and Jorge F. Perez-Lopez (eds.), *Labor Standards and Development in the Global Economy*, US Department of Labor, Bureau of International Labor Affairs, Washington, 1990. pp. 88–89.

15. See Papola, T. S., "International Labour Standards and Developing Countries," in Sengenberger, W. and Duncan Campbell (eds.), *International Labour Standards and Economic Interdependence*, International Institute for Labour Studies, Geneva, 1994, pp. 180–181.

16. Plant, R., *Labour Standards and Structural Adjustment*, International Labour Office, Geneva, 1994, pp. 192–193.

17. Torres, R., "Labour Standards and Trade," *The OECD Observer*, No. 202, October–November 1996, p. 10.

18. Sengenberger, W., "Restructuring at the Global Level: The Role of International Labour Standards," in Sengenberger, W. and Duncan Campbell (eds.), *Creating Economic Opportunities: The Role of Labour Standards in Industrial Restructuring*, International Institute for Labour Studies, Geneva, 1994, p. 410.

19. Langille, Brian A., "Eight Ways to Think about International Labour Standards," *Journal of World Trade*, Vol. 31, No. 4, August 1997, p. 32.

20. Sapir, A., "The Interaction Between Labour Standards and International Trade Policy," *The World Economy*, Vol. 18, No. 6, November 1995, p. 802.

21. Milner, C., " 'New Standards Issues' and the WTO," *The Australian Economic Review*, Vol. 30, No. 1, March 1997, pp. 91–92.

22. Servais, J.-M., "The Social Clause in Trade Agreements: Wishful Thinking or an Instrument of Social Progress?" *International Labour Review*, Vol. 128, No. 4, 1989, p. 430.

23. Hoekman, B. and Michel Kostecki, *The Political Economy of the World Trading System: From GATT to WTO*, Oxford University Press, Oxford, 1995, p. 263. ILO conventions, once they are signed and ratified, have the same authority and status as international treaties.

24. Herzenberg, S. A., Jorge F. Perez-Lopez and Stuart K. Tucker, "Labor Standards and Development in the Global Economy," in Stephen A. Herzenberg and Jorge F. Perez-Lopez (eds.), *Labor Standards and*

Development in the Global Economy, US Department of Labor, Bureau of International Labor Affairs, Washington, 1990, p. 4.

25. Jones, G., *The Evolution of International Business: An Introduction*, Routledge, London and New York, 1996, p. 303.

26. Myrdal, H.-G., "The ILO in the Cross-Fire: Would it Survive the Social Clause?" in Sengenberger, W. and Duncan Campbell (eds.), *International Labour Standards and Economic Interdependence*, International Institute for Labour Studies, Geneva, 1994, p. 342.

Chapter Ten

CONCLUSION

The post-war structure of international political economy was designed to prevent any resurgence of economic nationalism and destructive competitiveness. It represented a recognition of the futility of pre-war "beggar-thy-neighbor" economic policies, which instead of redistributing benefits as intended, resulted only in global depression. Under American leadership, regimes in international trade, finance, and monetary relations injected stability and order in international economic relations and ushered in a movement towards greater liberalization and openness. Regimes include rules and norms, which proscribe and prescribe particular behavioral alternatives, with the objectives of reducing transaction costs and enhancing liberal practices. The expectation that states would adhere to established rules was only ever partially fulfilled.

The postwar regimes in international economic relations were not perfect but they did initiate progressive liberalization and openness. By the 1970s, they had increased interdependence among countries and, coupled with technological advances and improved communications, laid the basis for economic globalization.

Globalization has tremendous potential for enhancing economic prosperity but also the potential or magnifying specific structural weaknesses to produce economic crises. The potential benefits of globalization can only be realized when states develop institutional structures that are consistent with the demands of a global economy. Not everyone, however, is convinced that globalization is a desirable process and critics have been most vocal in highlighting the threat to state sovereignty and autonomy. One way to rebalance the anomaly between a global economy and national polities would be to re-regulate aspects of the national economy but this is unlikely to be a satisfactory solution.

Assuming, that there is no immediate solution to the juxtaposition of economic globalization and political segmentation, the efficiency of a global economy requires a harmonization of the heterogenous regulatory structures across countries.

Harmonization of rules in a global economy is complex. While space has shrunk, interests remain diverse. It is true that some of the extreme divisions that characterized the international political economy in the 1970s — such as the New International Economic Order and views on foreign investment — have diminished, there is still no consensus on rule making for the global economy. There are also many more independent actors, states and non-governmental organizations, that have to be persuaded. The task of formulating rules in the early post-war period was not easy but it is going to be equally, if not more, difficult in the contemporary period, as evidenced by the failed negotiations on foreign investments. Difficulties in negotiating agreements may also be due to the "diminished giant" syndrome even if we agree that the United States has not lost its hegemonic position in the international system.

In dealing with the complex issues, one option for rule makers is to arbitrarily restrict the number of players in the hope of making rules that conform to high standards and which actually constrain state behavior. This was the approach taken in negotiating rules relating to foreign investments. The developed countries confined negotiations on the Multilateral Agreement on Investments to the OECD countries, consisting of advanced industrial economies. Excluded from the negotiating process were developing countries and multinational corporations but the criticisms that was raised related fundamentally to the charge that the developed countries were actually acting as agents of the multinational corporations, to the detriment of national sovereignty. Criticisms within the developed countries aborted the negotiations, and the issue of foreign investment rules has been held over to the next round of WTO trade negotiations.

The two main rules of the post-war liberal trade regime were most favored nation and national treatment. States were expected to govern their national economies in ways consistent with these rules. Globalization of business activities, however, has thrust forward additional considerations. With businesses investing in third countries not only to meet local demand, but as part of a global production network, the importance of uniform regulatory standards has become an important issue. Apart from the broad macro rules of GATT/WTO mentioned above, an efficient global economy demands regulations also on various other aspects of the production process, such as in labor market regulations and property rights. Alberto Tita observes that while there has been an increase in the network of relations internationally this, "... has not been accompanied by a corresponding increase in the global norms which should govern this phenomenon."[1] There exists a body of international law but these apply essentially to relations between states, whereas one consequence of globalization has been to expand the role of the private sector in deepening the networks of relations.

Finally, in terms of devising trade norms for the era of economic globalization, I will briefly consider the two issues of why we need new trade rules and the process of rule making. The first issue of need can be explained in terms of transaction costs. As mentioned in Chapter two, transaction costs were important in instigating regime creation and, similarly, transaction costs associated with globalized production within a segmented political/regulatory structures requires attempts at harmonization and uniformity of regulations. The transaction costs of complying with different regulatory environments in a single production process, as happens when production is globalized, is high and a source of inefficiency. Moreover, a multiplicity of regulatory environments may also mean that over time, global corporations will tend to transfer their activities to countries where the costs of regulatory compliance are least onerous. This possibility is, understandably, of some concern to countries with stringent regulations on, for example, labor standards, environmental protection etc. In order to minimize transaction costs, the rules of trade will have to adjust to the new circumstances.

Devising appropriate rules will be contentious but the process may be equally problematic. Conflicts are likely, not only between developed and developing economies, but also within and between developed countries. Thus, for example, developing countries denounced American plans to impose its labor standards on other countries or risk losing trade privileges, and Japan criticized the US for its attempts to restructure traditional societal values in Japan which the US identified as obstacles to doing business in Japan. The difficulties that states confront in achieving regulatory harmony do not diminish the responsibility for attempting this.

One extreme in the range of options concerning harmonization of regulatory norms is unilateralism. However, attempts to globalize domestic legislation, rules, and norms are unlikely to be very productive. This was the case, in mid-1996, when the United States decided to globalize its new anti-terrorism law proscribing substantive investment in "rogue states," like Iran and Libya, by private corporations. The passage of this legislation prompted immediate protest from other countries and the European Union, because the law infringed their own sovereignty. The EU warned the US that it would defend its rights and interests.

Another suggestion for regulatory harmonization is to borrow from models based on federal systems. Mark Barenberg suggested that in harmonizing norms within a global economy, the US system offered six different models below that might be considered.[2]

1. the first model is that of multistate uniformity and one where federal legislation preempts state legislation;
2. the second model is one of imposing minimum global standards but which still allow individual states to introduce higher standards;
3. a third model is one where the federal government offers financial incentives for heightened state standards;
4. the fourth model is that of state regulatory primacy, a situation exemplified by complete nonintervention by the federal government;
5. the fifth model is that of cooperative agreement among groups of states, such as regional economic development programs; and
6. the final model is one that allows states the rights to unilateral "tit for tat" strategies.

The federal approach is not entirely appropriate to the reality of globalization. As mentioned in Chapter one, globalization has created, or is in the process of creating, a unified economic structure alongside segmented political authority structures. This is more appropriately termed a confederal system. The absence of a supranational legal authority means that models derived from federal state structures provide only a rough guide to the response patterns.

In a confederated global political economy, a consultative and negotiated approach to rule making might be more applicable. Unilateralism, of course, is unproductive unless the real intent is to identity a problem area and force other countries to accept a specific approach. This may have been one consideration behind the US anti-terrorism legislation. The EU, while condemning the US legislation also stated that "it was ready to co-operate at a multilateral level to combat terrorist activity in all its forms and wherever its source."[3] US State Department officials expressed the hope that the disagreement might be resolved through quiet diplomacy. This may, in the end, produce regulatory harmony, but the unilateral approach can be counter-productive if it is relied upon excessively.

Ideally, as indicated above, the process should be consultative even if a consultative process still produces outcomes that favor particular interests of some countries. The history of multilateral negotiations provides many examples of dominance and the playing field of political power is rarely level. In early post-war negotiations on trade and monetary liberalization, for example, outcomes favored the United States but the process of negotiation and consultation did give legitimacy to those outcomes. As a general principle, in a confederated global political economy, harmonization will have to rise up from below rather than imposed from above. The principle of "bottom up" regulation and an inclusionary approach, even if time-consuming, holds the greatest promise of minimizing acrimony as states search for new rules for a global economy. In facilitating this, the WTO provides a ready forum for a global consensus to emerge.

The challenge for the future is to strike a balance between standards that appeal to the lowest common denominator and between standards that introduce real and meaningful constraints on state behavior. It is easy to achieve harmonization on the principle of the lowest common denominator but this may result in standards that are so loose as to be meaningless. On the other hand, in foreign investment, the OECD countries deliberately opted for a route of regulatory harmony in investments based on the highest and strictest standards possible to ensure that the new rules were "meaningful" in a real sense. This approach, however, excluded a majority of the countries and that, in itself, may undermine attempts at creating global treaties. The similarity here is with regionalism after the Second World War. Even though regionalism was at odds with multilateralism, they were countenanced in the expectation that these would progressively become global organizations but more than 50 years later, regional bodies are far from ushering in global free trade.

References

1. Tita, A., "A Challenge for the World Trade Organization: Toward a True Transnational Law," *Journal of World trade*, Vol. 29, No. 3, June 1995, p. 83.
2. Barenberg, M., "Law and Labor in the New Global Economy: Through the Lens of United States Federalism," *Columbia Journal of Transnational Law*, Vol. 33, No. 3, 1995, pp. 451–453.
3. *The Weekend Australian*, 10–11 August 1996, p. 15.

Bibliography

Books and Monographs

Abegglen, J. C. and George Stalk, Jr., *Kaisha: The Japanese Corporation* (Charles E. Tuttle, Tokyo, 1988).

Agmon, T., Robert Hawkins and Richard M. Levich (eds.), *The Future of International Monetary System* (Lexington Books, DC Heath and Co., Lexington, 1984).

Aslund, A. (ed.), *The Post-Soviet Economy: Soviet and Western Perspectives* (Pinter, London, 1992).

Axelrod, R., *The Evolution of Cooperation* (Penguin Books, New York, 1984).

Baldwin, R. E., *Trade Policy in a Changing World Economy* (Harvester-Wheatsheaf, London, 1988).

Banerjee, B. *et al.*, *Road Maps of the Transition: The Baltics, the Czech Republic, Hungary and Russia*, IMF Occasional Paper No. 127 (Washington, DC, September 1995).

Bartlett, C. J. (ed.), *Britain Pre-Eminent: Studies of British Influence in the Nineteenth Century* (Macmillan, London, 1969).

Barnet, Richard J. and Ronald E. Muller, *Global Reach: The Power of the Multinational Corporations* (Jonathan Cape, London, 1975).

Bergsten, C. Fred and Marcus Noland (eds.), *Pacific Dynamism and the International Economic System* (Institute for International Economics, Washington, DC, 1993).

Bhagwati, J. and Hugh T. Patrick (eds.), *Aggressive Unilateralism: America's 301 Trade Policy and the World Trading System* (University of Michigan Press, Ann Arbor, 1990).

Blackhurst, R. and Jan Tumlir, *Trade Relations Under Unfair Exchange Rates*, GATT Studies in International Trade, No. 8 (Geneva, 1980). Block, F. L., *The Origins of International Economic Disorder: A Study of United States International Monetary Policy from World War II to the Present* (University of California Press, Berkeley and Los Angeles, 1977).

Boyer, R. and Daniel Drache (eds.), *States Against Markets: The Limits of Globalization* (Routledge, London, and New York, 1996).

Brock, W. E. and Robert D. Hormats (eds.), *The Global Economy: America's Role in the Decade Ahead* (W. W. Norton, New York, 1990).

Chan, S. (ed.), *Foreign Direct Investment in a Changing Global Political Economy* (Macmillan, Houndmills, 1995).

Chechile, Richard A. and Susan Carlisle (eds.), *Environmental Decision Making: A Multidisciplinary Approach* (Van Nostrad Reinhold, New York, 1991).

Choucri, N. (ed.), *Global Accord: Environmental Challenges and International Responses* (MIT Press, Cambridge, Massachusetts, 1993).

Cipolla, C. M. (ed.), *The Fontana Economic History of Europe: The Sixteenth and Seventeenth Centuries* (Collins/Fontana, Glasgow, 1974).

Cline, William R., *Debt and the Stability of the World Economy* (Institute for International Economics, Washington, DC, September 1993).

Conybeare, J. A. C., *Trade Wars: The Theory and Practice of International Commercial Rivalry* (Columbia University Press, New York, 1987).

Cooper, R. N., Peter Kenen *et al.*, *The International Monetary System Under Flexible Exchange Rates: Global, Regional and National* (Ballinger, Cambridge, 1982).

Corbridge, S., Ron Martin and Nigel Thrift (eds.), *Money, Power and Space* (Blackwell, Oxford, 1994).

Corden, W. M., *Economic Policy, Exchange Rates, and the International System* (Oxford University Press, Oxford, 1994).

Dam, Kenneth W., *The Rules of the Game: Reform and Evolution in the International Monetary System* (University of Chicago Press, Chicago and London, 1982).

Dauvergne, P., *Shadows in the Forest: Japan and the Politics of Timber in Southeast Asia* (MIT Press, Cambridge, Massachusetts, 1997).

De Cecco, M., *The International Gold Standard: Money and Empire* (Pinter, London, 1984).

De la Motha, J. and Gilles Paquet (eds.), *Evolutionary Economics and the New International Political Economy* (Pinter, 1996).

De Vries, M. G., *The IMF in a Changing World, 1945–1995* (International Monetary Fund, Washington, DC, 1986).

Destler, I. M., Haruhiro Fukui and Hideo Sato, *The Textile Wrangle: Conflict in Japan–America Relations, 1969–1971* (Cornell University Press, Ithaca, 1979).

Dieren, Wouter van (ed.), *Taking Nature Into Account: A Report to the Club of Rome* (Springer-Verlag, New York, 1995).

Dornbusch, R. and Stanley Fischer, *Macroeconomics*, 3rd ed. (McGraw-Hill, Singapore, 1985).

Drummond, I. M., *The Gold Standards and International Monetary System 1900–1939* (Macmillan, Basingstoke, 1987).

Dunkley, G., *The Free Trade Adventure: The Uruguay Round and Globalism — A Critique* (Melbourne University Press, Carlton, Victoria, 1997).

The East Asian Economic Miracle: Economic Growth and Public Policy, A World Bank Policy Research Report (Oxford University Press, New York, 1993).

Eichengreen, B., *Elusive Stability: Essays in the History of International Finance, 1919–1939* (Cambridge University Press, Cambridge, 1990).

Feldstein, M. (ed.), *International Economic Cooperation* (University of Chicago Press, Chicago, 1988).

Fellner, W., *Emergence and Content of Modern Economic Analysis* (McGraw-Hill, New York, 1960).

Funabashi, J., *Managing the Dollar: From the Plaza to the Louvre*, 2nd ed. (Institute for International Economics, Washington, DC, 1989).

Furubotn, E. G. and Rudolf Richter (eds.), *The New International Economics* (J. C. B. Mohr, Tubingen, 1991).

Goddard, C. Roe, John T. Passe-Smith and John G. Conklin (eds.), *International Political Economy: State-Market Relations in the Changing Global Order* (Lynne Rienner, Boulder, 1996).

Goddin, Scott R., "Safeguards," *Business America* (1994).

Grilli, E. and Enrico Sassoon (eds.), *The New Protectionist Wave* (New York University Press, New York, 1990).

Haggard, S. and Chung-in Moon (eds.), *Pacific Dynamics: The International Politics of International Change* (Westview, Boulder, Colorado, 1989).

Hajnal, Peter I. (ed.), *The Seven Power Summit: Documents from the Summits of Industrialized Countries 1975–1989* (Krauss, New York, 1989).

Hansson, G., *Social Clauses and International Trade: An Economic Analysis of Labour Standards in Trade Policy* (Croom Helm, London and Canberra, 1983).

Harris, N., *The End of the Third World: Newly Industrializing Countries and the Decline of an Ideology* (Penguin, London, 1986).

Hatch, W. and Kozo Yamamura, *Asia in Japan's Embrace: Building a Regional Production Alliance* (Cambridge University Press, Cambridge, 1996).

Haus, Leah A., *Globalizing the GATT: The Soviet Unions' Successor States, Eastern Europe, and the International Trading System* (The Brookings Institution, Washington, DC, 1992).

Hellmann, Donald C. and Kenneth B. Pyle (eds.), *From APEC to Xanadu: Creating a Viable Community in the Post-Cold War Pacific* (M. E. Sharpe, New York, 1997).

Herzenberg, S. and Jorge F. Perez-Lopez (eds.), *Labor Standards and Development in the Global Economy* (US Department of Labor, Bureau of International Labor, Washington, 1990).

Hilf, M., Francis G. Jacobs and Ernst-Ulrich Petersmann (eds.), *The European Community and GATT* (Kluwer, The Netherlands, 1986).

Hoekman, B. and Michel Kostecki, *The Political Economy of the World Trading System: From GATT to WTO* (Oxford University Press, Oxford, 1995).

Hunter, David B. and Michelle Billig, "International economy and the environment," *Yearbook of International Environmental Law*, Vol. 7 (1996).

Jackson, John H., *Restructuring the GATT System* (Pinter, London, 1990).

Jackson, John H. and Alan O. Sykes (eds.), *Implementing the Uruguay Round* (Clarendon, Oxford, 1997).

Johnson, Stanley P., *The Earth Summit: The United Nations Conference on Environment and Development* (*UNCED*) (Graham and Trotman/ Martinus Nijhoff, London, 1993).

Jones, G., *The Evolution of International Business: An Introduction* (Routledge, London and New York, 1996).

Kahler, M. (ed.), *The Politics of International Debt* (Cornell University Press, Ithaca, New York, 1986).

Kapstein, Ethan B., *Governing the Global Economy: International Finance and the State* (Harvard University Press, Cambridge, Massachusetts, 1994).

Keohane, R. O., *After Hegemony: Cooperation and Discord in the World Political Economy* (Princeton University Press, Princeton, 1984).

Keohane, R. O., Joseph S. Nye and Stanley Hoffmann (eds.), *After the Cold War: International Institutions and State Strategies in Europe, 1989– 1991* (Harvard University Press, Cambridge, 1993).

Kitamura, K. and Tsuneo Tanaka (eds.), *Examining Asia's Tigers: Nine Economies Challenging Common Structural Problems* (Institute of Developing Economies, Tokyo, 1997).

Krauss, M. and R. D. Liebowitz (eds.), *Perestroika and East-West Economic Relations: Prospects for the 1990s* (New York University Press, New York, 1990).

Krueger, Anne O., *Economic Policy Reform in Developing Countries: The Kuznets Memorial Lectures at the Economic Growth Center, Yale University* (Blackwell Publishers, Massachusetts, 1992).

Krugman, P., *Peddling Prosperity: Economic Sense and Nonsense in the Age of Diminished Expectations* (W. W. Norton, New York, 1994).

Lall, S. and Paul Streeten, *Foreign Investment, Transnationals and Developing Countries* (Macmillan, London, 1977).

Leidy, M., "Antidumping: Unfair trade or unfair remedy," *Finance & Development*, Vol. 32, No. 1 (March 1995).

Leong, L., *The Chinese Economy in Transition: From Plan to Market* (Edward Elgar, Cheltenham, 1997).

Lieberman, S., *The Economic and Political Roots of New Protectionism* (Rowman and Littlefield, New Jersey, 1989).

Liew, Leong H., *The Chinese Economy in Transition: From Plan to Market* (Edward Elgar, Cheltenham, 1997).

Linden, C. and Jan S. Prybyla (eds.), *Russia and China on the Eve of a New Millenium* (Transactions, New Jersey, 1997).

Mander, J. and Edward Goldsmith (eds.), *The Case Against the Global Economy: And for a Turn Toward the Local* (Sierra Club, San Francisco, 1996).

Mastel, G., *The Rise of the Chinese Economy: The Middle Kingdom Emerges* (M. E. Sharpe, New York, 1997).

Mathias, P. and Sidney Pollard (eds.), *The Cambridge Economic History of Europe*, Vol. 8 (Cambridge University Press, Cambridge, 1989).

McMichael, T., *Planetary Overload* (Cambridge University Press, Cambridge, 1993).

Meier, G. M., *Problems of a World Monetary Order*, 2nd ed. (Oxford University Press, New York, 1982).

Mikdashi, Z. (ed.), *Bankers' and Public Authorities' Management of Risk* (Macmillan, London, 1990).

Milward, A. S., *The Reconstruction of Western Europe, 1945–1951* (Metheun, London, 1984).

Mokyr, J., *The Economics of the Industrial Revolution* (George Allen and Unwin, London, 1985).

Mungall, C. and Digby J. McLaren (eds.), *Planet Under Stress: The Challenge of Global Change* (Oxford University Press, Toronto, 1990).

Musson, A. E., *The Growth of British Industry* (Batsford, London, 1981).

Neelankavil, James P. and Yong Zhang (eds.), *Global Business: Contemporary Issues, Problems and Challenges* (McGraw Hill, New York, 1996).

Nester, William R., *Japan's Growing Power Over East Asia and the World Economy* (Macmillan, Basingstoke and London, 1990).

Nicholson, D. F., *Australia's Trade Relations: An Outline History of Australia's Overseas Trading Arrangements* (F. W. Cheshire, Melbourne, 1955).

Nolan, P., *China's Rise, Russia's Fall: Politics, Economics and Planning in the Transition from Stalinism* (Macmillan, Houndmills, 1995).

Odell, J. S., *US International Monetary Policy: Markets, Power and Ideas as Sources of Change* (Princeton University Press, Princeton, New Jersey, 1982).

Ohmae, K., *The Borderless World: Power and Strategy in the Interlinked Economy* (Fontana, London, 1990).

Oppenheim, P., *Trade Wars: Japan Versus the West* (Weidenfeld and Nicolson, London, 1992).

Our Common Future, The World Commission on Environment and Development (Oxford University Press Melbourne, Australia, 1990).

Pearson, Charles S. (ed.), *Multinational Corporations, Environment, and the Third World* (Duke University Press, Durham, 1987).

Peck, Merton J. and Thomas J. Richardson (eds.), *What is to be Done? Proposals for the Soviet Transition to the Market* (Yale University Press, New Haven and London, 1991).

Pitchford, R. and Adam Cox (eds.), *EMU Explained: Markets and Monetary Union* (Kogan Page, London, 1997).

Plant, R., *Labour Standards & Structural Adjustment* (International Labour Office, Geneva, 1994).

Porter, G. and Janet Welsh Brown, *Global Environmental Politics* (Westview, Boulder, Colorado, 1991).

Private Capital Flows to Developing Countries: The Road to Financial Integration, A World Bank Policy Research Report (Oxford University Press, New York, 1997).

Putnam, R. D. and Nicholas Bayne, *Hanging Together: The Seven Power Summits* (Heinemann, London, 1984).

The Results of the Uruguay Round of Multilateral Trade Negotiations: The Legal Texts (The GATT Secretariat, Geneva, 1994).

Rode, R. (ed.), *GATT and Conflict Management: A Transatlantic Strategy for a Stronger Regime* (Westview, Boulder, Colorado, 1990).

Rosenblatt, J. *et al.*, *The Common Agricultural Policy of the European Community: Principles and Consequences*, The International Monetary Fund, Occasional Papers No. 62 (Washington, DC, November 1988).

Sachs, J. and Andrew Warner, *Economic Convergence and Economic Policies*, NBER Working Paper No. 5039 (National Bureau of Economic Research, Massachusetts, 1995).

Salvatore, D., *The New Protectionist Threat to World Welfare* (North-Holland, New York, 1987).

Scammell, W. M., *International Monetary Policy: Bretton-Woods and After* (Macmillan, London and Basingstoke, 1975).

Schlagenhof, M., "Trade Measures Based on Environmental Processes and Production Methods," *Journal of World Trade*, Vol. 29, No. 6 (1995).

Schmidheiny, S., *Changing Course: A Global Business Perspective on Development and the Environment* (MIT Press, Cambridge, Massachusetts, 1992).

Schott, Jeffrey J. (ed.), *Completing the Uruguay Round: A Results-Oriented Approach to the GATT Trade Negotiations* (Institute for International Economics, Washington, DC, 1990).

Semmel, B., *The Rise of Free Trade Imperialism: Classical Political Economy, the Empire of Free Trade and Imperialism, 1750–1850* (Cambridge University Press, Cambridge, 1970).

Sengenberger, W. and Duncan Campbell (eds.), *Creating Economic Opportunities: The Role of Labour Standards in Industrial Restructuring* (International Institute for Labour Studies, Geneva, 1994).

_____, *International Labour Standards and Economic Interdependence* (International Institute for Labour Studies, Geneva, 1994).

Shelton, J., *Money Meltdown: Restoring Order to the Global Currency System* (Free Press, New York, 1994).

Shepherd, W. F., *International Financial Integration: History, Theory and Applications in OECD Countries* (Avebury, Aldershot, 1994).

Smith, D. (ed.), *Business and the Environment: Implications of the New Environmentalism* (Paul Chapman, 1993).

Steele, K. (ed.), *Anti-Dumping Under the WTO: A Comparative Review* (Kluwer, London, 1996).

Sterner, T. (ed.), *Economic Policies for Sustainable Development* (Kluwer, Dordrecht, 1994).

Strange, S., *States and Markets: An Introduction to International Political Economy* (Pinter, London, 1988).

Stubbs, R. and Geoffrey R. D. Underhill (eds.), *Political Economy and the Changing Global Order* (Macmillan, London, 1994).

Sung, W. and Rosaria Troia, *Developments in Debt Conversion Programs and Conversion Activities*, World Bank technical Paper No. 170 (The World Bank, Washington, DC, 1992).

Suzuki, Y., Junichi Miyake and Mitsuaki Okabe (eds.), *The Evolution of the International Monetary System: How Can Efficiency and Stability be Attained?* (University of Tokyo Press, Tokyo, 1990).

Thomas, Kenneth P., *Capital Beyond Borders: States and Firms in the Auto Industry, 1960–1994* (Macmillan, Houndmills, 1997).

Thurow, L., *Head to Head: The Coming Economic Battle Among Japan, Europe and America* (William Morrow, New York, 1992).

Todaro, Michael P., *Economic Development in the Third World*, 4th ed. (Longman, New York and London, 1989).

Tolba, Mostafa K., Osama A. El-Kholy *et al.* (eds.), *The World Environment, 1972–1992: Two Decades of Challenge* (Chapman & Hall, London, 1993).

Tuchman, B., *The Guns of August* (Macmillan, New York, 1962).

Van Dormael, A., *Breton Woods: Birth of a Monetary System* (Macmillan, London and Basingstoke, 1978).

Walter, A., *World Power and World Money: The Role of Hegemony and International Monetary Order* (Harvester Wheatsheaf, Hertfordshire, 1991).

Williamson, J. and Marcus H. Miller, *Targets and Indicators: A Blueprint for the International Coordination of Economic Policy* (Institute for International Economics, Washington, DC, 1987).

World Trade Organization, Annual Report (Geneva, 1996).

Yang, X., *Globalization of the Automobile Industry: The United States, Japan and the People's Republic of China* (Praeger, Westport, 1995).

Articles

Aggarwal, V. K., Robert O. Keohane and David B. Yoffie, "The dynamics of negotiated protectionism," *American Political Science Review*, Vol. 81, No. 2 (1987).

Andrews, S., "Slouching towards forgiveness," *International Investor*, Vol. 23, No. 6 (1989).

Auer, James E., "The imperative of US–Japanese Bond," *Orbis* (1995).

Bacani, C., "Ground zero in Asia's crisis," *Asiaweek* (February 6, 1998).

Barenberg, M., "Law and labor in the new global economy: Through the lens of United States federalism," *Columbia Journal of Transnational Law*, Vol. 33, No. 3 (1995).

Bhagwati, J. N., "Regionalism versus multilateralism," *The World Economy*, Vol. 15, No. 5 (1992).

Blackhurst, R., "The WTO and the global economy," *The World Economy*, Vol. 20, No. 5 (1997).

Blaine, M., "Déjà vu all over again: Explaining Mexico's 1994 financial crisis," *The World Economy*, Vol. 21, No. 1 (January 1998).

Blay, S. K. N., "New trends in the protection of the Antarctic environment: The 1991 Madrid protocol," *American Journal of International Law*, Vol. 86 (1982).

Bohnet, A., Zhong Hong and Frank Muller, "China's open-door policy and its significance for transformation of the economic system," *Intereconomics*, Vol. 28, No. 4 (1993).

Boltho, A., "The return of free trade," *International Affairs*, Vol. 72, No. 2 (1996).

Bonturi, M. and Kiichiro Fukusaku, "Globalization and intra-firm trade: An empirical note," *OECD Economic Studies*, Vol. 20, No. 1 (1993).

Bowles, P. and Brian MacLean, "Regional trading blocs: Will East Asia be next?" *Cambridge Journal of Economics*, Vol. 20, No. 4 (1996).

Bradshaw, Victoria W. and Ana-Maria Wahl, "Foreign debt expansion, the international monetary fund, and regional variation in Third World poverty," *International Studies Quarterly*, Vol. 35 (1995).

Bromley, S. and Ray Bush, "Adjustment in Egypt?: The political economy of reform," *Review of African Political Economy*, Vol. 21, No. 6 (1994).

Campanella, M. L., "The effect of globalization and turbulence on policy making processes," *Government and Opposition*, Vol. 28, No. 2 (1993).

Carlisle, Charles R., "Is the world ready for free trade?" *Foreign Affairs*, Vol. 75, No. 6 (1996).

Chowdury, A., "Soviet implosion paves the way for market economy," *Asian Finance*, Vol. 17, No. 9 (1991).

Clarke, T., "Mai-Day! The corporate rule treaty," http://www.nassist.com/mai/mai(2)x.html.

Collingsworth, T., J. William Goold and Pharis J. Harvey, "Time for a global new deal," *Foreign Affairs*, Vol. 73, No. 1 (1994).

Cooper, Richard N., "External adjustment: The proper role for the IMF," *Challenge* (1993).

Crabbe, L., "The international gold standard and US monetary policy from World War I to the new deal," *Federal Reserve Bulletin*, Vol. 75, No. 6 (1989).

Davies, B., "A balancing act on the road to reform," *Asiamoney*, Vol. 18, No. 10 (December 1997/January 1998).

Dorn, James A., "Economic liberty and democracy in East Asia," *Orbis*, Vol. 37, No. 4 (1993).

Dunning, John H., "How should national governments respond to globalization?" *The International Executive*, Vol. 35, No. 3 (1993).

Easterly, W. and Stanley Fischer, "What can we learn from the Soviet collapse?" *Finance & Development*, Vol. 31, No. 4 (1994).

Edwards, S., "The Mexican peso crisis: How much did we know? When did we know it?" *The World Economy*, Vol. 21, No. 1 (January 1998).

Ehrlich, P., "Too many rich people," *Our Planet*, Vol. 6, No. 3 (1994).

Etzioni, A., "How is Russia bearing up?" *Challenge* (1992).

Feinerman, J. V., "The quest for GATT membership," *The China Business Review*, Vol. 19, No. 3 (1992).

Fieleke, Norman, S., "One trading world, or many: The issue of regional trading blocs," *New England Economic Review* (Federal Reserve Bank of Boston) (1992).

Guitian, M., "The IMF as a monetary institution: The challenge ahead," *Finance & Development*, Vol. 31, No. 3 (1994).

Haas, Peter M., "Do regimes matter? Epistemic communities and the Mediterranean pollution control," *International Organization*, Vol. 43, No. 3 (1989).

Hardin, G., "The tragedy of the commons," *Science*, No. 168 (1968).

Hare, P., Saul Estrin, Mikhail Lugachyov and Lina Takla, "Russia's foreign trade: New directions and western policies," *The World Economy*, Vol. 21, No. 1 (January 1998).

Harris, R. G., "Globalization, trade and income," *Canadian Journal of Economics*, Vol. 26, No. 4 (1993).

Hart, M., "The WTO and the political economy of globalization," *Journal of World Trade*, Vol. 31, No. 5 (1997).

Henkoff, R., "Service is everybody's business," *Fortune*, Vol. 129, No. 13 (1994).

Hirst, P. and Grahame Thompson, "The problem of 'globalization': International economic relations, national economic management and the formation of trading blocs," *Economy and Society*, Vol. 21, No. 4 (1992).

Hoekman, Bernard M., "New issues in the Uruguay Round and beyond," *The Economic Journal*, Vol. 103, No. 421 (1993).

Hogbin, G., "Global warming: The mother of all environmental scares," *Policy*, Vol. 14, No. 1 (Autumn 1998).

Hough, J., "On the road to paradise again? Keeping hopes for Russia realistic," *The Brookings Review*, Vol. 11, No. 1 (1993).

Hutton, W., "Relaunching western economies: The case for regulating financial markets," *Foreign Affairs*, Vol. 75, No. 6 (1996).

Ipsen, E., "The Brady plan's enforcer," *Institutional Investor*, Vol. 23, No. 8 (1989).

Islam, S., "A deal, of sorts," *Far Eastern Economic Review* (1993).

Jager, H., "The global exchange rate system in transition," *The Economist* (The Netherlands), Vol. 139, No. 4 (1991).

Kapstein, Ethan B., "We are US: The myth of the multinational," *The National Interest* (1991–1992).

Katz, S. I., "Balance of payments adjustment, 1945–1986: The IMF experience," *Atlantic Economic Journal*, Vol. 17, No. 4 (1989).

Kawaharada, S., "Shin Jidai o Mukaeru Jidosha Kaigai Jigyo," *Tekko Kai*, Vol. 35, No. 9 (1989).

Kennedy, K. C., "The accession of the Soviet Union to GATT," *Journal of World Trade Law*, Vol. 21, No. 2 (1987).

Kostrzewa, W., Peter Nunnenkamp and Holger Schmieding, "A marshall plan for Middle and Eastern Europe," *The World Economy*, Vol. 13, No. 1 (1990).

Krueger, Anne O., "The political economy of the rent-seeking society," *American Economic Review*, Vol. 64, No. 3 (1974).

Krugman, P., "Is free trade passé?" *The Journal of Economic Perspectives*, Vol. 1, No. 2 (1987).

Krugman, P., "Does the new trade theory require a new trade policy?" *The World Economy*, Vol. 15, No. 4 (1992).

Krugman, P., "Competitiveness: A dangerous obsession," *Foreign Affairs*, Vol. 73, No. 2 (1994).

Krugman, P., "The myth of Asia's miracle," *Foreign Affairs*, Vol. 73, No. 6 (1994).

Langille, Brian A., "Eight ways to think about international labour standards," *Journal of World Trade*, Vol. 31, No. 4 (1997).

Lawrence, R. Z., "The reluctant giant: Will Japan take its role on the world stage?" *The Brookings Review*, Vol. 9, No. 3 (1991).

Lee, E., "Globalization and employment: Is anxiety justified?" *International Labour Review* (1996).

————, "Globalization and labour standards: A review of issues," *International Labour Review*, Vol. 136, No. 2 (1997).

Leong, L., "Chinese reform strategy: A unity of opposites," mimeo (February 1998).

Lindbaek, J. and Jean-Francois Rischard, "Agility in the new world economy," *Finance & Development*, Vol. 31, No. 3 (1994).

Lindzen, Richard S., "Global warming: The origin and nature of the alleged scientific consensus," *Regulation: The Cato Review of Business & Government* (http://www.cato.org/pubs/regulation/reg15n2g.html).

Loxley, J. "Structural adjustment in Africa: Reflections on Ghana and Zambia," *Review of African Political Economy*, Vol. 47 (1990).

Lipson, C., "International cooperation in economic and security affairs," *World Politics*, Vol. 37, No. 1 (1994).

Lustig, Nora C., "NAFTA: Setting the record straight," *The World Economy*, Vol. 20, No. 5 (1997).

Lutz, James M., "GATT reform or regime maintenance: Differing solutions to world trade problems," *Journal of World Trade*, Vol. 25, No. 2 (1991).

Main, Ann. M., "Dispute settlement understanding," *Business America*, (1994).

Marrese, M., "CMEA: Effective but cumbersome political economy," *International Organization*, Vol. 40, No. 2 (1986).

McCleary, W. A., "Policy implementation under adjustment lending," *Finance & Development* (1989).

McCulloch, R., "Investment policies in GATT," *The World Economy*, Vol. 13, No. 4 (1990).

McKenzie, P. D., "China's application to the GATT: State trading and the problem of market access," *Journal of World Trade*, Vol. 24, No. 5 (1990).

McMillan, J. and Barry Naughton, "How to reform a planned economy: Lessons from China," *Oxford Review of Economic Policy*, Vol. 8, No. 1 (1992).

Meyer, J. W., David John Frank, Ann Hironaka, Evan Schofer and Nancy Brandon Tuma, "The structuring of a world environmental regime, 1870–1990," *International Organization*, Vol. 51, No. 4 (1997).

Milner, C., " 'New standards issues' and the WTO," *The Australian Economic Review*, Vol. 30, No. 1 (1997).

Milner, H. V. and David B. Yoffie, "Between free trade and protectionism: Strategic trade policy and the theory of corporate trade demands," *International Organization*, Vol. 43, No. 2 (1989).

Neikirk, William B., "Mexico dropped like a bombshell," *Asian Finance*, (1987).

Noren, J. H., "The Russian economic reform: Progress and prospects," *Soviet Economy*, Vol. 8, No. 1 (1992).

Norton, R., "Back to Bretton-Woods," *Fortune* (1994).

Oberthur, S., "Montreal protocol: 10 years after," *Environmental Policy and Law*, Vol. 27, No. 6 (1997).

Prestowitz, Clyde V., "Playing to win," *Foreign Affairs*, Vol. 73, No. 4 (1994).

Qureshi, Z., "Globalization: New opportunities, tough challenges," *Finance and Development*, Vol. 33, No. 1 (1996).

Reich, R. B., "The economics of illusion and the illusion of economics," *Foreign Affairs*, Vol. 66, No. 3 (1987/1988).

Reich, R. B., "We need a strategic trade policy," *Challenge* (1990).

Robertson, D., "The global environment: Are international treaties a distraction?" *The World Economy*, Vol. 13, No. 1 (1990).

Roncesvalles, O. and Andrew Tweedie, "Augmenting the IMF's resources," *Finance & Development* (1991).

Ruggiero, R., "Growing complexity in international economic relations demand broadening and deepening of the multilateral trade system," *WTO Focus*, No. 6 (1996).

Ruggie, John G., "Multilateralism: The anatomy of an institution," *International Organization*, Vol. 46, No. 3 (1992).

Ruggie, John G., "Territoriality and beyond: Problematizing modernity in international relations," *International Organization*, Vol. 47, No. 1 (1993).

Ryrie, Sir William, "Where do we go from here?" *Euromoney* (1994).

Sachs, J., "The economic transformation of Eastern Europe: The case of Poland," *Economics of Planning*, Vol. 25, No. 1 (1992).

Sachs, J., "Strengthening western support for Russia," *International Economic Insights*, Vol. 4, No. 1 (1993).

Sapir, A., "The interaction between labour standards and international trade policy," *The World Economy*, Vol. 18, No. 6 (1995).

Schnoor, Jerald L., James N. Galloway and Bedrich Moldan, "East Central Europe: An environment in transition," *Environmental Science and Technology*, Vol. 31, No. 9 (1997).

Schonhardt-Bailey, C., "Lessons in lobbying for free trade in 19th-century Britain: To concentrate or not," *American Political Science Review*, Vol. 85, No. 1 (1991).

Servais, J. M., "The social clause in trade agreements: Wishful thinking or an instrument of social progress?" *International Labour Review*, Vol. 128, No. 4 (1989).

Simon, Dennis F., "The international technology market: Globalization, regionalization and the pacific rim," *Business & the Contemporary World*, Vol. 5, No. 2 (1993).

Soros, G., "The capitalist threat," *The Atlantic Monthly*, Vol. 279, No. 2 (1997).

Stegemann, K., "Policy rivalry among industrial states: What can we learn from models of strategic trade policy?" *International Organization*, Vol. 43, No. 1 (1989).

Summers L. H. and Lant H. Pritchett, "The structural adjustment debate," *American Economic Review*, Vol. 83, No. 2 (1993).

Tanzi, V. and Hamid Davoodi, "Roads to nowhere: How corruption in public investment hurts growth," *Economic Issues*, No. 12 (International Monetary Fund, Washington DC, 1998).

Tita, A., "A challenge for World Trade Organization: Toward a true transnational law," *Journal of World Trade*, Vol. 29, No. 3, (1995).

Torres, R., "Labour standards and trade," *The OECD Observer*, No. 202 (1996).

Tsang, S.-K., "Against 'Big Bang' in economic transition: Normative and positive arguments," *Cambridge Journal of Economics*, Vol. 20, No. 2 (1996).

Van Bael, I., "The GATT dispute settlement procedure," *Journal of World Trade*, Vol. 22, No. 4 (1988).

Wachtel, Howard M., "Taming global money," *Challenge* (1995).

Wang, Xinhua, "Trends towards globalization and a global think tank," *Futures*, Vol. 24, No. 3 (1992).

Wanniski, J., "The future of Russian capitalism," *Foreign Affairs*, Vol. 71, No. 2 (1992).

Wesson, R., "Wrapping up the debt problem," *PS; Political Science and Politics*, Vol. 23, No. 3 (1990).

Wiarda, Howard J., "The politics of Third World debt," *PS: Political Science and Politics*, Vol. 23, No. 3 (1990).

Witherell, William H., "An agreement on investment," *The OECD Observer*, No. 202 (1996).

Zeitz, J., "Negotiations on GATT reform and political incentives," *The World Economy*, Vol. 12, No. 1 (1989).

INDEX